Operational
Urban
Models

AN INTRODUCTION

To my mother and father

Operational Urban Models

AN INTRODUCTION

David Foot

Methuen
London and New York

First published in 1981 by
Methuen & Co. Ltd
11 New Fetter Lane, London EC4P 4EE

Published in the USA by
Methuen & Co.
in association with Methuen, Inc.
733 Third Avenue, New York, NY 10017

Printed in Great Britain by
Richard Clay (The Chaucer Press) Ltd
Bungay, Suffolk

British Library Cataloguing in Publication Data

Foot, David
Operational urban models.
1. Cities and towns – Mathematical models
I. Title
307.7'6'0724   HT153

ISBN 0-416-73320-4
ISBN 0-416-73330-1 Pbk (University paperback 749)

Contents

Contents

Acknowledgements

I wish to thank all those people who developed the operational urban models quoted in this book, and in particular the publishers and authors who allowed me to use diagrams or tables from their work.

Figures 2.1 and 5.7 from Piasentin, Costa and Foot (1978) *Regional Studies*

Figure 3.4 from Davies, Jackson and Robinson (1964) Manchester University

Figure 3.11 and Table 3.15 from McLoughlin, Foot and Nix (1966) Manchester University

Figure 3.12 from Lewisham Borough Council (1978) London Borough of Lewisham

Figure 3.14 from Moseley (1977) The Unit for Retail Planning and Information

Table 3.16 from Gilligan, Rainford and Thorne (1974) *European Journal of Marketing*

Figures 5.5 and 5.6 from Cripps and Foot (1970) *Environment and Planning*

Figure 6.5 from Foot (1974) University of Reading

Figure 6.6 from Hill (1965) *Journal of the American Institute of Planners*

Figure 7.4 from Brotchie and Sharpe (1975) Construction Press

List of figures

List of tables

Preface

I should have written this book several years ago. As well as researching into urban modelling I have been teaching urban models for many years, but without what I regard as the right sort of text book. Some of the books explain the models with simple hypothetical examples, others use advanced mathematics, but none in my view put sufficient emphasis on the practical application of the models. What I have tried to do in this book is to stress the practical side of modelling by explaining in quite simple terms the different types of models, applying them to small actual regions and then describing numerous operational models to show how they have been applied. The book is intended for undergraduate students and for practising planners and urban analysts wishing to know about urban models and how they are currently applied.

There are a number of people that I would like to mention that have helped me since I became involved with urban modelling. It was in 1965 at Manchester University that Brian McLoughlin, Keith Nix and myself learnt about the practical application of urban modelling during the development of a retail shopping model to study the impact of a new regional shopping centre in north-west England. This was followed by a short period in local government at Bedfordshire working with Eric Cripps; then to Reading University and the Geography Department under Peter Hall which has provided a pleasant place for working and where a lot of research has been undertaken. In particular there has been my good friend Mike Batty to provide a non-stop source of discussion and information on modelling.

A great deal of work by people other than the author goes into producing a book, and as far as this book is concerned there are some that I would particularly like to thank: Mike Batty and

Norman Stothers for reading through an earlier draft of the book and making a number of useful suggestions; Jacquie Lewis, Mary Esslemont and Chris Holland for all the hard work typing the first draft and final manuscript; Sheila Dance for producing such an excellent set of diagrams; also Mary Ann Kerman at Methuen for being so helpful and obliging. It has taken a great many late nights working to write the book and so a special thanks to my wife Celia and children Lynne, Karron and Robin for putting up with my absence. I hope this proves a useful book and then all the effort will have been worthwhile.

David Foot
Reading
February 1981

1 Modelling the urban system

This book is an introduction to the various urban models that have been developed and applied in practical planning situations. A model is a simplified abstraction of a real-world phenomenon and the urban models considered here describe different aspects of the urban system using mathematical equations. They are mathematical models of cities and regions designed for solution on a computer. The models attempt to simulate the spatial structure of urban areas where a simulation can be regarded as an imitation or representation of the behaviour occurring in urban areas with relation to the allocation and interaction of landuse activities. The urban areas might relate to a town, city, subregion or region. The particular aspects of the urban system under investigation might be, for example, the residential location pattern in a region dealing with the distribution of population and employment and the journey to work travel pattern, or it might be the retail shopping pattern in a region dealing with the distribution of the residential population and shopping centres, together with the shopping trip pattern and retail expenditure. The urban models are operational in the sense that they have been successfully developed and applied in actual planning studies in many parts of the world, rather than being developed for theoretical or academic reasons. The book does not cover models specifically used for forecasting activities such as population, employment and housing, and indeed this information at a regional level is generally input into the spatial urban models which then determine the most likely distribution of these activities over the region. Similarly non-spatial and aspatial models that do not deal with the distribution and allocation of activities over a study region are also excluded.

All operational urban models are different in detail, but they do conform to a certain broad classification, and the three main types are based on gravity, linear and optimizing mathematics. All the models are formulated and explained by applying them to small study regions in different parts of Britain. A number of operational models of each type are then described to show how they have been applied in practical planning situations. At the same time the practical and theoretical problems involved with developing each model are described and an assessment made of their usefulness. There is also a fourth group of models that can be called hybrid models which are described briefly in the last chapter and are formulated by using some of the other model types linked together by a set of accounting equations. In the last chapter there is a general discussion of the criticism of the modelling approach and an appraisal of its value. Because of the nature of urban models, the book necessarily contains a large number of mathematical equations. However, the mathematical formulation of the different models and the calculations involved in solving them are fully described, and the level of mathematics required to follow the book and to understand the models is really just a basic knowledge of algebra. The algebraic notation of activities such as population and employment and trip patterns such as journey to work, are fully explained in Chapter 2. In Chapters 6 and 7, the basic ideas of linear regression and linear programming are explained, and though not essential, it would help if the reader had a little prior knowledge of these two techniques.

Since this book is specifically about urban modelling, there are some aspects of the way urban areas function that are only very briefly discussed. Good complementary reading can be gained from two other books in this same Methuen series: Daniels and Warnes (1980) on movement in cities, and Rhind and Hudson (1980) on landuse; and also from Hall (1974) on urban and regional planning and Needham (1977) on how cities work. For a general outline of the systems view of planning and the role of urban modelling see Chadwick (1971) and McLoughlin (1969). There are also several books that deal with a broad range of analytical techniques in urban and regional planning and these cover statistical and quantitative techniques (Baxter 1976, Dickey and Watts 1978), regional science techniques (Krueckeberg and Silvers 1974, Catanese 1972, Oppenheim 1980, Openshaw 1978) and general planning techniques (Helly 1975, Roberts 1974, Chapin and Kaiser 1979). This book on operational urban models is intended as a highly practical introduction to urban modelling techniques, and the reader can then proceed to more advanced books such as Batty (1976) and Wilson (1974). However, before the models are covered in any detail, this first chapter will provide the general background by considering the nature of urban models, their role in planning, the history of their development, and their basic characteristics.

URBAN MODELS

Urban models attempt to describe the urban system using mathematical equations. They provide a simplified and abstract view of some aspect of the urban system and deal with the allocation and interaction of landuse activities in cities and regions. Urban areas display certain patterns and urban models are developed in order to gain both an understanding of the urban system and to predict future changes. These mathematical models generally deal with the spatial problems of urban areas for use in physical or strategic planning, and are developed to look at different aspects of the spatial distribution of landuse activities within the urban system. The landuse activities might be, for example, the distribution of residential population, employment, shops, offices or recreational sites, and the interactions might be the journey to work trip pattern or the journey to shop trip pattern.

Urban modelling is a practical approach to urban analysis which seeks firstly to understand and describe the mechanisms which govern the structure and behaviour of the urban system and secondly to predict the outcome of future policy decisions. The models are policy oriented and the overriding influence on their development has been their application to practical planning problems. An urban area is a highly complex system of interrelated activities and components but for simplicity of understanding and ease of manipulation it can be divided into subsystems. Urban models can then be developed to represent the main relationships within a subsystem and the mathematical formulation of the model can be based on both theoretical and empirical evidence. In order to make the models workable, they are going to be considerably simplified representations of real-world subsystems and they will not deal with many of the complex links that exist between the subsystems. However, the models do provide a structure for problem solving and for comparing alternative planning policies.

Any changes in the landuse pattern of a city or region will have

3

repercussions on its present urban structure. These changes might be in the form of new urban development resulting from the redevelopment of an area, or from building on a new site. The development of a large hypermarket would certainly have an effect on the pattern of retailing in the surrounding area, and similarly a new airport sited in a rural area is bound to have considerable consequences for its surrounding region. Landuse changes can also be generated through non-spatial urban factors. For example, an increase in car ownership would increase population mobility and by altering the travel pattern of individuals so generate pressure for landuse changes, such as greater suburban residential development or new transport routes. In order to look at the consequences of all these changes, a detailed planning study of the area will very often be undertaken, and increasingly over recent years urban modelling techniques have been used as part of this process of analysis.

Any urban area is a complex, dynamic system with innumerable factors continuously altering its form. Even though the urban system has been studied quite extensively, there is still no adequate description of its structure. Theories do exist about certain parts of the system and urban models attempt to test these theories. However, any model can usually only contain the main features of a theory since an urban model has to be set out in the form of mathematical equations that can be solved on a computer. Urban models are therefore being developed against a background of rather limited theoretical knowledge. They can only hope to try and represent in a fairly rudimentary way, what appear to be the main factors in a small part of the urban system. This should always be borne in mind when evaluating the usefulness of an urban model which expresses a small number of variables in a set of mathematical equations.

URBAN MODELS AND PLANNING

The traditional procedure for carrying out a planning study of 'survey analysis plan' has now been considerably expanded although the basic ideas still hold. Most importantly the systems approach to planning (Chadwick 1971, McLoughlin 1969) introduced new concepts which added a number of further steps to this three-stage process, and showed it to be highly interconnected with feedbacks and links between all the various stages. This expanded procedure involves formulating goals and objectives for the study area and identifying particular problems, making a full analysis of the past and present situation and forecasting future levels of all the different activities, and generating and evaluating several alternative future policies in order to obtain some preferred plan for the future. Within this process there is continual feedback and movement between the various stages as new problems become apparent or new insight into the urban structure of the area is gained.

During this change in approach to planning studies there has been a large increase in the use of analytical techniques (e.g. see Batey and Breheny 1978). Since no one model is general enough to cover all aspects of the planning process, there are now a whole range of techniques that are available. Urban models are just one group of techniques, which are particularly relevant in the generation and evaluation stages. Other models will be used to estimate future activity levels and generate alternative strategies, but then urban models can test and evaluate the effect of these strategies on the study region. This procedure can in turn generate further development strategies which are then evaluated. These results could possibly feedback to other stages in the planning process as new regional problems are highlighted, leading to changes in future activity estimates or even amendments to the original objectives of the study. Among the other techniques that can be used are methods for forecasting future levels of different activities such as population and employment through cohort survival population models, migration models and employment models. To generate alternative strategies for an area potential surface analysis or threshold analysis can be used, while at evaluation there are goals-achievement and planning balance sheet methods. A number of other methods of analysis are also available and several books dealing with the different planning techniques have already been referenced (e.g. Helly 1975, Roberts 1974, Chapin and Kaiser 1979).

Urban models are used to evaluate the effects of changes in relation to certain landuse activities, dealing particularly with residential development, industrial development, retail development, the provision of services and the transport network. They relate mainly to spatial aspects of the urban system although they do attempt to estimate the spatial consequences of changes in non-spatial variables. In particular, they can test the impact of new development or redevelopment, compare alternative schemes of development, and show the effect of different planning policies on an urban area. They are generally operated at a fairly aggregate level, both spatially and in terms of the landuse variables, and each model only deals with a part of the whole urban system. The models also involve only the main landuse activities, although further submodels can easily be incorporated to consider such things as environmental impact with regard to noise and pollution, or changes in accessibility. The urban models are therefore providing the planner with information about the likely outcome of future policy actions. The results can be considered along with output from other techniques and other forms of analyses to provide an overall synthesis of the strengths, weaknesses and likely outcome from different planning policies.

It can be seen that urban models do fill a specific role within the planning process and this is well explained in Batty (1978). For example in the Nottinghamshire – Derbyshire Subregional Study three urban models were developed, a retail shopping model, a transport model, and then a Garin – Lowry model which linked together the service, residential and transport sectors of the urban system. Other non-spatial models of employment, population and migration were developed, and plans were generated through the potential surface technique. The whole technical planning process was carried through four cycles, with the planning team constantly intervening, in order to arrive at a preferred strategy for development in the region.

A BRIEF HISTORY OF URBAN MODELLING

Urban models have quite a short history of development because they deal with large quantities of data which can only be processed by computer. As the computer has been developed, increased in size and become generally available to all urban analysts, so urban modelling has followed a similar course. Prior to the advent of the computer there was some significant work by Reilly in the 1930s looking at the way cities attract retail trade from a surrounding area and on the theoretical side in the 1930s and 1940s there were also certain location theories proposed, for example, by Christaller and Losch. However it was not until 1945 that the first electronic computer was developed and it was the mid-1950s before computers were large enough and available for urban modelling.

The early developments in urban modelling were in transportation planning in the USA in order to try and study in a scientifically organized way the traffic problems arising from the enormous increase in car ownership. These transport models were applied to a large number of North American cities in the late 1950s dealing with trip generation and trip attraction for small zones within an urban area, the flow of trips between zones, and then the assignment of trips to the transport network. The trip distribution model was generally based on the gravity model which was a reformulated version of the retail model used by Reilly. The transport planning techniques were taken up and applied in many other countries, particularly in Britain where many towns and cities developed models in the 1960s.

Meanwhile in the USA, the problem of looking at the transport system without sufficient regard for the landuse pattern was being realized. This led to the development of large-scale integrated landuse transportation models to generate and test landuse plans for a number of metropolitan areas such as Boston, Baltimore, Connecticut, Penn Jersey, Pittsburgh and San Francisco (see Harris 1968). They were nearly all developed in practical planning situations, and used a variety of different methods based on gravity, linear and optimizing mathematics. These models tended to be extremely large and consequently rather expensive to develop and although several of them did become operational, others were abandoned before they could be fully developed.

In Britain in the late 1960s and early 1970s after the majority of the transportation studies had been completed, and having witnessed the North American modelling experience, relatively modest, small-scale, low-cost, urban models were developed, largely based on an extension to the Lowry model (Lowry 1964). Again these were mainly developed in practical planning situations and were generally fairly successfully applied (see Batty 1975). Their introduction usefully coincided with a number of subregional studies and local authority structure planning exercises, which were interested in applying new methods of analysis.

While urban modelling was rapidly spreading to many other countries during the 1970s, in North America there was a general decrease in interest in this form of analysis and indeed some sharp criticism (Lee 1973). However, in the late 1970s and early 1980s, there is a renewed interest in urban modelling and Pack and Pack (1977) show that planning agencies are in fact using the models and finding them useful methods of analysis.

7

SOME BASIC CHARACTERISTICS OF URBAN MODELS

Operational urban models fall into four broad types. Three of the groups are covered in detail and are based on gravity, linear and optimizing mathematics. A fourth group of hybrid models will only be discussed briefly and these contain elements of the other three types linked together by a series of equations. No two operational models are ever the same but they can quite reasonably be grouped into this general classification. However, it is worth considering further, some of the general characteristics of the urban models that are discussed later in the book.

Almost all operational urban models are deterministic and predictive. They are deterministic in that the part of the urban system being modelled is represented as a fixed mathematical relationship, and the output from the model is completely determined by this set of equations. A few stochastic models have been developed where a probabilistic element is incorporated into the mathematical relationship, but these have been of a largely experimental nature. Operational models are also predictive rather than purely descriptive, in that not only do they describe part of the urban system, but more importantly they can be used predictively to provide estimates of the future situation. A series of planning policies can be compared in order to assist in the physical planning of an area.

Another feature of operational urban models is that they are static or comparative static equilibrium models. Many of the models deal with data for one point in time and the model operates as though this is an equilibrium state of the system. Similarly the results at prediction provide information on the equilibrium situation at some future date. Some models, however, can be considered comparative static models since they deal with incremental changes in activities over a time period of say five years, rather than a total allocation of activities at one point in time. Also many of the models perform recursive predictions which can be considered as a form of quasi-dynamic prediction. Here a series of predictive runs of the model is made, for example at five year intervals over a twenty-five year projection period, and the output from one future point in time is used as additional information for input into the following predictions. This is obviously not an ideal position, since an urban system is clearly dynamic and never in equilibrium. However, there are insufficient theories to explain the dynamic working of the urban system and enormously complex problems are encountered in trying to develop even a simple dynamic urban model. For this reason truly dynamic models have really only been developed as academic research exercises. The urban dynamics model of Forrester (1969) was a non-spatial model of a theoretical city and will not therefore be considered. All operational models have been static or comparative static models with at best recursive predictions.

Operational models are also macro-models, both spatially and in terms of the variables. The level of aggregation does differ between models, but at no point do they become micro-models dealing with an individual's behaviour pattern. Urban models deal with data from an area divided into zones, which for a regional model might be a whole town, or for a city might be as small as an enumeration district or street block. The models deal with the aggregate behaviour patterns within and between zones. An example might be the journey from work to home pattern for all workers or there could be some degree of disaggregation of the variables to study the movement of different types of workers to different types of house.

It is quite useful to make a further distinction amongst these operational models in three ways. Firstly between partial and general models. Partial models deal with one part or subsystem of the overall urban system, such as retail shopping or residential location or transport distribution. General models on the other hand consider a number of subsystems, such as the Garin–Lowry model described in Chapter 5 which deals with the allocation of services to urban centres as well as the residential location of workers. Both partial and general models have been developed and successfully applied. A second useful distinction can be drawn between optimizing and non-optimizing models. The majority of operational models are non-optimizing and try to reflect the actual real-world situation. A smaller number of optimizing models have been developed which generate an optimal location pattern under various conditions, for example to minimize new development costs or transport costs in a region or to maximize consumer benefit. The third distinction is between linear and non-linear models and this is determined by the nature of the mathematical equations in the model. Linear models comprise one of the four main groups of urban models while optimizing models involving linear programming are also of a linear form.

The broad groups of model mentioned earlier can now be considered in relation to these characteristics. The most widely applied urban model is the gravity or entropy maximizing model. It is basically a spatial distribution model and on its own can be used as a partial model to study retail shopping (Chapter 3), residential location and transport distribution (Chapter 4). More general models can be formulated by linking together two or more gravity models dealing with different subsystems, such as the Garin–Lowry model (Chapter 5), or by incorporating the gravity model in a system of accounting equations that consider other aspects of the urban system (Lowry 1964). The second group of urban models consists of linear models based on linear regression techniques. They can be general or partial depending on the nature of the equation system and the landuse activities included. Several alternative versions of this type of model are given in Chapter 6. Thirdly, there are the optimizing models, which are usually based on mathematical programming methods and again can be partial or general depending on the variables being included. The more straightforward linear optimizing models are based on linear programming techniques, but there are also some non-linear optimizing models which include non-linear interaction functions and have to be solved by an iterative procedure (Chapter 7). The fourth group of hybrid models consists of models of many different forms and covers the whole range of model characteristics.

It is intended that the reader gains a thorough understanding of the model building procedure, the form of the different types of model and how operational models have been applied in practice. Chapter 2 describes the general procedure involved in developing an urban model for a region, dealing with the modelling process and the practical problems involved. This sets the background for the next five chapters which cover the three main types of urban models outlined above. The last chapter deals very briefly with hybrid models which is followed by a general discussion on the strengths and weaknesses of urban modelling, and an assessment of the success and failure of their application in practical planning situations.

2 Building an operational urban model

Before looking at the different urban models in detail, it is helpful to have an understanding of the general procedure involved in developing a model for a study region. This procedure is similar no matter which model is to be developed and involves defining the objectives of the study, deciding on the study region and zoning system, the collection of data, the calibration of the model and then lastly using the model predictively.

OUTLINING THE PURPOSE OF THE MODEL

The reasons for wanting to develop an urban model must be clearly formulated at the beginning of the model building exercise. The questions relating to the study area that need to be investigated can be defined, together with the overall objectives. The modelling exercise will be part of a larger overall investigation and the model builder must be very clear about the role that the model can play within the study. Since the urban models deal with landuse activities, they are developed particularly to study aspects of residential location, employment location and retailing, and the interaction between these activities in terms of the transport system.

There are a whole range of questions that could be investigated using urban models:

(1) How would a large area of new residential development or inner city redevelopment affect the journey to work trip pattern and general accessibility of a region?

(2) How would a large increase in employment resulting from the development of a new airport affect the surrounding

11

region and what other housing and transport policies would be needed?

(3) How would the development of a new hypermarket affect the shopping pattern of the region, particularly the other nearby shopping centres?

(4) How would the transport pattern of an area change in response to a change in the transport system such as the building of a new motorway?

(5) How would constraints on residential and industrial development in areas of high environmental quality affect the residential distribution of the region and the transport pattern, particularly for journey to work?

(6) How would a general change in accessibility due to a large increase in petrol prices affect the region?

(7) How would a series of alternative future residential and industrial development policies affect the region and which of these policies would provide the best future planning strategy for the region?

(8) What relationships can be identified within the urban system which can be used to assist in estimating the future level of landuse activities in a region?

(9) What would be the most efficient division of a region into school or hospital catchment areas in order to minimize travel costs?

(10) What would be the best urban development and transport policies for the future in order to conserve the consumption of oil?

(11) What would be the effect on a city region of a decentralization of basic employment from the central area to a suburban location?

(12) What would be the cumulative effect of a general decline in the economy of a region in terms of population and employment changes?

There are any number of similar questions that could be posed, either at this aggregate level or dealing with more disaggregated activities. Urban models can be developed to help provide information on the most likely outcome of these policies, and later in the book operational models are described that deal with many of these questions. There are two main types of situation when the models will be used, although in both situations the models themselves are applied in a similar way. Firstly, for conditional prediction in a general strategic planning exercise, such as a structure plan, a development plan or a subregional or regional study, where the models are used to consider alternative forms of new development for the future in order to arrive at some preferred plan for the region. Secondly, for impact analysis to look at a specific policy when an application has been made for some major landuse change, such as the development of a new hypermarket, and a model is used to try and evaluate the effects of this change.

This process of setting out the purpose of the study and defining the objectives will indicate the type of model that could be developed and the activities and other variables that need to be included. Those variables that seem to have a strong relationship with the activities in the planning problem should be considered, looking at both theoretical and empirical evidence. For example, the basic minimum information that would be required to look at the impact of a new hypermarket would be information on the nature of the other shopping centres in the region, the residential population distribution and retail expenditure, and the pattern of trips to the shopping centres. This information can be at various levels of aggregation with retail sales considered as one total figure or disaggregated into durable and consumer goods, or into an even finer division. Obviously many other variables do affect shopping behaviour and could be included, but it all depends on how complex a model is required; a quick, cheap, aggregate model, or a more expensive but detailed disaggregated model. This problem is discussed in Chapter 3 in relation to retail models developed by various local authorities in Britain.

All studies, therefore, have to define their purpose very clearly by setting out the questions that need answering, which in turn will indicate the type of model that is most appropriate, and the information on the activities and other variables that will be required to build the model. These data would almost certainly be collected no matter what the form of the analysis, so that urban models can often be developed on available information to provide additional insight into a planning problem.

DEFINING THE STUDY REGION AND ZONING SYSTEM

Once it has been decided to build a mathematical model for a part of the urban system, it is then necessary to define the boundary of the study region. This is the area to be investigated by an urban model and can refer to a region of a country, a subregion or even a city or town. There are numerous examples presented in the book, but it is useful to consider the general rules involved. There is usually a particular area of interest and for modelling purposes a rather larger area is generally used as the study region. This is in order to find a study region that is as enclosed and self-contained as possible. The boundary is drawn so that the interaction across the boundary is minimized, covering interactions such as journey to work, journey to shop or to use service facilities, and commercial and industrial journeys. It is not sensible, therefore, to have a town on the edge of the study region otherwise the model will not be able to deal with that part of its interaction which takes place with areas outside the model region.

For example, in a study of the problems of Venice which is described in Chapter 5 (Piasentin, Costa and Foot 1978), the main area of interest was that covered by a special law for Venice, the *Piano Comprensoriale*, and in particular the historical city in the lagoon (figure 2.1). However, a preliminary analysis of the area showed that the Venice urban system extended further into the mainland and so an enlarged region was prescribed for modelling purposes. This region was still influenced by two large urban areas, Padova and Treviso, and so they were included as special external zones, when only their interaction with the main study region is modelled. The alternative would have been to include the two towns within the model region together with a much extended area around them, but this might then have led to problems over their interaction with other towns and so on. Before long the whole of northern Italy could have been included, but instead a sensible compromise was reached to give the boundary shown in figure 2.1.

The study region then has to be divided into zones and the size and nature of these zones will differ between a region (north-west England, figure 3.11), a subregion (Berkshire, figure 3.14) and a city or town (London Borough of Lewisham, figure 3.12). However, there is a set of factors that influences the zoning system. Probably the most important factor is that the zones have to be compatible with the areal unit for which data are available. Since the data describe the average landuse characteristics of each zone, it is important to collect data for the finest possible spatial unit, so that if an aggregation into a coarser zoning system is required, then data units with similar characteristics can be combined (see

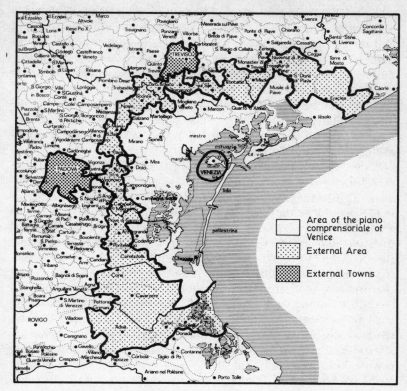

Figure 2.1 The Venice region

Masser, Batey and Brown 1975). Also, zones must not be too large otherwise too much of the interaction will take place within the zone rather than between zones, which is very often the purpose of the exercise. Conversely, the zones should not be too small otherwise the interaction flows between the zones become so small that the aggregate models have difficulty in describing the trip patterns. Another factor is that if the study region has too many zones, then it can become difficult to interpret and understand the model output. On the other hand, if there are too few zones, then there are bound to be many zones on the edge of the model region and again the models will have difficulty in describing the trip patterns since, as already explained, interaction cannot take place across the boundary. It is also useful to try and have zones of roughly similar size and so neutralize the land area variable. There may also be computer limitations to the number of zones allowed, because for most models both the computer storage requirements and the runtime increase at a greater rate than the increase in the number of zones. However, this is becoming a much less important point, since most model builders will have access to large, very fast computers. Lastly, the nature of the zoning system and the number of zones can affect the performance of certain models (Batty 1976), but since the same zoning system is being used to study the base year situation and the future predictions, the problem can be minimized.

Some compromise has to be obtained between all these conflicting problems in order to devise a zoning system. Experience suggests that a reasonable number of zones for an operational model would be between eighty and a hundred zones. There are many examples of zoning systems throughout this book for many different parts of the world, for example Bedfordshire in England (figure 5.5), Venice in Italy (figure 5.7), Boston in the USA (figure 6.6) and Melbourne in Australia (figure 7.4). Amongst these examples there is considerable variation in the number of zones used in the study. Also detailed transport models that assign trips to particular road links in the network (Chapter 4) have tended to use very many more than a hundred zones. Almost all operational models have irregular shaped zones because of the constraint on the areal unit of available data which refers to local authority boundaries. There have been some attempts at developing models for regions divided into zones of grid squares (Echenique, Crowther and Lindsay 1969), but this can only be achieved if a special set of data has been obtained. Some other studies have used a hierarchical zoning system where interaction between activities is modelled at a coarse level with each zone representing some spatial system, and then the system within each coarse zone is modelled (Broadbent 1971). This type of model is explained in Chapter 3 for the Berkshire shopping model (Moseley 1977), and was also used in a Garin–Lowry model of Cheshire (Barras *et al.* 1971).

As each of the different urban models is introduced in the following chapters, a small study region in Britain is used as an example to help explain the procedure involved. The location of these study regions is shown in figure 2.2, and most of the data for the models have been taken from the Census of Population for England and Wales.

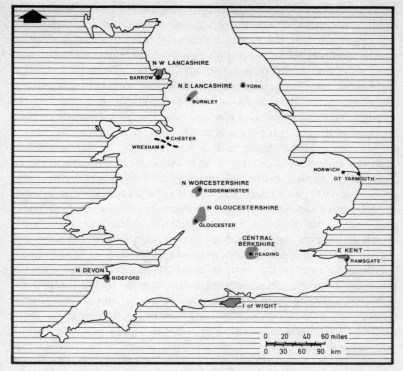

Figure 2.2   The location of study regions that are used to explain the urban models

DATA COLLECTION

There is a strong link between all the previous stages in the model building process and the collection of data. Data availability can strongly influence the definition of the study region and its division into zones, the type of urban model to be built and the scope of its application. One of the first tasks is to determine the availability of data from all possible sources. This will include published information such as the Census of Population Reports and other government publications, together with additional information from the local authorities, such as their updated intercensus estimates and the results from any other surveys. If this does not provide sufficient data for the model, then it will have to be supplemented by data collected from further surveys. Many urban models have been developed from available data together with a small amount of survey work, although some of the larger transport and landuse transport models developed particularly in North America have used data collected from extensive surveys. So if a planning study is being undertaken, either to look at a particular planning policy or to perform a strategic planning study, large amounts of data have to be assembled, and many urban models have relied on this information and have been developed as part of the overall planning analysis.

All countries will have quite a large amount of published data that can be collected initially. For example, in Britain there is a full population census every ten years, the most recent being 1961, 1971 and 1981, and there was also a 10% sample census in 1966. Local authorities keep up to date estimates on the main variables between these census years and also carry out local surveys on particular topics. The Census of Population provides detailed data on residential population, their economic activity and housing for small areal units, but employment at place of work and the journey to work trip movements are only given for larger local authority areas. However, many local authorities obtain special census information for their area which provides even more detailed information by small area for the main variables. There are also a number of more frequent government reports that provide data. For example the Annual Census of Employment gives employment at workplace for a fine industrial grouping, but for employment exchange areas which do not correspond to local authority boundaries. The Census of Distribution provides data on shopping floorspace and retail sales, while the Family Expenditure Survey shows the level of consumer retail expenditure for different socio-economic groups. There are many other publications that can be consulted, but none of them provide information on personal incomes. Another source of data is the ongoing research studies carried out by local authorities which involve such things as traffic surveys, shopping surveys and employment surveys.

A large quantity of data can be assembled, therefore, from a number of different sources. There will nearly always be problems in using these data in that they will probably refer to several different points in time, to different spatial units, and there may be slight differences in the definition of certain variables. All that can be done, however, is to arrange the data into the best possible form and accept their limitations. This might well prove to be sufficient data for modelling purposes, but if this is not the case, then either the scope of the modelling exercise has to be reduced and the data limitations accepted, or extra data have to be collected from new survey work. These new surveys will generally be quite expensive and increase the overall duration of the project. If the extra data were in any case going to be collected as part of the overall planning analysis, then it can be used in the urban modelling exercise at no significant extra expense. On the other hand, if they are to be collected purely for use in the model, then the cost of the modelling exercise is going to be considerably increased. There comes a point when the model builder has to decide on the trade-off between accepting certain data limitations by running a slightly more aggregate model but saving time and expense, as against using a more detailed urban model which requires considerable extra data and results in a much larger and more expensive project. Since the nature of each project is different, the answer to the dilemma might well be different for every modelling exercise.

THE MATHEMATICAL PRESENTATION OF LANDUSE ACTIVITIES AND TRIP PATTERNS

To explain the modelling procedure outlined above and to introduce the mathematical notation that will be used throughout the book, consider a small study region in north-west Lancashire around Barrow-in-Furness (figure 2.3). Since it is a promontory of land with sea on three sides, the study region is a highly self-contained area with less than 4% of the journey to work interaction taking place across the northern boundary. The region is divided into three zones based on the three urban areas of Barrow-in-Furness (zone 1), Dalton-in-Furness (zone 2) and Ulverston (zone 3), although obviously any worthwhile operational model would involve very many more zones. Most of the data are adapted from the Census of Population Reports.

Zonal activities

Data on the main landuse activities of population, employment and housing are given in table 2.1 for the three zones. To represent the data in algebraic terms, let the population in zone i be denoted by P_i where i is a subscript which is indexed 1, 2 or 3, depending on the zone number. The population in Barrow, which is zone 1, will be $P_1 = 64,860$, the population in Dalton, zone 2, will be $P_2 = 11,540$ and the population in Ulverston, zone 3, will be $P_3 = 13,820$.

19

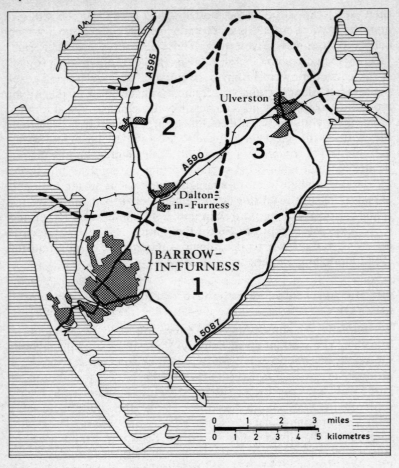

Figure 2.3   The north-west Lancashire study region

The total population in the study region will be the sum of the population in the three zones:

$$\text{total population} = P_1 + P_2 + P_3 = \sum_{i=1}^{3} P_i = 90{,}220 \quad (2.1)$$

This can be represented by the summation sign of equation (2.1) which means that i takes on the values 1, 2 and 3 and the values P_1, P_2 and P_3 are summed to give the overall total population. The number under the summation sign is the first zone number and the

Table 2.1 Zonal activity data for north-west Lancashire

	Barrow (zone 1)	Dalton (zone 2)	Ulverston (zone 3)	Study region total
Population in each zone	$64,860 = P_1$	$11,540 = P_2$	$13,820 = P_3$	90,220
Employment in each zone	$31,980 = E_1$	$2,390 = E_2$	$5,590 = E_3$	39,960
Number of houses in each zone	$22,350 = H_1$	$3,960 = H_2$	$4,770 = H_3$	31,080

summation takes place for all zones up to and including the zone number above the summation sign.

Employment and housing data can be represented in a similar way. If E_i represents the level of employment in zone i and H_i represents the number of houses in zone i, then for Barrow (which is zone 1) and therefore $i = 1$, $E_1 = 31,980$ and $H_1 = 22,350$. Similarly for Dalton (zone 2) and Ulverston (zone 3), where $i = 2$ and 3 respectively. The total employment and total number of houses in the study region can be calculated:

$$\text{total employment} = \sum_{i=1}^{3} E_i = E_1 + E_2 + E_3 = 39,960$$

$$\text{total number of houses} = \sum_{i=1}^{3} H_i = H_1 + H_2 + H_3 = 31,080 \tag{2.2}$$

The subscript used here is i but it could have been any other letter of the alphabet since it is only a general identification of an activity. It is the zone number that is assigned to the subscript i that is important because only then does it refer to the population or employment or housing in a particular zone. For example, in a residential location model in Chapter 4, H_j represents the number of houses in a zone j, where j takes on the values from 1 to the number of zones in the study region.

Trip patterns

Nearly all urban models deal with the interaction of activities between zones. Some, such as the linear models described in Chapter 6, while not having spatial interaction within the

Table 2.2 The journey to work trip matrix for north-west Lancashire

Work zone i	Residential zone j			Total employment
	Barrow (zone 1)	*Dalton (zone 2)*	*Ulverston (zone 3)*	
Barrow (zone 1)	$28{,}010 = T_{11}$	$2{,}340 = T_{12}$	$1{,}630 = T_{13}$	$31{,}980 = O_1$
Dalton (zone 2)	$270 = T_{21}$	$2{,}070 = T_{22}$	$50 = T_{23}$	$2{,}390 = O_2$
Ulverston (zone 3)	$550 = T_{31}$	$520 = T_{32}$	$4{,}520 = T_{33}$	$5{,}590 = O_3$
Total employed residents	$28{,}830 = D_1$	$4{,}930 = D_2$	$6{,}200 = D_3$	$39{,}960$

structure, have to be linked to an interaction model at a later stage in the analysis.

The journey to work trip matrix for the study region is given in table 2.2 and shows the number of employed persons' daily trip movements from work zone i to residential zone j. In this matrix let T_{ij} represent the number of persons working in zone i and travelling to live in zone j. With this double subscript, the number of persons working in Barrow (zone 1) and living in Barrow (zone 1) is $T_{11} = 28{,}010$, the number of persons working in Barrow and living in Dalton (zone 2) is $T_{12} = 2340$, and the number of persons working in Barrow and living in Ulverston (zone 3) is $T_{13} = 1630$.

Because the study region is a closed system, the sum of the employed persons travelling from Barrow to all the zones in the study region will give the total number of persons in employment in Barrow:

$$\text{total employment in Barrow} = T_{11} + T_{12} + T_{13}$$

$$= \sum_{j=1}^{3} T_{1j} = 31{,}980 = O_1 \qquad (2.3)$$

Here the first subscript refers to work zone 1 (Barrow), and the summation takes place over the second subscript, the residential zones j for $j = 1$, 2 and 3. In a trip matrix the row totals are generally represented by O_i, the total activity being distributed from the origin zones i. In this case it is the total number of employed persons in each zone, so that $O_1 = E_1$, where E_1 has been previously defined as the total employment in zone 1 (Barrow) (table 2.1). The journey from work trip movements leaving Dalton and Ulverston are represented in a similar form:

total employment
in Dalton
$$= T_{21} + T_{22} + T_{23}$$
$$= \sum_{j=1}^{3} T_{2j} = 2390 = O_2 = E_2$$

$$(2.4)$$

total employment
in Ulverston
$$= T_{31} + T_{32} + T_{33}$$
$$= \sum_{j=1}^{3} T_{3j} = 5590 = O_3 = E_3$$

The number of employed persons living in a zone can also be calculated from this trip matrix by summing a column of the matrix. The employed residents of Barrow (zone 1) come from working in Barrow (T_{11}), Dalton (T_{21}) and Ulverston (T_{31}), hence

total employed
residents in
Barrow
$$= T_{11} + T_{21} + T_{31}$$
$$= \sum_{i=1}^{3} T_{i1} = 28,830 = D_1 \qquad (2.5)$$

Here it is the second subscript, the residential zone number that remains constant at zone 1 for Barrow, while the summation takes place over all work zones i, for $i = 1, 2$ and 3. In a trip matrix the column totals are generally represented by D_j, the total activity being located at the destination zone j. This would have to be multiplied by a population to employment activity rate in order to obtain the zonal population P_i (table 2.1). The movements of employed persons to live in Dalton and Ulverston are calculated in a similar way:

total employed
residents in
Dalton
$$= T_{12} + T_{22} + T_{32}$$
$$= \sum_{i=1}^{3} T_{i2} = 4930 = D_2$$

$$(2.6)$$

total employed
residents in
Ulverston
$$= T_{13} + T_{23} + T_{33}$$
$$= \sum_{i=1}^{3} T_{i3} = 6200 = D_3$$

The overall total number of employed persons in the region can be calculated by summing the whole of the trip matrix T_{ij} or by summing the total zonal employment in each zone O_i or by summing the total zonal employed residents in each zone D_j:

$$\sum_{i=1}^{3} \sum_{j=1}^{3} T_{ij} = \sum_{i=1}^{3} O_i = \sum_{j=1}^{3} D_j = 39{,}960 = \sum_{i=1}^{3} E_i \qquad (2.7)$$

This double summation sign means that all permutations of $i = 1$ to 3 and $j = 1$ to 3 for T_{ij}, the nine trip flows in the matrix, are summed to give the overall total.

The travel distance between zones

Some measure of the distance between zones is required in order to model the interaction between activities in the region. This can take several different forms, such as the road distance, or travel time or some generalized cost. In some countries this information can be obtained from published sources. For example, the Italian Census of Population asks a question on the time taken in travelling to work and the mode of travel, and these returns can be analysed to give an average journey to work travel time between zones. In many other countries, such as Britain, this information is not available and it is therefore necessary to use detailed maps of the road network to calculate the data.

Firstly, zone centroids have to be determined and then distances measured between these points. The centroid is the centre of the urban development in each zone. In most cases this is quite easy since most zones will have a centre, as in this study region where the centroids are at the town centres of Barrow, Dalton and Ulverston. There are occasionally problems when the urban development is scattered over the zone, and this happens particularly within rural areas.

The most basic measure is the road distance between zone centroids which can be taken from a detailed road map (figure 2.3), and this information for the study region is given in table 2.3 in miles. It can be represented as d_{ij}, the distance from origin zone i to destination zone j, and is measured in any units of distance, for example miles (table 2.3) or kilometres (table 3.2). It is a symmetrical distance matrix in that the distance from zone i to zone j is the same as the distance from zone j to zone i. The distance from Barrow to Dalton, d_{12}, is 4.05 miles, and similarly

Table 2.3 The distance matrix (miles) for north-west Lancashire

	Barrow (zone 1)	Dalton (zone 2)	Ulverston (zone 3)
Barrow (zone 1)	$1.50 = d_{11}$	$4.05 = d_{12}$	$9.25 = d_{13}$
Dalton (zone 2)	$4.05 = d_{21}$	$0.50 = d_{22}$	$5.20 = d_{23}$
Ulverston (zone 3)	$9.25 = d_{31}$	$5.20 = d_{32}$	$0.70 = d_{33}$

the distance from Dalton to Barrow, d_{21}, is 4.05 miles. Only in a system of very fine zones would these distances not be equal to take account of one-way streets. The main problem in calculating the matrix is in measuring the intrazonal distances, here d_{11}, d_{22} and d_{33}. This is generally determined in a fairly subjective way by measuring what appears to be the 'most reasonable', average distance from points within the zone to the zone centroid. A more objective method is to try and represent the urban development of the zone as a circle and use two thirds of the radius as the intrazonal distance measure, although this procedure is rather difficult to apply. In this study region Barrow has a much larger urban development than the other centres and so has a larger intrazonal distance of $d_{11} = 1.5$ miles.

The travel time between zones is a better measure than the actual distance, because different travel speeds can be assumed on different classes of roads. The travel times for the study region are shown in table 2.4 where a simple division is made between urban roads and other main roads, and average speeds of 20 mph and 40 mph assumed respectively. The trip between Barrow and Dalton of 4.05 miles involves 2.25 miles on urban roads at 20 mph and 1.8 miles on other main roads at 40 mph, giving a total time of 9.45 minutes. Anything other than distance is represented in a matrix as c_{ij}, the time or cost of travel from zone i to zone j (table 2.4). For an operational model a finer division of the road network would have to be made, for example into motorways, other main roads, rural country roads, suburban roads and inner urban roads, and a decreasing set of speeds assumed.

This type of travel time data have often been used for aggregate urban models, but it must be remembered that they refer to

Table 2.4 The travel time matrix (minutes) for north-west Lancashire

	Barrow (zone 1)	Dalton (zone 2)	Ulverston (zone 3)
Barrow (zone 1)	$4.50 = c_{11}$	$9.45 = c_{12}$	$19.125 = c_{13}$
Dalton (zone 2)	$9.45 = c_{21}$	$1.50 = c_{22}$	$9.675 = c_{23}$
Ulverston (zone 3)	$19.125 = c_{31}$	$9.675 = c_{32}$	$2.10 = c_{33}$

standardized average model times between zones by private car. They could be improved by including a trip end time for parking and walking to the destination, and also by incorporating other methods of transport such as bus and train. The usual procedure has been to calculate only the times between adjacent zones and then a shortest route algorithm can be used to determine the full travel matrix. Transport models which study regions containing a large number of fine zones, deal with a far more detailed network and assign trips by different modes of travel to particular road links. An alternative measure to the travel time between zones is a generalized cost of travel, but this proves difficult to determine and has therefore only been attempted for very detailed transport work.

The average travel time for the region

For a trip interaction matrix it is useful to determine the average journey to work travel time for employed persons in the study region. This can be calculated from the trip matrix (table 2.2) and the travel time matrix (table 2.4):

$$\text{average travel time} = \frac{\text{total travel time for all workers}}{\text{total number of workers}}$$

$$= \frac{\sum_{i=1}^{3} \sum_{j=1}^{3} T_{ij} c_{ij}}{\sum_{i=1}^{3} \sum_{j=1}^{3} T_{ij}}$$

$$= \frac{(28,010)(4.5) + (2340)(9.45) + \ldots}{28,010 + 2340 + \ldots}$$

$$= 5.27 \text{ minutes} \tag{2.8}$$

The average work trip travel time for workers in the study region is 5.27 minutes which might seem rather low but it has already been pointed out that this is a standardized model time. This information is useful for testing how well the output from a model compares with a known base year situation.

One last general point about the mathematical notation is the generally accepted convention that if a summation takes place over all zones, then the limits to the subscript are not given. So for this study region of three zones

$$\sum_{i=1}^{3} E_i \text{ can be written as } \sum_{i} E_i$$

$$\sum_{i=1}^{3} \sum_{j=1}^{3} T_{ij} \text{ can be written as } \sum_{i} \sum_{j} T_{ij}$$

CALIBRATING AN URBAN MODEL

Most urban models contain parameters or coefficients within their mathematical structure which will differ when a model is applied to different parts of the world or even to different regions within a country, and so they have to be determined for each study region. A complete set of data is assembled for a base year at some past point in time not only for all the input variables, but also for the output variables of the model. The calibration process then involves finding the 'best' values of the parameters or coefficients that reproduce as closely as possible the known results for the base year.

The calibration procedure does differ with the type of urban model. The gravity or entropy maximizing models (Chapters 3, 4 and 5) contain parameters on certain variables, particularly distance, and calibration involves finding the best parameter values that reproduce both the trip pattern and the zonal activity totals. This can be performed on a trial and error basis, or preferably by using a numerical or analytical search procedure on the computer. Linear regression models (Chapter 6) use the least squares regression procedure for calibration in order to determine the coefficients in the mathematical equations. This is a very widely applied technique and so calibration is a reasonably straightforward process. Optimizing models (Chapter 7), on the other hand, are not usually calibrated since they are generally used to determine the optimum situation under certain conditions, and are not therefore trying to reproduce the actual situation, although the two can be compared.

There are certain methods that can be used at calibration to test for the goodness of fit between actual data and the estimated results from the model. For a spatial interaction model on the north-west Lancashire study region around Barrow, the best calibration test would be to find the parameter values that make the actual and the estimated average journey to work travel time as nearly equal as possible. There are also several tests that can be performed between the actual and estimated zonal activity totals resulting from a gravity model or a linear model. Table 2.5 shows the actual population totals P_i for the three zones in the north-west Lancashire study region, the estimated population totals P_i^* from the application of an urban model, together with two methods for testing the goodness of fit, the absolute deviation and the squared deviation:

$$\text{absolute deviation} = \sum_{i=1}^{3} |P_i^* - P_i| = 500$$

$$(2.9)$$

$$\text{squared deviation} = \sum_{i=1}^{3} (P_i^* - P_i)^2 = 93{,}800$$

These tests merely consider the differences between the estimated and the actual zone totals, and need to be minimized at calibration. The coefficient of determination which will be explained in Chapter 6, can also be used although it is really a measure of the strength of association between two variables with a value of $r^2 = 1.0$ representing a perfect fit. It is not a very satisfactory measure for goodness of fit, although it is very often used, the object being to maximize the value at calibration.

Calibration is not just a mechanical procedure for obtaining the best fit between model output and actual values, but it also allows the model builder to gain an understanding of the way the region functions, as well as indicating the strengths and shortcomings of the models themselves. There are almost certain to be difficulties occurring at calibration with, for example, the form of the data, the nature of the zoning system, and more particularly a poor model representation of certain zonal activity totals or trip movements. These problems have to be thoroughly investigated and, if at all possible, overcome. It is highly informative to know which zonal activity totals and trip movements do not conform to the general pattern specified by the model, and to investigate why this is happening. At the same time it is important to look at the actual

Table 2.5 Tests for goodness of fit between actual and estimated populations for north-west Lancashire

	Actual population, P_i	Estimated population, P_i^*	Deviation $(P_i^* - P_i)$	Absolute deviation, $|P_i^* - P_i|$	Squared deviation $(P_i^* - P_i)^2$
Barrow (zone 1)	64,860	64,610	−250	250	62,500
Dalton (zone 2)	11,540	11,660	+120	120	14,400
Ulverston (zone 3)	13,820	13,950	+130	130	16,900
Totals	90,220	90,220	0	500	93,800

mathematical model to see how well it represents the workings of the urban system and to investigate how is could be improved.

There is a problem in knowing just how good a performance of the models is required at calibration. In fact this part of the calibration process is carried out in a fairly subjective way with the model builder deciding on a satisfactory level of performance, all the time remembering that general mathematical models are being used to represent behavioural movements and locations, and therefore a perfect fit can never be expected. All the various tests for goodness of fit can usefully be considered, although certain tests are preferred on each of the models, and these will be explained as the models are introduced later in the book. It is also important to plot, both graphically and spatially, the differences between actual and estimated results in order to determine if any patterns are present, which again would have to be investigated. There are particular problems with the three zone regions that are used in this book because the tests are not really applicable with so few observations, although the tests are included in order to explain the procedure. The calibration process will be covered in more detail in the following chapters as the various urban models are explained and particularly in the next chapter on the retail shopping model.

PREDICTING INTO THE FUTURE WITH AN URBAN MODEL

In most cases the main purpose of a modelling exercise is to use the models predictively in order to gain an insight into and try and find answers for the questions posed at the beginning of the study. The method of prediction involves updating the variables or activities within the model that are not being forecast, and then by running the model with this information, predictions made about the future level of the other activities and their interactions. The initial predictions are generally based on the most likely future growth pattern and then the effects on the study region from a whole series of alternative planning strategies or planning policies are studied. The types of predictions performed depend on the purpose of the study, but they could include looking at the location of new residential development, new employment, and new shopping facilities, as well as new road networks, general changes in transport and accessibility, and environmental constraints on developing in certain areas.

These predictions follow two forms. Firstly, there are 'one shot' predictions which refer to one date in the future, say twenty years forward, where all the updated data and all the model output refer to the equilibrium situation at this point in time. The second and more favoured method is to perform 'recursive' predictions. This involves carrying out a series of predictive runs of the model over the forecast period, for example at five year intervals over a twenty year projection period. Output from each prediction is used as additional information in determining input data for the next prediction. This does add a dynamic element into the prediction stage, for although each five year prediction represents a static equilibrium situation of the urban system, the overall model can be regarded as quasi-dynamic. A number of operational examples of both types of prediction procedure are described later.

In using the different types of urban model predictively all the assumptions underlying their use have to be taken into account and these will be discussed as each model is explained. The main general assumption at prediction is that when the parameters and coefficients of the models are held constant at their calibration values, which is usually the case, then it is assumed that the general pattern of activity allocation and interaction which held at the base year will also hold in the future. This does give a basis for studying the likely effect of changes in the urban system although the activity patterns are obviously going to change in the future and in fact the parameters and coefficients can be altered at prediction. The results from the models must, therefore, be interpreted in an intelligent way with the problems and limitations of the models fully recognized.

The final stage in the analysis of urban problems using mathematical models is to use the predictions to help formulate future planning policies. The models provide conditional predictions that look at the consequences resulting from certain actions, and test and compare alternative policies. These predictions should be interpreted in a rather broad and general way, rather than looking for very detailed specific answers. They can suggest ways in which the urban system might respond to landuse changes in the future, help to focus on critical factors, and structure ideas concerning future policies. Throughout the book many applications are described in order to show how the results at prediction have been used in practical planning situations.

3   Retail shopping models

Many of the operational urban models that have been developed are based on the concept of the gravity model. It is referred to as the gravity model because of its analogy with the physical and conceptual ideas of Newton's law of universal gravitation in physics. Newton's gravity model was adapted and used as a spatial interaction model as early as the mid-nineteenth century, and a good description of the history of the gravity model is contained in Carrothers (1956). This original formulation and the family of urban models based on the gravity principle will be considered in the next chapter. However, to gain an understanding of the method of analysis, it is most useful to look at its application to retailing beginning with the work of William J. Reilly (1931) and tracing the development of the retail shopping gravity model from his law of retail gravitation through to the present day shopping models.

REILLY'S LAW OF RETAIL GRAVITATION

Using Newton's gravity principles, Reilly (1931) proposed two simple rules that would help to describe the flow of retail trade between towns and cities. The first rule was that the larger the city the more retail trade it would draw from towns in the surrounding region. From his empirical work he discovered that retail trade increased at about the same rate as the population of a city increased. A city with about twice the population of another city would draw about twice as much retail trade from the surrounding region. The second rule was that a city draws more trade from nearby towns than it does from more distant ones. Again from his empirical work he found that retail trade decreased approximately in inverse proportion to the square of the distance from the city.

Combining these two rules, Reilly's law states that 'A city will attract retail trade from a town in its surrounding territory, in direct proportion to the population size of the city and in inverse proportion to the square of the distance from the city'. In algebraic terms the attraction of the shopping centre of city i, R_i, with population P_i, to individuals living in a town k, distance d_{ki} from city i, will be

$$R_i = \frac{P_i}{d_{ki}^2} \qquad (3.1)$$

Reilly was very concerned with the relative attractiveness of two shopping centres to those people living between the centres. This can be calculated by applying the above formula (equation (3.1)) to find the attraction of each of the shopping centres and then the relative magnitude of these two values will give the proportion of the retail trade attracted to each centre from the population living between the two centres. Consider city i with population P_i and city j with population P_j. The population living in a town k, distance d_{ki} from city i and d_{kj} from city j, according to Reilly's law, would be attracted to the two cities in the ratio $R_i : R_j$ where

$$R_i = \frac{P_i}{d_{ki}^2} \text{ and } R_j = \frac{P_j}{d_{kj}^2} \qquad (3.2)$$

To show how this might be applied, consider an area of Norfolk in East Anglia (figure 3.1) using 1971 Population Census data. Let Norwich with a population of 122,083 be city i and Great Yarmouth with a population of 50,236 be city j. Norwich and Great Yarmouth are 20 miles apart on the A47 road, and the village of Acle with a population of 1584 is 9 miles from Great Yarmouth and 11 miles from Norwich. Reilly's law can be used to calculate the relative attractiveness of the two shopping centres to the people living in Acle (village k):

attraction of Norwich, $R_i = \dfrac{P_i}{d_{ki}^2} = \dfrac{122{,}083}{11^2} = 1008.95$

$$(3.3)$$

attraction of Great Yarmouth, $R_j = \dfrac{P_j}{d_{kj}^2} = \dfrac{50{,}236}{9^2} = 620.20$

33

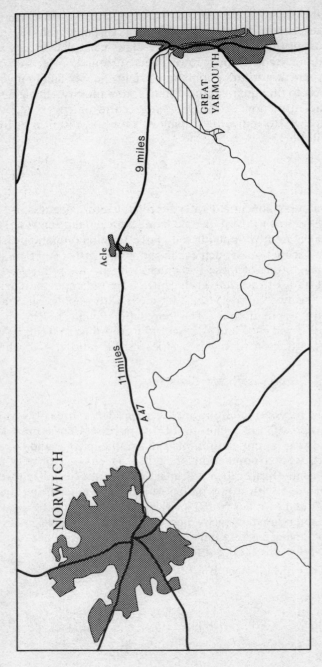

Figure 3.1 The Norfolk study region

Retail sales from Acle will therefore be attracted to Norwich and Great Yarmouth in the ratios 1008.95 to 620.20. This can be expressed more meaningfully as a percentage of retail sales attracted to each of the centres:

$$\text{to Norwich } \frac{1008.95}{1008.95 + 620.20} \times 100 = 61.9\%$$

$$\text{to Great Yarmouth } \frac{620.20}{1008.95 + 620.20} \times 100 = 38.1\%$$

(3.4)

Consumer expenditure from Acle will be attracted to Norwich and Great Yarmouth in the ratio 61.9% to 38.1%.

This process can be extended to look at the actual flow of consumer expenditure. If it is assumed that the population of Acle spends an average of £100 per person per year on goods in Norwich and Great Yarmouth, then the total annual expenditure can be calculated:

$$\text{population} \times \text{expenditure per head} = 1584 \times 100 = £158,400$$

According to Reilly's law, this total expenditure will be divided in the ratio 61.9% to 38.1% between Norwich and Great Yarmouth. Therefore, the consumer expenditure going to the two centres will be

$$\text{to Norwich} \quad £158,400 \times 0.619 = £98,050$$

$$\text{to Great Yarmouth} \quad £158,400 \times 0.381 = £60,350$$

(3.5)

Reilly, however, did not look at the actual flow of retail sales between areas. He was more concerned with the relative attraction of two retail centres, and more particularly the position of the breaking point between two cities and defining a city's retail trade hinterland.

The breaking point between two centres

The breaking point between two cities is defined as a point to which one city exercises the dominating retail trade influence, and beyond which the other city dominates. It is the equilibrium point between city i and city j where the attraction of city i is equal to the attraction of city j. In terms of equation (3.2), this is where $R_i = R_j$, such that when equations (3.4) are calculated, 50% of the retail trade will be attracted to city i and 50% to city j.

In mathematical terms it is a quite straightforward process to calculate the position of the breaking point k from equation (3.2).

It is where $R_i = R_j$ and therefore:

$$\frac{P_i}{d_{ki}^2} = \frac{P_j}{d_{kj}^2} \qquad (3.6)$$

Let the distance between city i and city j be d_{ij}, and therefore $d_{ki} = d_{ij} - d_{kj}$. By substituting for d_{ki} in equation (3.6) and then manipulating the equation, the distance from city j to the breakpoint k, the distance d_{kj}, can be calculated as follows:

$$d_{kj} = \frac{d_{ij}}{1 + \sqrt{(P_i/P_j)}} \qquad (3.7)$$

This equation can be applied to the previous example of Norfolk (figure 3.1), where Norwich is city i and Great Yarmouth is city j. In this case

$$d_{kj} = \frac{20}{1 + \sqrt{(122{,}083/50{,}236)}}$$

$$= \frac{20}{1 + 1.559} = \frac{20}{2.559} = 7.82 \text{ miles}$$

The position of the breaking point between Norwich and Great Yarmouth is 7.82 miles from Great Yarmouth and therefore 12.18 miles from Norwich. This can be seen from figure 3.2 which shows the proportion of retail sales attracted to each centre from the residents living between the two centres who are going to spend their money in either Norwich or Great Yarmouth. The graph shows the position of the breaking point, where 50% of the retail expenditure is attracted to each centre, and hence the areas dominated by the two centres. This indicates that Norwich is the dominant centre for people living up to 12.18 miles from Norwich while Great Yarmouth is the dominant centre for people living beyond that distance. Within the area dominated by Norwich, residents will still spend some of their money in Great Yarmouth, but this will be less than 50% of their expenditure. Similarly, in the area dominated by Great Yarmouth, residents will spend less than 50% of their expenditure in Norwich. Also shown in figure 3.2 is the position of the village of Acle, which is clearly within the area dominated by Norwich, although, as previously calculated (equation (3.4)), 38.1% of its expenditure will be attracted to Great Yarmouth. This type of analysis is dealing with just the retail expenditure leaving an intermediary town or village that is to be spent in either of the two shopping centres, in this case Norwich and Great Yarmouth. Reilly's law can be used to determine the

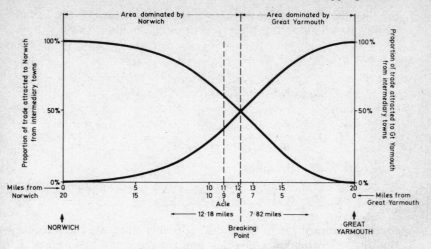

Figure 3.2   Reilly's law applied to the Norfolk region

percentage of this expenditure attracted to each shopping centre, and the breaking point between the two centres which shows the retail trade area dominated by each of the centres.

Reilly carried out extensive empirical work to demonstrate that the 'law' actually worked. He studied the breaking point between large cities all over the USA and in each case the field study result was very close to that obtained by applying the law of retail gravitation. These applications, however, were for a particular situation, dealing with only the largest American cities, generally over 100 miles apart.

Shopping centre hinterlands

The method of finding the breaking point between two centres can be extended to find the breaking point along different routes between the two centres. Consider an example on the England-Wales border, the relative retail attraction of Chester and Wrexham to the population living between the two centres. Figure 3.3 shows three routes between Chester and Wrexham and by finding the breaking point on each route, a hinterland boundary can be drawn between the two centres. If Chester is town i with population $P_i = 62,911$ and Wrexham is town j with population $P_j = 39,052$, and the distance between the two centres, d_{ij}, is 11 miles for route 1, 14 miles for route 2 and 15 miles for route 3, then d_{kj}, the distance from Wrexham (town j) to the breaking point k, can be calculated along the three routes using equation (3.7):

route 1 $d_{ij} = 11$ miles

$$d_{kj} = \frac{11}{1 + \sqrt{(62{,}911/39{,}052)}} = \frac{11}{2.27} = 4.85 \text{ miles}$$

route 2 $d_{ij} = 14$ miles

$$d_{kj} = \frac{14}{1 + \sqrt{(62{,}911/39{,}052)}} = \frac{14}{2.27} = 6.17 \text{ miles}$$

route 3 $d_{ij} = 15$ miles

$$d_{kj} = \frac{15}{1 + \sqrt{(62{,}911/39{,}052)}} = \frac{15}{2.27} = 6.61 \text{ miles}$$

Plotting the position of the breaking points along the three routes (figure 3.3) provides a dividing line for the retail hinterlands of Wrexham and Chester. Other routes could be considered in order to extend this hinterland boundary.

If this analysis is extended and these calculations performed between a number of centres in a region, then retail hinterlands can be drawn showing the area over which a centre has a dominant retailing influence. As previously explained, some retail sales from a centre's hinterland will be attracted to other centres, but this will be less than 50% of retail purchases by hinterland residents.

Reilly looked at the retail trade hinterland for a city, but not for a group of centres in a region. However, this method was used quite extensively, particularly in the USA in the 1950s and early 1960s to look at trade areas within a city. Probably the most thorough application of this method of analysis was undertaken by Davies, Jackson and Robinson (1964) at the University of Manchester in a study of shopping centres in north-west England. The input variables were modified, with an average retail sales for different grades of centre replacing population, and travel times between centres replacing distances. A three grade hierarchy of centres was constructed with the very large city centres of Manchester and Liverpool grade I, the twenty-one large town centres grade II, and the twenty-four smaller town centres which contained no specialized shops or department stores grade III. This division can reflect the different shopping patterns that occur for the type of goods sold in the different grade of centre, with people making shorter trips to more local centres for convenience goods and longer trips to larger centres for durable goods. Using

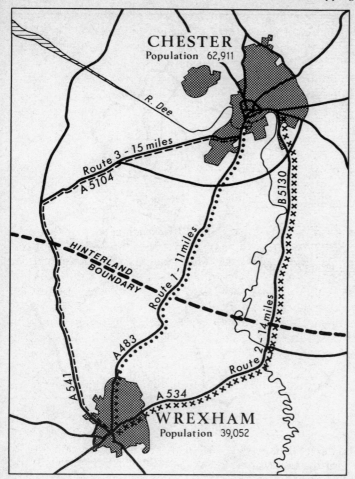

Figure 3.3 The hinterland boundary between Chester and Wrexham

1961 information, hinterlands were constructed for these different grades of centre and figure 3.4 shows the shopping hinterlands for the grade II retail trade. In the south-west of the region can be seen the hinterland boundary between Chester and Wrexham previously calculated. This method of retail analysis then assumes that as an approximation, all the retail expenditure from the population within each hinterland is spent in the hinterland centre. Total annual retail sales for each centre is calculated by multiplying the population of the hinterland by an average annual

39

Figure 3.4   Shopping centre hinterlands for north-west England

expenditure per head. These results were compared to the actual
retail sales in each centre for 1961, to gain an understanding of the
hierarchical and spatial structure of retail sales in the region. The
main purpose of the study was to evaluate the effect of a proposed
new out-of-town shopping centre at Haydock, which is midway
between Manchester and Liverpool. Input information was
updated to 1971 and a new system of retail hinterlands constructed
in a similar way, firstly without a new centre at Haydock, and then

secondly with a new centre at Haydock. A comparison of these two situations suggested the kind of impact that the new centre might have on the region. An alternative retail modelling analysis of this proposal will be described in more detail later in this chapter.

Limitations to Reilly's work

There are several limitations to the formulation of the retail gravity model developed so far.

(1) Reilly's law was originally used to compare the attractiveness of two centres to the population living in between them. In reality people will have a choice of several competing centres and the retail analysis should be comparing the attractiveness of all these competing centres. In the example of the Norfolk region the residents of Acle can do their shopping in a number of centres including Acle itself, Norwich, Great Yarmouth, Lowestoft, other smaller centres nearby and a number of other larger centres further away. However, it will be shown in the next section that Reilly's ideas can be extended to analyse a full choice of shopping centres to the population living within a region.

(2) The calculation of breaking points between centres in order to delimit retail trade hinterlands for shopping centres, conveys the idea of a fixed trading area. Also in determining the retail trade sales at each centre, the population of each hinterland is assumed to spend all its expenditure in its own shopping centre. In fact the true retail pattern of a region consists of a set of shopping centres competing with each other for retail trade and with overlapping retail sales and overlapping shopping trip patterns. These patterns will vary for different types of retail goods, with consumer goods having a shorter and more local pattern than durable goods.

(3) The distance decay function used in this earlier work on retail shopping patterns was the inverse of the squared distance. Reilly's empirical evidence for using a parameter of 2 was derived from a study of the breaking point between large American cities, mostly over 100 miles apart. However, further empirical work has shown that for other situations this parameter can vary between about 1.5 and 3.0. The actual parameter value for a study region will depend upon a number of factors. Firstly, the type of retail trade; the consumer goods trade produces a higher parameter than the durable goods trade, because of its shorter trip pattern.

Secondly, the type of study area; with different parameters being derived for the shopping pattern within an urban area than from a regional shopping pattern studying trips between urban shopping centres. Thirdly, the country in which the retail analysis is being conducted, when for example Britain will reveal different shopping characteristics from North America and hence a different parameter. Fourthly, car ownership levels within a country will affect shopping mobility and therefore alter the parameter.

(4) There is very little theory or behavioural content underlying the ideas of the gravity model. Reilly considered the gravity model to be a 'law' rather than a theory; a law summarizing existing conditions for one aspect of retail trade based on empirical evidence. It has been used therefore as a useful tool to determine trade flows rather than looking at shopping behaviour.

In addition to these conceptual limitations there are also a number of operational problems, which have already been covered in the last chapter, or will be dealt with as small worked examples are explained and applied operational models described.

A PROBABILISTIC APPROACH TO THE GRAVITY MODEL

The major development of the retail gravity model came with the work of Casey (1955) and was expanded by Huff (1963) which overcame some of the limitations outlined above. Using Reilly's ideas, a probabilistic approach was proposed for using the gravity model as a distribution model, with attention focused on the consumers and how they are attracted to shopping centres in an area. Obviously there is a whole range of factors influencing shopping behaviour and these factors will vary by consumer. However, there are just two factors considered within a gravity model, the attractiveness of a shopping centre and the travel distance to a shopping centre.

Firstly, the attractiveness of a shopping centre; showing the quality, quantity and variety of shops will draw people into a shopping centre. A good index of attraction, and one that has often been used, is the total retail floorspace, F_j, in each centre. This information is relatively easy to obtain, but there is no reason why other factors should not be incorporated into this index, such as the amount of car parking space or the environmental quality of the shopping centre; the larger the retail floorspace in a shopping centre, the more people will be attracted to that centre. The index of attraction is generally assumed to be linearly related to

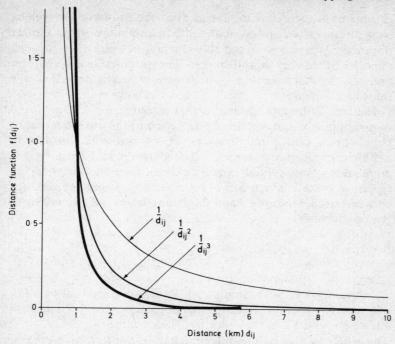

Figure 3.5   The effect of changing the parameter of the distance function

floorspace, with a shopping centre having twice as much retail floorspace as another centre being twice as attractive.

Secondly, the distance a consumer has to travel to a shopping centre, d_{ij}, will considerably influence the number of shoppers drawn to the centre; the shorter the distance the more people will be attracted to the centre. Both the effort and expense of travelling means that there is a definite distance decay function that is certainly not linear, but can be considered as the inverse of the distance raised to a power γ. The value of γ in the distance function $1/d_{ij}^{\gamma}$ can be found at calibration. Whereas Reilly assumed $\gamma = 2$, here γ is allowed to vary to fit the data. Ignoring the differences in the attractiveness of shopping centres, and considering just the effect of travel distance on shopping patterns, then figure 3.5 demonstrates the changes in the shopping pattern of the region resulting from varying the value of γ. The area under the curve represents the relative proportion of people travelling various distances. With a parameter $\gamma = 1$ and a distance function $1/d$, then a large number of people travel long distances. As the parameter is increased to $\gamma = 2$, then the proportion travelling long distances is reduced, and consequently more travel shorter distances. When $\gamma = 3$ and the function is $1/d_{ij}^{3}$, then the vast majority travel only short distances. The general rule is, therefore, that as the parameter γ gets larger, shopping trips become shorter.

The overall hypothesis asserts that consumers will be attracted to a shopping centre in direct proportion to the attractiveness of the shopping centre and in inverse proportion to the distance to the shopping centre raised to some parameter. Therefore, the population of residential zone i will be attracted to the shopping centre of zone j which has a floorspace F_j, where the distance between residential zone i and shopping centre j is d_{ij}, according to the relationship

$$\text{attractiveness} = \frac{F_j}{d_{ij}^{\gamma}} \tag{3.8}$$

This formula is very similar to Reilly's original ideas. The differences are that Reilly used population as the index of attraction, and a fixed distance parameter value of $\gamma = 2$.

In order to gain a full understanding of the following calculations, an area of Gloucestershire will be used as an example. In operating a simple retail distribution model, the region needs to be considered as a closed system, with all residents spending their retail expenditure within the region. The regional boundary is defined so that the shopping trips across the boundary are minimized. The region then has to be divided into a number of zones and in this part of Gloucestershire, the towns of Gloucester, Cheltenham and Tewkesbury, together with their surrounding areas, will be considered as a three zone region (figure 3.6). This is done purely to make the explanation as realistic as possible, because obviously a division into many more zones would generally be required. Data have been collected for 1971, floorspace (table 3.1) from the Census of Distribution Report, and distances between zones (table 3.2) calculated from the ordnance survey map.

Using this information, and because the model deals with a closed region the residents of Gloucester (zone 1) have just three opportunities to spend their retail expenditure. These residents are attracted to the three centres of Gloucester (zone 1),

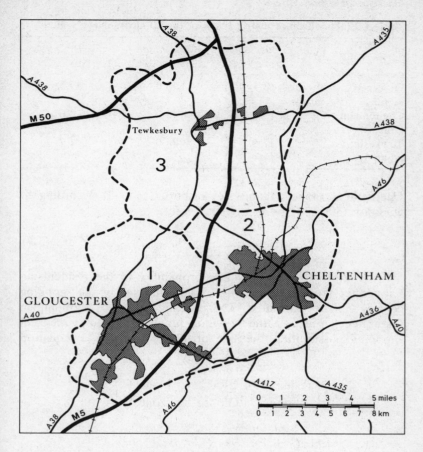

Figure 3.6   The Gloucestershire study region

Table 3.1   Retail floorspace for shopping
centres in the Gloucestershire region

Shopping centre	Retail floorspace (m^2)
Gloucester (zone 1)	82,000
Cheltenham (zone 2)	86,500
Tewkesbury (zone 3)	7,500

Table 3.2 The distance matrix (km) for the Gloucestershire region

	Gloucester (zone 1)	Cheltenham (zone 2)	Tewkesbury (zone 3)
Gloucester (zone 1)	3.4	13.0	17.5
Cheltenham (zone 2)	13.0	3.0	14.0
Tewkesbury (zone 3)	17.5	14.0	1.7

Cheltenham (zone 2) and Tewkesbury (zone 3) according to equation (3.8):

$$\frac{F_1}{d_{11}^{\gamma}} : \frac{F_2}{d_{12}^{\gamma}} : \frac{F_3}{d_{13}^{\gamma}} \tag{3.9}$$

From these relationships, the probability of the residents in Gloucester (zone 1) travelling to shop in each of the shopping centres can be calculated. The probability, Pr, of shopping in Gloucester (zone 1) is the individual function divided by the total shopping possibilities, the sum of all the functions in equation (3.9):

$$\Pr \begin{bmatrix} \text{residents of Gloucester (zone 1)} \\ \text{shopping in Gloucester (zone 1)} \end{bmatrix}$$

$$= \frac{F_1/d_{11}^{\gamma}}{F_1/d_{11}^{\gamma} + F_2/d_{12}^{\gamma} + F_3/d_{13}^{\gamma}} \tag{3.10}$$

Similarly the probabilities of shopping in Cheltenham (zone 2) and Tewkesbury (zone 3) can be calculated:

$$\Pr \begin{bmatrix} \text{residents of Gloucester (zone 1)} \\ \text{shopping in Cheltenham (zone 2)} \end{bmatrix}$$

$$= \frac{F_2/d_{12}^{\gamma}}{F_1/d_{11}^{\gamma} + F_2/d_{12}^{\gamma} + F_3/d_{13}^{\gamma}} \tag{3.11}$$

$$\Pr \begin{bmatrix} \text{residents of Gloucester (zone 1)} \\ \text{shopping in Tewkesbury (zone 3)} \end{bmatrix}$$

$$= \frac{F_3/d_{13}^{\gamma}}{F_1/d_{11}^{\gamma} + F_2/d_{12}^{\gamma} + F_3/d_{13}^{\gamma}} \tag{3.12}$$

Table 3.3 The calculation of the probabilities of residents in Gloucester (zone 1) shopping in each of the shopping centres in the Gloucestershire region

For residential zone i	Shopping centre zone j			
Gloucester (zone 1)	Gloucester (zone 1)	Cheltenham (zone 2)	Tewkesbury (zone 3)	Sum-mation
Function				
$\dfrac{F_j}{d_{ij}^2}$	$\dfrac{82{,}000}{(3.4)^2} = 7093.4$	$\dfrac{86{,}500}{(13)^2} = 511.8$	$\dfrac{7500}{17.5} = 24.5$	7629.7
Probability function				
$\dfrac{F_j/d_{ij}^2}{\sum_j F_j/d_{ij}^2}$	$\dfrac{7093.4}{7629.7} = 0.9297$	$\dfrac{511.8}{7629.7} = 0.0671$	$\dfrac{24.5}{7629.7} = 0.0032$	1.0

Since these equations represent the total shopping possibilities for the residents of Gloucester, the sum of the three probabilities will equal 1.0.

In a retail shopping model, therefore, the probability that people from a residential zone will go to a particular shopping centre, will be the overall attractiveness function for that shopping centre compared with the overall attractiveness functions of all the shopping centres in the region, and this calculation can be written in a general form:

$$\Pr \left[\begin{array}{l} \text{a resident of zone } i \\ \text{shopping in zone } j \end{array} \right] = \frac{F_j/d_{ij}^\gamma}{\sum_j F_j/d_{ij}^\gamma} \qquad (3.13)$$

This procedure is similar to that set out by Reilly (equations (3.3) and (3.4)), except that Reilly only considered two centres, and did not deal with a closed region containing all the shopping oportunities. This method of analysis is therefore just an extension of Reilly's original ideas.

Returning to the actual data, table 3.3 shows the calculations required to find the above probabilities. An initial estimate $\gamma = 2$ will be used in these calculations, and then possibly revised in the light of the results. In exactly the same way, the probabilities of the residents in Cheltenham (zone 2) and the residents in Tewkesbury (zone 3), shopping in the three zones can be calculated. The full probability matrix for the Gloucestershire region is given in table 3.4 and shows the probability of the residents of each zone shopping in each of the shopping centres.

Table 3.4 The shopping probability matrix for the Gloucestershire region

Residential zone i	Shopping zone j		
	Gloucester (zone 1)	Cheltenham (zone 2)	Tewkesbury (zone 3)
Gloucester (zone 1)	0.9297	0.0671	0.0032
Cheltenham (zone 2)	0.0479	0.9483	0.0038
Tewkesbury (zone 3)	0.0810	0.1336	0.7854

Now, if these probabilities on each row of the matrix are multiplied by the retail expenditure generated by the population of each residential zone i, C_i, this will give a new matrix S_{ij} showing the flow of retail expenditure from each residential zone i to each shopping centre j:

$$S_{ij} = C_i \frac{F_j/d_{ij}^\gamma}{\sum_j F_j/d_{ij}^\gamma} \tag{3.14}$$

The consumer retail expenditure from zone 1, C_1, will be divided amongst the shopping centres in the proportions outlined in equations (3.10), (3.11) and (3.12) and similarly for other residential zones.

For the Gloucestershire region, further data are required, again for 1971 (table 3.5). The total population in each zone can be

Table 3.5 Retail sales and consumer expenditure for the zones in the Gloucestershire region

	Population	Retail Sales £000s	Population x average retail expenditure per head	Total consumer retail expenditure (£000s)
Gloucester (zone 1)	113,163	39,219	113,163 × 355 =	40,173
Cheltenham (zone 2)	104,652	40,362	104,652 × 355 =	37,152
Tewkesbury (zone 3)	16,373	3,556	16,373 × 355 =	5,812
Totals	234,188	83,137		83,137

Table 3.6 The distribution of consumer expenditure for the residents of Gloucester (zone 1) to the shopping centres in the Gloucestershire region

Retail expenditure from Gloucester (zone 1)	Shopping zone			Total retail Expenditure (£000s)
	Gloucester (zone 1)	Cheltenham (zone 2)	Tewkesbury (zone 3)	
Probability × retail expenditure	0.9297 × 40,173	0.0671 × 40,173	0.0032 × 40,173	
Calculated value (£000)	37,349	2,696	128	40,173

obtained from the Population Census, and the total retail sales at each shopping centre can be obtained from the Census of Distribution. By assuming an average annual consumer retail expenditure per head of population in 1971 of £355, the total consumer expenditure for each zone can be calculated by multiplying the total zonal population by the average retail expenditure per head. From these data it can be seen that Cheltenham (zone 2) is the largest shopping centre, but has a lower resident population than Gloucester (zone 1). Cheltenham must therefore attract a higher proportion of the consumer expenditure from other zones in the region than its loss to other centres from its own resident population. Tewkesbury is a much smaller shopping centre, and the resident population spends a large proportion of its retail expenditure in other zones.

The residents of Gloucester (zone 1) will distribute their retail expenditure of £40,173,000 (table 3.6) in the proportions previously calculated in table 3.3. Similar calculations are performed to distribute the consumer retail expenditures from Cheltenham (zone 2) and Tewkesbury (zone 3), in the proportions set out in table 3.4. The results are summarized in table 3.7 to provide a matrix showing the distribution of retail expenditure from the zones of residence i to the shopping centres j (S_{ij} of equation (3.14)).

Also included in table 3.7 is the total annual retail sales for each shopping centre, estimated by this retail gravity model. This is calculated by summing the column of the matrix for each shopping centre. For example, the retail sales attracted to Gloucester (zone 1) are obtained from the residents of Gloucester (zone 1) £37,349,000, Cheltenham (zone 2) £1,780,000 and Tewkesbury

Table 3.7 The distribution of consumer expenditure from residential zones to shopping centres ($\gamma = 2.0$) in the Gloucestershire region

Residential zone i	Shopping zone j			Total retail expenditure (£000)
	Gloucester (zone 1)	Cheltenham (zone 2)	Tewkesbury (zone 3)	
Gloucester (zone 1)	37,349	2,696	128	40,173
Cheltenham (zone 2)	1,780	35,231	141	37,152
Tewkesbury (zone 3)	471	776	4,565	5,812
Total retail sales (£000)	39,600	38,703	4,834	83,137

(zone 3) £471,000, which gives a total of £39,600,000. The total retail sales for Cheltenham (zone 2) and Tewkesbury (zone 3) are calculated in a similar way. The total retail sales S_j for shopping centre j will be

$$S_j = \sum_i C_i \frac{F_j/d_{ij}^{\gamma}}{\sum_j F_j/d_{ij}^{\gamma}} \qquad (3.15)$$

This is the final output from a retail distribution gravity model, the total sales in each shopping centre and a matrix showing the flow of consumer expenditure from each residential zone to every shopping centre.

To make these equations less cumbersome, it is useful to use the mathematical definition $d_{ij}^{-\gamma}$

$$\frac{1}{d_{ij}^{\gamma}} = d_{ij}^{-\gamma} \qquad (3.16)$$

Equations (3.14) and (3.15) can be written more conveniently as

$$S_{ij} = C_i \frac{F_j d_{ij}^{-\gamma}}{\sum_j F_j \, d_{ij}^{-\gamma}} \qquad (3.17)$$

and

$$S_j = \sum_i C_i \frac{F_j d_{ij}^{-\gamma}}{\sum_j F_j d_{ij}^{-\gamma}} \qquad (3.18)$$

These equations for the retail expenditure flows (equation (3.17)) and for the shopping centre sales totals (equation (3.18)), represent the retail distribution gravity model. The variables in the equations refer specifically to the retail shopping model. However, this model is a particular application of a singly constrained spatial interaction gravity model which can also be applied to residential location, service location and transportation. It is more usually written in a general form which will be set out at the beginning of the next chapter along with a discussion of the different ways of measuring the variables in a retail shopping model.

THE CALIBRATION OF A RETAIL SHOPPING MODEL

It has already been explained using figure 3.5 that the distribution of shopping trips will vary with the parameter γ on the distance function; the lower the value of γ the more interaction there will be between residential zones and shopping centres. The procedure for varying the value of γ in order to find the best fit between the model output and the actual base year situation is called calibration. The first run of the model on the Gloucestershire region used a parameter value of $\gamma = 2$. These results can now be compared to the actual situation in 1971 in order to observe how close a fit has been obtained, and also to see if an improved value of γ could be found which would give an even closer result.

Looking firstly at zone totals, and taking the actual retail sales from table 3.5 and the estimated retail sales from table 3.7, the results are compared in table 3.8, and mapped in figure 3.7. The

Table 3.8 A comparison of the actual and estimated retail sales ($\gamma = 2.0$) for the shopping centres in the Gloucestershire region

Shopping centre	Total retail sales (£000)			
	Model estimate	*Actual sales*	*Absolute error (estimate − actual)*	*Error as % of actual*
Gloucester (zone 1)	39,600	39,219	+ 381	1.0%
Cheltenham (zone 2)	38,703	40,362	−1659	4.1%
Tewkesbury (zone 3)	4,834	3,556	+1278	35.9%
Totals	83,137	83,137	0	

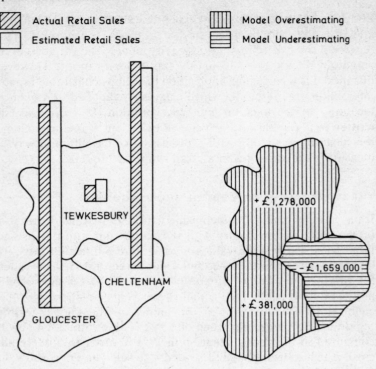

Figure 3.7   A comparison of the actual and estimated retail sales (γ = 2.0)

results are reasonably close, as shown in the bar graph of figure 3.7, although there do appear to be systematic errors that could be improved upon. Cheltenham (zone 2) is just not attracting sufficient retail sales from the other two zones and is over £1½ million below its actual 1971 retail sales. Tewkesbury (zone 3) on the other hand is retaining far too much expenditure from its own residents for its total retail sales is more than £1¼ million above its actual 1971 figure of £3½ million. The estimated retail sales for Gloucester (zone 1) is very close. It can also be seen from table 3.8 how the percentage error can be very large for zones such as Tewkesbury with small zone totals. The error of £1,659,000 for Cheltenham represents 4% of its actual sales while a smaller absolute error of £1,278,000 for Tewkesbury represents 36% of its actual sales.

At calibration it is also essential to study the distribution matrix

Table 3.9 Retail expenditure flows as a percentage of residential zone totals ($\gamma = 2.0$)

Residential zone	Shopping zone			Totals
	Gloucester (zone 1)	Cheltenham (zone 2)	Tewkesbury (zone 3)	
Gloucester (zone 1)	93.0	6.7	0.3	100
Cheltenham (zone 2)	4.8	94.8	0.4	100
Tewkesbury (zone 3)	8.1	13.4	78.5	100

S_{ij} showing the flow of money from the residential zones to the shopping centres (Openshaw 1973), in a similar way to the analysis of zone totals above. The problem can arise where the shopping centre retail sales totals are very close to the actual situation, but with a distribution matrix that is completely incorrect. The money flow matrix estimated by the model should be compared with the actual distribution which has been derived from a shopping survey of the region. However, this information is not always available, for although most local authorities conduct shopping surveys, the information might not be in a comparable form to the model output, or the survey might not have been for the whole study region. In this case, either the information has to be collected from a new shopping survey, or the money flow matrix is analysed to see whether it appears 'reasonable', which is a rather unsatisfactory situation. The model builder generally has the option of either making do with available information accepting its limitations, or carrying out a large shopping survey.

The estimated money flow matrix for the Gloucestershire region is shown in table 3.7 and mapped in figure 3.8. It is also useful to look at the percentage of consumer expenditure from each zone travelling to the shopping centres (table 3.9), and alternatively the percentage of retail sales of each shopping centre attracted from the residential zones (table 3.10). It would appear from this information that there is too little interaction between the residential zones and the shopping centres, with too much retail sales being spent by the residents of each zone in their own shopping centre. In particular, Cheltenham (zone 2) should be

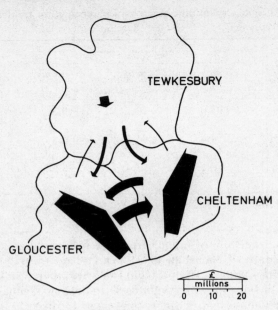

Figure 3.8   Retail expenditure flows ($\gamma = 2.0$)

attracting far more retail sales from the other zones, and Tewkesbury (zone 3) needs to disperse far more of its consumer expenditure to other shopping centres. It also seems possible that the very close fit of retail sales for Gloucester (zone 1) has been achieved from an incorrect distribution matrix of consumer expenditure.

Table 3.10   Retail expenditure flows as a percentage of shopping centre sales totals ($\gamma = 2.0$)

| Residential zone | *Shopping zone* | | |
	Gloucester (zone 1)	Cheltenham (zone 2)	Tewkesbury (zone 3)
Gloucester (zone 1)	94.3	7.0	2.7
Cheltenham (zone 2)	4.5	91.0	2.9
Tewkesbury (zone 3)	1.2	2.0	94.4
Totals	100	100	100

Table 3.11 The distribution of consumer expenditure from residential zones to shopping centres ($\gamma = 1.5$) for the Gloucestershire region

Residential zone i	Shopping zone j			Total retail expenditure (£000)
	Gloucester (zone 1)	Cheltenham (zone 2)	Tewkesbury (zone 3)	
Gloucester (zone 1)	34,966	4,933	274	40,173
Cheltenham (zone 2)	3,506	33,359	287	37,152
Tewkesbury (zone 3)	1,058	1,559	3,195	5,812
Total retail sales (£000)	39,530	39,851	3,756	83,137

From this analysis, it would seem that there is insufficient interaction between residential zones and shopping centres. It was shown in figure 3.5 that the lower the parameter value γ on the distance function the further people will travel to do their shopping. In the Gloucestershire region it would seem reasonable to lower the parameter value from $\gamma = 2.0$ to $\gamma = 1.5$, which will generate more interaction within the model, and should provide a closer fit to the actual situation. The retail gravity model can now be recalculated using a distance parameter of $\gamma = 1.5$. The new distribution of consumer expenditure from the residential zones to the shopping centres is given in table 3.11 together with the retail sales in each shopping centre. This output can be compared with the actual situation and table 3.12 shows the results for the three shopping centres which are also presented graphically in figure 3.9. It is very clear that the errors have been considerably reduced. Cheltenham is still not attracting sufficiently high retail sales, and consequently Gloucester and Tewkesbury are attracting too much retail sales, but on this run of the model, the shopping centres are in the correct order of magnitude with Cheltenham being shown as a slightly larger centre than Gloucester. The percentage errors have also been considerably reduced, particularly the small shopping centre of Tewkesbury which now has an error of less than 6%. The money flow matrix also shows considerable improvement. Tables 3.13 and 3.14 and figure 3.10 represent these results in a similar form as before. The flows between residential zones and other shopping centres have been roughly doubled, and

Table 3.12 A comparison of the actual and estimated retail sales ($\gamma =$ 1.5) for shopping centres in the Gloucestershire region

Shopping centre	Total retail sales (£000)			
	Model estimate	Actual sales	Absolute error (estimate−actual)	error as % of actual
Gloucester (zone 1)	39,530	39,219	+311	0.8
Cheltenham (zone 2)	39,851	40,362	−511	1.3
Tewkesbury (zone 3)	3,756	3,556	+200	5.6
Totals	88,137	83,137	0	

Table 3.13 Retail expenditure flows as a percentage of residential zone totals ($\gamma = 1.5$)

Residential zone	Shopping zone			
	Gloucester (zone 1)	Cheltenham (zone 2)	Tewkesbury (zone 3)	Totals
Gloucester (zone 1)	87.0	12.3	0.7	100
Cheltenham (zone 2)	9.4	89.8	0.8	100
Tewkesbury (zone 3)	18.2	26.8	55.0	100

Table 3.14 Retail expenditure flows as a percentage of shopping centre sales totals ($\gamma = 1.5$)

Residential zone	Shopping zone		
	Gloucester (zone 1)	Cheltenham (zone 2)	Tewkesbury (zone 3)
Gloucester (zone 1)	88.4	12.4	7.3
Cheltenham (zone 2)	8.9	83.7	7.6
Tewkesbury (zone 3)	2.7	3.9	85.1
Totals	100	100	100

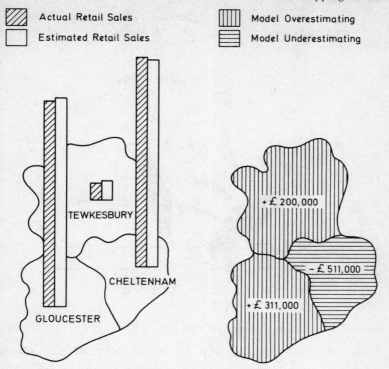

Actual Retail Sales

Estimated Retail Sales

Model Overestimating

Model Underestimating

TEWKESBURY

CHELTENHAM

GLOUCESTER

+ £ 200,000

- £ 511,000

+ £ 311,000

Figure 3.9 A comparison of the actual and estimated retail sales (γ = 1.5)

this result seems much closer to the true situation. Overall, therefore, by reducing the parameter value from γ = 2.0 to γ = 1.5, the model gives a much more realistic simulation of the actual situation.

This retail gravity model of Gloucestershire will not be taken any further, but the model could be calculated several more times until the best value of γ is obtained which gives the closest fit between the actual situation and the output from the model, both for zone totals and for the distribution matrix. It might well be that the parameter value γ should be even lower than γ = 1.5 but before proceeding any further, some information would be required on shopping trips and money flows in the region. A very thorough analysis should therefore be performed at calibration to detect errors in the data, difficulties with certain zones or systematic variations in the differences between actual and

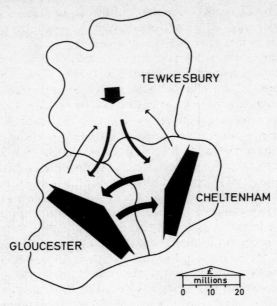

Figure 3.10   Retail expenditure flows ($\gamma = 1.5$)

estimated zone totals and trip movements. Considerable effort should be made to minimize these problems, and this process will provide a further understanding of the nature of shopping in the region. However, it must be recognized that a perfect fit should not be expected from a model of this form. It is a general aggregate model which assumes that people are attracted to a shopping centre in direct proportion to the size of the centre and in inverse proportion to the distance from the shopping centre, raised to some power, and is being used to distribute retail sales over a whole region. Although these might appear to be the most important factors, there are obviously a large number of other factors influencing shopping behaviour which will prevent shopping patterns conforming perfectly to this general model. This analysis has provided an insight into the structure of shopping in the Gloucestershire region, although far more could be gained if the region was divided into a large number of zones.

PREDICTING WITH THE MODEL

Once the model has been successfully calibrated to a base year situation, the input data are updated and the model run predictively for some future date. Over a short period, say five to seven years, this can be performed quite successfully, but over a longer period it is far more speculative.

Using the retail model set out in equation (3.17), then for each zone, future estimates of retail floorspace, F_j, and consumer expenditure, C_i, have to be determined. Shopping centre floorspace changes over the short period can be estimated reasonably accurately, although there are problems in that changes can take place within a zone which are not reflected in zonal floorspace changes, since each zone is considered as a single unit, and also it is difficult to allow for increased efficient use of floorspace, where, for example, a new supermarket would attract larger retail sales than older, more traditional shops of the same floorspace. Consumer expenditure changes can prove more difficult. The population levels in each zone are relatively straightforward, but determining the future level of retail expenditure per head can be a problem. Here assumptions have to be made about changes in absolute and real income levels, the proportion of income spent on retail commodities and inflation rates in order to gain an estimate of future retail expenditure per head. The other input information required is the matrix of distances or times between zones, d_{ij}, and any changes in the transport network since the calibration date can be taken into account. There are likely to be more changes if travel time between zones has been used rather than distance.

With this updated input information, and retaining the calibration parameter value γ, the retail model can be run to estimate the shopping pattern over the region at the future date. An important point to remember is that in using the calibration value of γ, the parameter on the distance function, it is being assumed that the shopping behaviour observed at the base year will persist in the future. Again, in the short period this is not too unrealistic, and is probably the best estimate that can be made. The parameter value could be changed in the future, but it is very difficult to know by how much it should be changed. Another point to remember is that this is a static equilibrium model that refers to one point in time. For a given set of input data, the model estimates the distribution of retail sales in each centre and the flow of money between residential zones and shopping centres. It shows nothing about the way the system will change during the projection period, instead it just gives the equilibrium situation when the changes have worked through the system to the prediction date.

Having considered and evaluated the effects of the most likely

59

changes to occur by some future date, the model can then be used further to simulate alternative planning policies for the region by altering one or more of the input variables:

(1) To simulate shopping centre policy alternatives the size and location of new or expanded shopping centres can be changed by altering the index of attraction F_j.

(2) To simulate either alternative distributions of population over the region or alternative assumptions about the level of future retail expenditure per head, alter the zonal distribution of consumer spending power C_i.

(3) To simulate new road alternatives, the transport network can be modified by changing the distance matrix d_{ij}.

(4) To simulate changes in accessibility to shopping centres, alter the parameter value γ on the distance function. An increase in γ would simulate a decrease in accessibility which could be caused by increased petrol prices and bus fares, while a decrease in γ would simulate an increase in accessibility caused for example by increased car ownership and increased use of the car for shopping.

In the three zone Gloucestershire region, after the model has been calibrated to the 1971 base year situation, then it is best to rerun the model for some more recent data, probably obtained from a shopping survey, in order to test that the model is predicting the recent past situation reasonably accurately. These new data could be used as the new base year, and then predictions made of the future shopping pattern for the region. This is the system used by Lewisham in developing their shopping model and is described in the next section. The Gloucester region, divided into three zones, would be rather insensitive to changes in the variables because of its aggregate nature, but a more realistic situation where the region is divided into 100 zones would provide a model sensitive enough to simulate marginal changes in parts of the system. However, before becoming too involved in the mathematical calculation, theoretical concepts and further extensions to the basic model, a number of operational retail models will be described in order to explain how they have been applied in practice.

OPERATIONAL RETAIL SHOPPING MODELS

The first retail model to be built using the probabilistic gravity model concept was for the Baltimore region in the USA

(Lakshmanan and Hansen 1965). In this study, several alternative forms of future retail development were compared in terms of the retail trade attracted to each centre, the retail sales per square foot, and the average lengths of shopping trips for the study region. This demonstrated how a fairly simple urban model could usefully be applied in studies of retailing and very quickly shopping models were developed for other areas of North America and in many other countries. In Britain, a model was developed to study the effect of building a regional shopping centre at Haydock in north-west England (McLoughlin, Foot and Nix 1966) and this was immediately followed by a number of shopping models developed by local authorities and planning consultants. Articles in journals initially showed how shopping models could be developed and applied. Later work has tended to be more theoretical, dealing with such topics as calibration procedures, constraint procedures, disaggregation of activities and behavioural theory, although all the new ideas have been empirically tested. Retail shopping models continue to be widely used within an overall shopping analysis, and have now been extensively applied in many parts of the world.

In order to explain in more detail how retail models have been used in practice, four British studies will be described. Firstly the Haydock study, although now rather dated, does still provide an excellent example of how the model can be applied. Then two of the models at present in use in local authorities in Britain will be described: the Lewisham and Berkshire shopping models. Lastly, a study which looked at the effects of a new hypermarket on shopping behaviour (Gilligan, Rainford and Thorne 1974) and compared output from the model with the results from a shopping survey carried out two and a half years after the hypermarket was opened. This comparison provides some information as to the effectiveness of retail models. There are of course a number of problems and limitations in using a retail model, and some of these points will be covered when dealing with the various operational models, but a more comprehensive consideration will be made in Chapter 4 when an overall assessment is made of spatial interaction models.

The Haydock shopping model

This study was set up to investigate the proposal to build a regional shopping centre at Haydock which is situated between Manchester

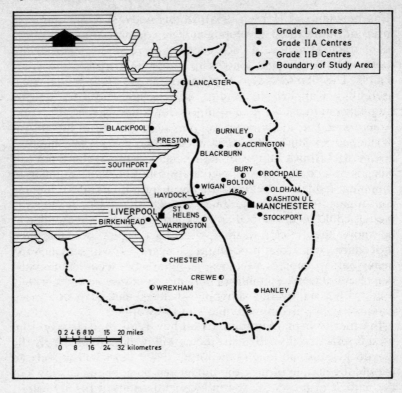

Figure 3.11   Principal shopping centres in north-west England

and Liverpool at the junction of the M6 and the A580 (see figure 3.11). Since the proposal was to build the shopping centre with a range of shopping facilities that would compete with Manchester and Liverpool, it was decided to study the shopping pattern of the whole of north-west England. The objectives of the study were threefold. Firstly, to investigate if there was a need for a regional shopping centre. Secondly, if the area could support a regional shopping centre, then was Haydock the best location? Thirdly, what would be its effect on the other shopping centres in the region?

A first report (Davies, Jackson and Robinson 1964) carried out a comprehensive study covering all aspects of shopping in the North-West and has already been described as an example of a shopping centre hinterland approach to shopping analysis. A second report (McLoughlin, Foot and Nix 1966) used the same set of data and studied the same problem using a retail shopping model similar to the one shown in equation (3.18). Only durable goods sales were considered since these account for well over 90% of the sales in any large centre such as Manchester or Liverpool. The area was divided into 244 residential zones which were local authorities or divisions of rural areas, but retail sales in only the forty-seven largest shopping centres were considered.

The model was calibrated for 1961 data and inevitably certain problems arose. There was a problem in finding a suitable index of attraction for each of the shopping centres. Retail floorspace for each centre was not available, so an index of the number of different types of shops in each centre was constructed. In running the model, there was a problem with holiday trade which inflated the actual sales of shopping centres such as Blackpool, Southport and Morecambe with expenditure by consumers from outside the region. Poor fits were also obtained in a few other centres near the boundary, particularly near the southern boundary. Eventually the best results were obtained between actual and estimated 1961 retail sales, which also gave a reasonable money flow pattern between residential zones and shopping centres. To study the effect on the region of another centre offering similar facilities to Manchester and Liverpool, data were updated to 1971 and the model run predictively to estimate retail sales in each of the shopping centres, firstly without any new centre in the region and secondly with a new centre at Haydock (table 3.15).

An attempt could then be made to answer the questions set out above. It was predicted that Haydock could expect to attract about £47.5 million retail sales at 1961 prices, not as much as Manchester or Liverpool, but nevertheless it did seem to show that the area could support a regional shopping centre and would be a worthwhile investment for the developers. However, there are several towns within 8 or 10 miles of Haydock which would be drastically affected. Wigan could expect to lose nearly half its expected 1971 sales to the new centre at Haydock, while Warrington and St Helens could expect to lose about one third of their expected 1971 sales. Other smaller centres like Leigh would also be considerably affected. All this is hardly surprising since the proposal was to build a huge regional shopping centre only a few miles from these towns. Alternative sites for the shopping centre were also tested. Other new centres on the M6 motorway at Risely, Leyland and Knutsford were considered, along with large developments in existing towns at Preston, Wigan and Warring-

Table 3.15 Estimated retail sales 1971 from the Haydock shopping model (£millions 1961 prices)

| Central areas | Total durable goods sales 1961 | Total durable goods sales 1971 | | | Sales captured as % of 1971 sales |
		Without Haydock	With Haydock	Sales captured by Haydock	
Liverpool	53.69	77.63	69.45	8.18	10.5
Manchester	50.84	70.00	62.92	7.08	10.1
Haydock	—	—	47.46	—	—
Birkenhead	7.44	9.88	9.48	0.40	4.0
Blackburn	5.96	8.83	7.93	0.90	10.2
Blackpool	13.46	18.99	18.35	0.64	3.4
Bolton	11.63	18.18	15.91	2.27	12.5
Burnley	4.49	5.98	5.69	0.29	4.8
Chester	10.68	14.82	13.51	1.31	8.8
Hanley	9.02	12.52	11.28	1.24	9.9
Preston	10.91	18.41	15.50	2.91	15.8
Southport	7.29	9.63	9.06	0.57	5.9
Stockport	7.05	11.76	11.15	0.61	5.2
Warrington	6.02	10.74	6.84	3.90	36.3
Wigan	6.65	11.13	5.84	5.29	47.5
Altrincham	3.27	5.40	4.62	0.78	14.4
Ashton-under-Lyne	3.78	4.45	4.34	0.11	2.5
Bury	3.38	5.58	5.37	0.21	3.8
Crewe	3.53	5.42	4.48	0.94	17.3
Lancaster	4.19	5.75	5.35	0.40	7.0
Oldham	6.34	8.56	8.26	0.30	3.5
Rochdale	4.88	6.10	5.87	0.23	3.8
St Helens	5.99	7.82	5.17	2.65	33.9
Wrexham	5.35	7.06	6.83	0.23	3.3

ton. However, in terms of the attraction of retail trade, Haydock seemed the best site if a regional shopping centre was to be built in the region.

One problem with using the retail model to predict the impact of a large out-of-town shopping centre is that having calibrated the model to a shopping behaviour for the base year 1961, at prediction it is being assumed that the same pattern of behaviour will persist. The output from the model is, therefore, showing the effect on north-west England of developing a large shopping centre at Haydock, assuming that shopping behaviour does not change. However, if a shopping centre was constructed, this would of course change the shopping behaviour, particularly in relation to the new centre with people probably making longer trips to the new centre. Because of this, retail sales attracted to Haydock are most likely being underestimated by the retail model, and probably the drastic influence on nearby centres is being overemphasized. It is extremely difficult to overcome this problem, although decreasing the distance parameter value from the calibrated value would have the effect of increasing shopping mobility, but the problem is by how much should it be decreased, and the effect would be felt over the whole region.

Here then a retail model gave a general picture and broad outline of the likely effects of building a new centre at Haydock. There are of course many other factors to be taken into consideration before coming to a planning decision. In this case, after a long public inquiry, the application to build the centre at Haydock was rejected largely on the grounds of the effect it would have on other nearby towns, and also because of the problem of traffic accessibility to the centre.

The Lewisham and Berkshire shopping models

Two local authority planning departments in Britain that have developed and are currently using retail shopping models are the London Borough of Lewisham (Lewisham Borough Council 1978) and Berkshire County Council (Moseley 1977). These two models, though, are of a rather different nature with Lewisham using a fairly basic straightforward model while Berkshire use a much more disaggregated model.

The Lewisham model has been developed in the planning department using the basic model already described (equation (3.18)) except that retail commodities have been disaggregated

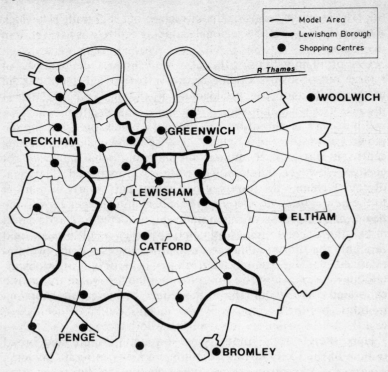

Figure 3.12   The London Borough of Lewisham shopping model study region

into consumer goods (food goods) and durable goods (non-food goods). This division is made because shopping behaviour is different for the two groups, with generally longer, less frequent trips to purchase durable goods and shorter, more frequent trips to purchase convenience goods. The effect is to run two shopping models of the type described for the three zone Gloucestershire region, one for consumer goods and the other for durable goods. A London borough is rather an awkward area to model because of the problem of boundary closure since a retail model deals with a closed system. However, with the help of three large shopping surveys in 1965, 1973 and 1977 which indicated the movement of shoppers over the area, a study region extending outside Lewisham (figure 3.12) was delineated with 69 residential zones and 31 shopping centres of which 26 residential zones and 12 shopping centres are in the Borough of Lewisham. Calibration was originally for 1971 and then updated and checked with 1976 data, which then formed the base year for later forecasts. A great deal of work went into collecting data and a very thorough analysis was made of shopping in Lewisham and the surrounding area. Lewisham decided on a relatively simple model in order to make it readily available for use in the planning department. It has been developed on a desktop computer and can therefore be run quite quickly and used very frequently. It has been used in the preparation of the Lewisham Structure Plan, and to provide short-term shopping forecasts for the area, which are continually being revised as new information becomes available. The model is used to estimate the impact of future population and expenditure levels on shopping provision, and also the impact of any new retail development on existing shopping provision.

The Berkshire shopping model, developed jointly by the unit for retail planning information and the planning department, contrasts sharply with the Lewisham model. Starting with the same basic information, this model is highly disaggregated throughout, as shown in figure 3.13. Retail commodities are disaggregated into durable and convenience goods, but in this case there is some link between the two models to take account of the fact that people on a principally durable goods shopping trip will most probably spend some money on convenience goods as well. These two commodity types are further disaggregated by mode of travel to the shopping centre, distinguishing between private transport and public transport which also includes walking. Shopping behaviour by these two modes shows different patterns and a shopping survey of Berkshire indicated that about half of the total consumer expenditure of the region went by each mode. The model also contains spatial disaggregation, with the study area divided into subareas, each of which is modelled separately. These are chosen so that most retail activity takes place within each subarea. For convenience goods trade, Berkshire is divided into eight subareas, whereas for durable goods trade the division is into three subareas (figure 3.14). This reflects the different types of goods, shorter trips to purchase convenience goods and longer trips to purchase durable goods.

The study area, which also contained small parts of the neighbouring counties (figure 3.14) was finally divided into 186 durable goods expenditure zones and 377 convenience goods expenditure zones. The zoning systems were relatively fine in the urban areas, but much coarser in the rural areas. Every conven-

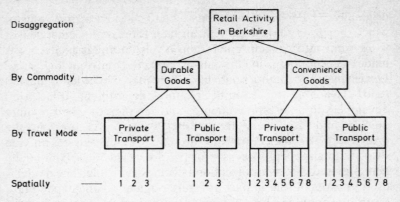

Figure 3.13   The structure of the Berkshire shopping model

ience goods zone was considered to contain a shopping centre, whereas only thirty-six durable goods shopping centres were defined. Also, since this is a densely populated part of Britain, with considerable retail interaction over the area, a number of external expenditure zones and external shopping centres had to be included. Central London, which is only 40 miles from Reading and 20 miles from Slough and Windsor on the east of the county, proved to be a particular problem.

The Berkshire shopping model is basically a probabilistic gravity model, except that a negative exponential distance function is used rather than the power function in equation (3.18). However, in this model there are 22 parameters on 22 submodels because of the disaggregation by commodity, by mode of travel and into subareas (figure 3.13), although there are links between some of the submodels. Most of the data requirements for a disaggregated model of this type can only be obtained from an extensive shopping survey. In 1974, Berkshire carried out a questionnaire survey of 10,000 adult shoppers and also 5500 adults kept a diary on their shopping trips for one week, showing the origin and destination of each trip, mode of travel, expenditure on different types of goods, as well as personal information such as age, sex, social class, if they owned a car, etc. Information obtained from this sample survey, together with some published information, provided sufficient data to calibrate the model. Berkshire have developed, therefore, a highly disaggregated model which required a large amount of data for calibration, and now requires considerable additional information at prediction. It has been

CONVENIENCE GOODS SHOPPING SYSTEM

DURABLE GOODS SHOPPING SYSTEM

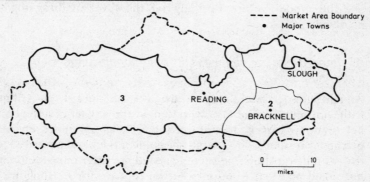

Figure 3.14   The Berkshire shopping model study region

developed on the local authority computer, and since 1976 the
planning department has been using it to evaluate alternative
shopping strategies for the county's three structure plans, and also
to assess the impact of proposals for major out-of-town shopping
developments.

These two retail models show the dilemma facing local
authorities. Should they follow the Lewisham example and build a
straightforward fairly aggregate model with limited data requirements, which can be developed on a desktop computer and
therefore used very frequently and almost at a moment's notice?
Alternatively, should they follow the Berkshire example and build
a highly disaggregated model with large data requirements that
can only be obtained from an extensive shopping survey, which
has to be developed on a large computer and is therefore run
rather infrequently? One fact that might have affected the
decisions of these two local authorities on the level of disaggrega-

tion, is that they are quite different types of area; Lewisham is an Inner London Borough and Berkshire a Shire county. Obviously more output information is being obtained from the Berkshire model, but this has to be balanced against the considerable extra cost, time and effort involved. There is also a problem with a disaggregated model in that retail sales flows between residential zones and shopping centres become quite small and therefore more difficult to model. There are really no right or wrong answers to these problems and many of the points raised here will be discussed later. However, any local authority contemplating developing a retail model should be clear about how it wishes to use the model before deciding on the level of disaggregation involved.

A comparison between the results of a shopping model and a shopping survey

A particularly interesting study was conducted by Gilligan, Rainford and Thorne (1974) to look at the impact of a hypermarket shopping centre. It is one of the very few examples where the predicted results from a retail shopping model are compared with the results of a shopping survey carried out after the development has taken place. It is an out-of-town centre with a selling area of 50,000 square feet and parking for 500 cars, and is situated on the edge of an unspecified city of just over half a million people in south Yorkshire, near to another large town and commanding a large hinterland. The shopping centre was opened in 1970 and the shopping survey carried out two and a half years later, giving it time to reach its maximum operating capacity. A study was made of its impact on the city centre, twenty-seven district centres within the city boundary, eight hinterland centres outside the city boundary and local shops.

The retail shopping model was developed and calibrated, and predictions made for early 1973, firstly without the centre and then including the new centre, in exactly the same way as for the Haydock study. The shopping survey collected information on the number of customers using the store each week, the amount spent by customers, the areas from which the customers came, and the alternative shopping centres available to the customers. This survey provided information to determine the turnover of the store, the areas from which this turnover had been derived and the effect on previously established shopping centres. For comparison

Table 3.16 Retail turnover diverted to the hypermarket shopping centre: a comparison of survey estimates and model predictions as percentages of the total turnover

		Survey	*Model prediction*
City centre		25.9	28.1
District centres	1	4.1	3.6
	2	1.2	1.8
	3	1.7	1.5
	4	0.1	0.3
	5	1.7	1.5
	6	—	0.6
	7	5.5	5.0
	8	0.9	0.9
	9	—	0.4
	10	—	0.5
	11	0.1	0.3
	12	0.3	0.7
	13	0.3	0.4
	14	0.2	0.3
	15	0.2	0.4
	16	—	0.3
	17	0.1	0.2
	18	—	0.2
	19	1.3	1.5
	20	0.2	0.1
	21	0.2	0.3
	22	—	0.3
	23	—	0.3
	24	0.1	0.2
	25	—	0.3
	26	6.8	6.3
	27	1.1	1.0
Total		26.1	29.2
Hinterland centres	1	10.8	9.3
	2	2.4	2.0
	3	2.1	1.7
	4	1.6	1.6
	5	2.4	2.0
	6	1.9	1.7
	7	2.5	2.3
	8	2.0	1.1
Total		25.7	21.7
Local shops		22.3	21.0
Totals		100.0	100.0

purposes, both the results from the model and from the survey are presented as the proportion of the store's total turnover derived from the other shopping centres in the region (see table 3.16).

There is a close fit between the results of the survey and the predictions from the model for the city centre, district centres and hinterland centres. The model did estimate that rather more would be captured from the city centre, but the difference is quite small and well within the sampling error of the survey. As one would expect, there is a big impact on the district centres close to the new store, centres 1, 7 and 26 (table 3.16). Care has to be exercised though in interpreting these results. The 25.9% of the new store's sales that is captured from the city centre represents only about 1½% of the city centre retail turnover, the sort of increase in spending power that might be expected in a year. However, the 6.8% of the new store's sales captured from the district centre 26, which is only one mile from the new store, represents 18% of the sales of this district centre, and hence the impact will be far greater.

The biggest problem concerned the impact on local shops. The new shopping centre becomes the local shop for those residents living within a mile or two, and this has considerable effect on existing local shops. This was clearly shown in the survey but the retail model just cannot be specific enough to deal with individual local shops, since it simulates the shopping pattern at a much more aggregated level. The overall aggregate total sales captured from local shops show the model estimates to be close to the survey result. However, as it is impossible to look at the effect on individual shops using the retail model, the aggregate results would have to be interpreted with a more in-depth study immediately around the store.

Overall, however, there is a close fit between the retail model estimates and the results from the survey, which would seem to support the use of retail models in studying the impact of new shopping centres. There are problems in looking at the very local shops near to the new store, and as mentioned in the Haydock study, problems of changing shopping behaviour in the future, but it does seem that the retail model can produce a broad outline of the likely effects of building a new shopping centre.

4 Spatial interaction models

This type of model simulates for a part of the urban system the interaction between landuse activities and in most cases also allocates activities to zones. These interactions might be journey to work trips, journey to school trips, shopping trips, recreation trips or the movement of industrial goods. The retail shopping model which has been covered in detail in the last chapter is a spatial interaction model of the retail sector, and now residential location and transport models will be introduced. The retail model was expressed in equation (3.17) in the form

$$S_{ij} = C_i \frac{F_j d_{ij}^{-\gamma}}{\sum_j F_j d_{ij}^{-\gamma}} \qquad (4.1)$$

where S_{ij} is the flow of retail expenditure between residential zone i and shopping centre j, C_i is the total consumer expenditure generated from residential zone i, F_j is an index of attraction for the shopping centre in zone j, d_{ij} is a measure of the distance between residential zone i and shopping centre j, and γ is a parameter to be determined at calibration. This model can be reformulated in more general terms to represent a model of spatial interaction and allocation. The generalized model is in fact a singly constrained gravity model, just one of a whole family of spatial interaction gravity models which will now be introduced.

THE SINGLY CONSTRAINED MODEL

A singly constrained model of spatial interaction and allocation based on the gravity concept can be expressed by the following equation:

$$T_{ij} = A_i O_i D_j f(c_{ij}) \qquad (4.2)$$

where

$$A_i = \left[\sum_j D_j f(c_{ij}) \right]^{-1}$$

and with

T_{ij} = the interaction taking place between origin zone i and destination zone j

O_i = the activity to be distributed from origin zone i

D_j = an attraction index for destination zone j

c_{ij} = the cost of travel between origin zone i and destination zone j, which could be measured in terms of distance, travel time or some generalized cost

$f(c_{ij})$ = some function of travel cost, generally an inverse power function or a negative exponential function

A_i = the competition term or balancing factor.

In the model there is a fixed level of activity O_i in the origin zones to be distributed to destination zones and this distribution takes place such that $O_i = \Sigma_j T_{ij}$ (see figure 4.1). It is an allocation interaction model, with an activity being allocated to destination zones and with the interaction matrix T_{ij} also being produced. The amount of activity allocated to each destination zone is calculated by summing a column of the trip matrix $\Sigma_i T_{ij}$. It is referred to as a singly constrained model because the quantities generated from the origin zones are fixed and the model is free to allocate and then determine the level of activity in each destination zone. The competition term or balancing factor in the equation, A_i, is equivalent to the bottom line (denominator) of equation (4.1). It ensures that the origin zone totals O_i are at the given fixed level for each zone by setting the sum of the probabilities of movement from each origin zone to all the destination zones equal to 1.0 (as in equations (3.10) to (3.12)). The calibration process involves finding the best parameter value in the travel cost function to reproduce known base year information for the trip matrix and destination zone totals.

This singly constrained model of equation (4.2) is equivalent to the retail shopping model of equation (4.1) when

$$\begin{aligned} T_{ij} &= S_{ij} & O_i &= C_i \\ D_j &= F_j & f(c_{ij}) &= d_{ij}^{-\gamma} \end{aligned} \qquad (4.3)$$

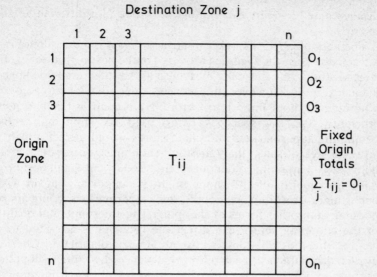

Figure 4.1 A singly constrained trip matrix

and therefore

$$A_i = \left(\sum_j F_j d_{ij}^{-\gamma} \right)^{-1}$$

The variables within a singly constrained model can take on a number of different forms. In the retail shopping model of the Gloucestershire region, T_{ij} represented the flow of retail expenditure (S_{ij}) between residential zone i and shopping centre j and O_i the consumer expenditure (C_i) generated by the population in zone i. Total consumer retail expenditure for each zone was calculated outside the model using population and average expenditure figures and fed into the model as an input variable (C_i). An alternative procedure which was used for example in the Berkshire study, is to model person trips by setting O_i as the residential population in each zone i and with T_{ij} the person trips from residential zone i to shopping zone j. In this case the resultant trip matrix T_{ij} gives the number of trips with destination in each shopping centre. The shopping centre retail sales can be calculated by multiplying the number of trips reaching the shopping centre by either an overall average expenditure per person or at a more disaggregated level by expenditure per person for different length of trip.

The variable D_j is the index of attraction and is a measure of the attractiveness of the facilities provided in the destination zones. In a retail study, this is usually measured as the total retail floorspace in each zone F_j. However, this measure does not take into account a number of other important factors. No account is taken of how efficiently the floorspace is being used. A shopping centre containing supermarkets and chain stores would attract a higher level of retail sales than another shopping centre of similar floorspace containing older more traditional and smaller shops. Also the quality of the shops might be important, again with department stores, chain stores and supermarkets being more popular than other forms of shopping. The environmental quality of the shopping centre can affect the retail sales attracted to a centre. In the Haydock study previously described, Chester attracted retail sales from a longer distance than other shopping centres in the area because it is a pleasant, environmentally attractive centre in which to shop. The provision of car parking can also be important. Certainly shopkeepers will generally complain if parking is restricted near their retail establishments because of the adverse effect on retail sales. Overall, however, there are tremendous problems in measuring these other factors and it is for this reason alone that retail floorspace has often been used as the index of attraction in shopping studies.

Some models have contained a non-linear relationship for the attractiveness of a shopping centre, as for example in the Haydock study, $D_j = F_j^\theta$. Here floorspace for each shopping centre was not available and since the index used combined the number of certain types of retail establishments, it did not give sufficient distinction between the smaller and larger centres. With a value of θ greater than one, larger centres became proportionately more attractive than smaller centres. In the Haydock study, because the original index contained such small values (Manchester = 45), then the best fit was obtained at calibration with $\theta = 3$. However, most studies have used retail floorspace as the index of attraction because it gives sufficient distinction between shopping centres and hence dispenses with the need for a second parameter θ in the model which obviously simplifies the calibration process.

In the travel cost function of the singly constrained model, $f(c_{ij})$, the variable used to measure the cost of travel between zones in the region (c_{ij}) can be distance, travel time or a generalized cost as

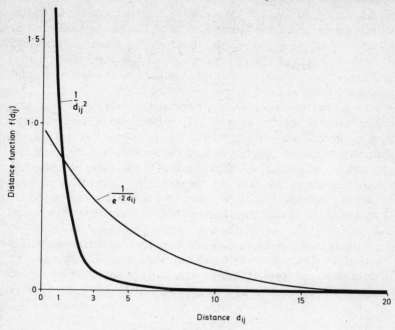

Figure 4.2   A comparison of distance functions

was explained in Chapter 2. The actual travel cost function $f(c_{ij})$ can take on a number of forms. Originally an inverse power function $1/c_{ij}^{\gamma}$ or $c_{ij}^{-\gamma}$ was used, as in equation (4.1), but this has since been replaced by a negative exponential function $1/\exp(\lambda c_{ij})$ or $\exp(-\lambda c_{ij})$ where exp is the exponential function of natural growth and λ is a parameter to be found at calibration. These two functions show rather different levels of decrease in interaction as distance or cost increases. If the cost of travel between zones (c_{ij}) is measured as travel distance d_{ij} then figure 4.2 gives an example of the two functions using $\gamma = 2$ in the inverse power function and $\lambda = 0.2$ in the negative exponential function. It can be seen that the inverse power function curve falls off very rapidly as travel time increases, whereas the negative exponential function curve falls off more gently. In a mobile western society the negative exponential function is the better function to use in that it reproduces the actual trip pattern better than the inverse power function. However, there are sometimes problems when the travel times between zones are very short but the system of zoning can be arranged such that this is avoided. In addition, the entropy maximization procedure for deriving spatial interaction models which will be explained later, shows that the most probable form of the travel function is the negative exponential function. Therefore, although the inverse power function was used to derive and explain the basic gravity model in the last chapter, almost all studies now use the negative exponential function.

This model has been widely applied to study retail shopping patterns and residential location. There have also been attempts to develop recreation models where the population of an area is distributed from residential zones to recreation sites in the region (Mansfield 1971, Baxter and Ewing 1979). It has also been applied to archaeology (Hodder and Orton 1976) where the area of influence or market areas of ancient towns are determined by considering the spatial distribution of the archaeological finds such as pottery.

There is an alternative form of the singly constrained model where the destination zone totals are fixed and the model is used to determine the level of activity generated from the origin zones:

$$T_{ij} = B_j D_j O_i f(c_{ij}) \qquad (4.4)$$

where

$$B_j = \left(\sum_i O_i f(c_{ij}) \right)^{-1}$$

Again with i as the origin zone and j as the destination zone, then D_j is the fixed level of activity to be allocated to the destination zones such that in the trip matrix $\Sigma_i T_{ij} = D_j$. Also O_i is the index of attraction for the origin zones and B_j the competition term, while T_{ij} and $f(c_{ij})$ are as before. This method has very rarely been used as a singly constrained model on its own because it can always be transformed into the identical situation of fixed origin zone totals. However, it has been used in the development of more general models, such as the Garin–Lowry model which links an origin constrained model and a destination constrained model within an overall modelling framework, and will be described in the next chapter. Here again though, two origin constrained models could have been used just as easily.

A residential location model

The general spatial interaction allocation model of equation (4.2) can be used as a residential location model to distribute employed persons from their place of work to their place of residence. The given activity to be distributed, O_i, is the total number of employed persons in each zone, E_i, and the model then distributes these employed persons to their zones of residence.

Adapting equation (4.2) to represent a residential location model:

$$T_{ij} = A_i E_i H_j f(c_{ij}) \qquad (4.5)$$

where

$$A_i = \left(\sum_j H_j f(c_{ij}) \right)^{-1}$$

and with

T_{ij} = the number of workers travelling from work zone i to residential zone j

$E_i = O_i$ = the activity to be allocated, the number of employed persons in each work zone

$H_j = D_j$ = an index of attraction for each residential zone taking the quantity and quality of housing into account

c_{ij} = the cost of travel between work zone i and residential zone j

$f(c_{ij})$ = some function of spatial interaction

A_i = the competition term or balancing factor.

In this case, from a given distribution of employment at place of work (E_i), the model will distribute these employed persons to their residential zones. Using exactly the same principles as explained in detail in the last chapter for the retail distribution model, the probabilities of people working in zone i and living in all the residential zones are calculated, and then the employed persons distributed to their zones of residence. The resultant trip matrix T_{ij} shows the number of workers travelling from each work zone i to each residential zone j.

The measure of travel cost over the region, c_{ij}, and the travel function $f(c_{ij})$ are similar to those used in the retail distribution model discussed above in some detail. The other variable in the model, the residential attraction index, H_j, measures the quantity and quality of housing in the residential zones. The total housing stock in each zone is often used but it is far better if this is combined with an index of housing prices or housing rents since these can vary quite markedly over the study area. In the Venice model to be described in the next chapter, house prices vary considerably over the region with extremely expensive housing in the historical centre of Venice, but much cheaper and often a better standard of housing on the mainland. These variations in house prices and house rents had to be taken into account within the attraction index when building a residential location model for the region since the low house prices make certain areas highly attractive to workers employed in the historical centre of Venice. These are probably the two main factors to include in the attractor H_j, the stock of housing and the price of housing or cost of rents, although environmental quality might also be important. For example, the part of Worcestershire used to explain the transport model (figure 4.6) contains Kidderminster which is an industrial town and Bewdley which is a small, very pleasant, old-world market town. If a residential location model had been developed for this area, then the variation in environmental quality would have had to be taken into account within the attraction index with Bewdley weighted quite strongly against Kidderminster. This higher level of environmental quality is reflected in higher house prices in Bewdley. The residential attractor, therefore, needs to take account of the lower house prices in Kidderminster, and the greater environmental quality of the housing in Bewdley, and it can be difficult to find the right balance between the weightings.

The output from the model is the journey from work to home trip matrix, T_{ij}, showing the number of workers employed in work zone i travelling to live in residence zone j, and the number of employed persons resident in each zone $\Sigma_i T_{ij}$. To find the population in each zone, P_j, multiply the number of employed persons resident in each zone by a regional activity rate α where

$$\alpha = \frac{\text{total population in the region}}{\text{total employment in the region}} \qquad (4.6)$$

and

$$P_j = \alpha \sum_i T_{ij} \qquad (4.7)$$

By using this general activity rate, the overall actual and estimated regional population totals will be equal and so the estimated and actual zone population totals can be directly compared. Here α is an average activity rate for the region, but some studies have used a different activity rate α_j for each zone j. This leads to a problem at calibration of having to adjust the estimated zonal population totals so that the actual and estimated regional population totals are equal. At prediction there is the additional problem of having to estimate the future activity rate for each individual zone.

At calibration this estimated population in each zone, P_j, is compared to the actual population, and the estimated journey from work to home trip matrix, T_{ij}, is compared to the actual trip matrix in order to find the best parameter value on the travel cost function $f(c_{ij})$. Data are more readily available for the residential location model than the retail distribution model. Information on population and employment is contained in Population Census Reports, generally to quite a fine spatial level, although the journey to work trip matrix might not be for such small areas.

Consider modelling the residential location and journey to work trip pattern for a small area in east Kent, the three towns of Margate, Broadstairs and Ramsgate (figure 4.3). They are all seaside holiday centres with Margate a highly commercialized holiday town, and Broadstairs catering more for the elderly. Ramsgate is also a small port for both commercial boats and leisure craft. This three zone model is used purely to demonstrate the model building methodology, since a true model for the area would involve a large number of zones. The residential location model of equation (4.5) will be developed, with an exponential function $\exp(-\lambda c_{ij})$ as the travel cost function.

At this aggregate level, the basic information for these towns can be obtained from the workplace reports of the 1971 Population Census, which provides the following journey to work matrix (table 4.1). This represents a very large proportion of the work trips in the area, with over 93% of those working in the three centres also living in one of the three centres. This workforce accounts for over 82% of the employed residents of the area, with the other employed residents working outside the three towns,

Table 4.1 The journey to work trip matrix for the east Kent region

Work zone	Residential zone			Totals
	Margate	*Broadstairs*	*Ramsgate*	*Totals*
Margate	12,350	1,200	1,460	15,010
Broadstairs	1,040	3,360	1,600	6,000
Ramsgate	1,260	1,250	8,210	10,720
Totals	14,650	5,810	11,270	31,730

81

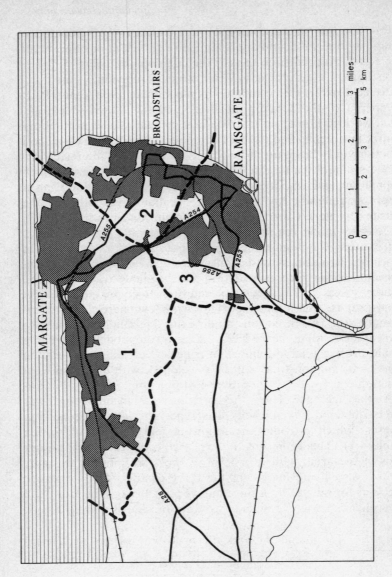

Figure 4.3   The east Kent study region

Table 4.2 The number of occupied dwellings in each zone of the east Kent region

	Margate	*Broadstairs*	*Ramsgate*
Occupied dwellings	18,755	8,025	14,435

either in nearby employment centres or in London which is about 70 miles away on a direct rail service. The overall population to employment ratio for the area calculated using equation (4.6) is $\alpha = 2.846$, which is quite high because of the large number of retired people who live in the area. The index of attraction used in this model is the number of occupied dwellings in each zone (table 4.2). It would be better to include other variables within the index of attraction, although the type of housing and cost of housing does not vary too much between these three towns. The cost of travel between zones is in terms of travel time (table 4.3) which assumes a speed of 20 mph on urban roads and 40 mph on other main roads, and gives an overall average travel time of 5.2 minutes. It can be shown (see Batty 1976) that if a negative exponential travel cost function is used in the model, the parameter value λ will lie within the range

$$\frac{1}{\text{average travel time}} \leqslant \lambda \leqslant \frac{2}{\text{average travel time}} \quad (4.8)$$

In order to calibrate the model quickly, the best initial estimate for the parameter λ is the midpoint of this range:

$$\text{initial parameter} = \frac{1.5}{\text{average travel time}} = \frac{1.5}{5.2} \simeq 0.29 \quad (4.9)$$

The residential location model is calculated in exactly the same way as the retail shopping model of the last chapter, except here the negative exponential function is used rather than the inverse

Table 4.3 The travel time matrix (minutes) for the east Kent region

Work zone	Residential zone		
	Margate	*Broadstairs*	*Ramsgate*
Margate	4.5	10.125	12.00
Broadstairs	10.125	2.10	7.65
Ramsgate	12.00	7.65	3.00

Table 4.4 The estimated journey to work trip matrix ($\lambda = 0.29$) for the east Kent region

Work zone	Residential zone			Totals
	Margate	*Broadstairs*	*Ramsgate*	
Margate	12,816	1,073	1,121	15,010
Broadstairs	862	3,779	1,359	6,000
Ramsgate	826	1,248	8,646	10,720
Totals	14,504	6,100	11,126	31,730

power function. The full trip matrix, T_{ij}, is given in table 4.4 and the deviations from the actual trip pattern of table 4.1 are given in table 4.5. These results clearly show that with a parameter of $\lambda=0.29$, there is too little interaction taking place over the area, with too many workers living in their work zone. However, the estimated number of employed persons resident in each zone is very close to the actual situation, but this is because there are compensating errors in the trip matrix. This shows that at calibration, both the zone totals and the trip matix must be compared with the actual base year information. It is most certainly not sufficient to compare just the number of employed residents in each zone. It is the trip matrix that is the vital piece of information, and the actual journey to work trip pattern is far easier to obtain for a residential location model than the retail expenditure flow pattern for a retail shopping model.

To generate more interaction in the area, and so disperse more workers away from their work zone, the parameter value λ on the travel cost function needs to be lowered, as explained earlier (figure 4.2). Automatic calibration procedures could be used

Table 4.5 A comparison of the actual and estimated journey to work trip matrices ($\lambda = 0.29$) for the east Kent region

Work zone	Residential zone			Totals
	Margate	*Broadstairs*	*Ramsgate*	
Margate	+466	−127	−339	0
Broadstairs	−178	+419	−241	0
Ramsgate	−434	−2	+436	0
Totals	−146	+290	−144	0
%errors	1.0	5.0	1.3	

Table 4.6 The effect of parameter changes on the average travel time (minutes) for the east Kent region

	Parameter value λ			Actual average travel time
	0.29	0.25	0.2	
Average travel time	4.868	5.174	5.692	5.181

(Batty 1976) which search for the best parameter value when the estimated average travel time in the region is equal to the actual average travel time. These procedures will be covered in the next chapter, and so for this model the parameter value was gradually reduced until a good fit was obtained at $\lambda=0.25$ where the estimated average travel time of 5.174 was very close to the actual average travel time of 5.181 minutes. Table 4.6 shows how the average travel time changed with the parameter value. Other tests for goodness of fit could have been used, although trying to obtain an estimated average travel time equal to the actual value is probably the best measure.

The output from the model with a parameter $\lambda = 0.25$ is given in tables 4.7, 4.8 and 4.9. The trip matrix is very close to the actual trip pattern, with only very small errors over the whole of the matrix. The errors in the total number of employed persons resident in each town have hardly changed from the previous result with $\lambda = 0.29$. Here, therefore, a correct trip pattern is producing small errors in the zone totals, whereas before an incorrect trip pattern with compensating errors was producing a good fit in terms of zone totals. By multiplying by an average regional population to employment ratio of $\alpha = 2.846$, the estimated population in each centre can be determined. A very close fit has been obtained, although Broadstairs is attracting slightly too many employed persons to live in the town. This is

Table 4.7 The estimated trip matrix ($\lambda = 0.25$) for the east Kent region

	Residential zone			
Work zone	Margate	Broadstairs	Ramsgate	Totals
Margate	12,274	1,287	1,449	15,010
Broadstairs	1,070	3,402	1,528	6,000
Ramsgate	1,120	1,422	8,178	10,720
Totals	14,464	6,111	11,155	31,730

Table 4.8 A comparison of actual and estimated trip matrices ($\lambda = 0.25$) for the east Kent region

Work zone	Residential zone			Totals
	Margate	Broadstairs	Ramsgate	
Margate	−76	+87	−11	0
Broadstairs	+30	+42	−72	0
Ramsgate	−140	+172	−32	0
Totals	−186	+301	−115	0
% errors	1.3	5.2	1.0	

Table 4.9 A comparison of the actual and estimated populations for the east Kent region ($\lambda = 0.25$)

	Residential zone			Totals
	Margate	Broadstairs	Ramsgate	
Estimated population	41,171	17,394	31,752	90,317
Actual population	41,700	16,538	32,079	90,317

probably because no allowance is taken within the index of attraction for the fact that a higher proportion of retired people live in Broadstairs than in the other two centres.

Now that calibration has been successfully completed, this residential location model can be run predictively and input data estimated for some future date. Changes in the transport network, and net changes in the numbers of dwellings in each zone are reasonably straightforward to estimate in the short term. More difficult is the size and distribution of employment in the region. However, using the most likely estimates of variables, and the calibration parameter, the model can be run to evaluate the effects of these changes on the region. Then further alternative planning policies can be tested by altering the variables within the model to simulate residential, employment and transport policies:

(1) To simulate residential growth alternatives the size and location of new residential development can be changed by altering the zonal attraction indexes H_j, the number of dwellings in each zone.
(2) To simulate economic growth alternatives alter the zonal distribution of employment E_i.

(3) To simulate new road alternatives modify the transport network by changing the travel cost matrix c_{ij}.

(4) To simulate changes in accessibility to residential areas, the parameter value λ on the travel cost function can be varied.

(5) To simulate environmental policy apply capacity constraints on the level of residential location allowed in certain zones with any excess population re-allocated to unconstrained zones. The model developed to test the impact of the third London airport which will be described in the next chapter, applied severe constraints on new residential development in zones that would experience high aircraft noise levels.

This type of residential location model has been used extensively within the Garin–Lowry model which is a more general urban model that will be explained in Chapter 5. In some operational Garin–Lowry models, such as the model of the Venice region, it has been used in this fairly simple form, while in other studies, such as those developed by Echenique, an expanded version of the model has been applied. Also disaggregated residential location models have been developed for a number of study regions, including Reading and Leeds, and these will be described later. In these models, employees are separated into different types of workers and housing is separated into different house types based on price, and the allocation then takes place between these disaggregated activities.

THE DOUBLY CONSTRAINED TRANSPORT MODEL

Transport models deal with the situation where not only is the level of activity generated from the origin zones fixed, but the level of activity attracted to each destination zone is also fixed. In figure 4.4 therefore $\Sigma_j T_{ij} = O_i$ and $\Sigma_i T_{ij} = D_j$. This model is purely an interaction model, the trip ends O_i and D_j are fixed and the model finds the trip pattern T_{ij} to satisfy these constraints. It is therefore rather different from the singly constrained model which is an allocation interaction model, since it allocates activities to zones as well as determining the interaction between zones.

In order to constrain the level of activity at both origin zones and destination zones, a model combining equations (4.2) and (4.4) is formulated:

$$T_{ij} = A_i B_j O_i D_j f(c_{ij}) \qquad (4.10)$$

87

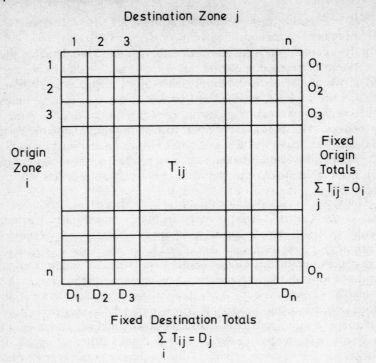

Figure 4.4 A doubly constrained trip matrix

where

$$A_i = \left(\sum_j B_j D_j f(c_{ij}) \right)^{-1} \tag{4.11}$$

$$B_j = \left(\sum_i A_i O_i f(c_{ij}) \right)^{-1} \tag{4.12}$$

and with

T_{ij} = the trips from origin zone i to destination zone j
O_i = the trips generated from origin zone i
D_j = the trips attracted to destination zone j
c_{ij} = some measure of the cost of travel between zone i and j
$f(c_{ij})$ = some function of travel cost, generally $\exp(-\lambda c_{ij})$ where λ is a parameter.

The competition term or balancing factor, A_i, ensures that the activity leaving origin zone i is equal to O_i, and the competition term or balancing factor, B_j, ensures that the activity attracted to destination zone j is equal to D_j.

To calibrate the model at some base year, with a given set of origin zone totals O_i and destination zone totals D_j, a parameter value on the travel cost function $f(c_{ij})$ has to be found that 'best' reproduces the known base year trip pattern T_{ij}. Because the balancing factors A_i and B_j form a set of non-linear simultaneous equations, an iterative procedure is used to solve the model (figure 4.5). For a given parameter value on the travel cost function, all B_j values can be initially set at 1.0 and then equation (4.11) solved to give values for A_i. These initial values for A_i can then be substituted into equation (4.12) to find new values for B_j at the second iteration. These new B_j values are again substituted into equation (4.11) and then A_i values substituted back into equation (4.12) to obtain revised B_j values. This iterative procedure continues until the values for A_i and B_j show no changes between iterations. At this stage, the output from the model, the trip distribution pattern T_{ij} (equation (4.10)), can be compared with the actual trip pattern and tests carried out to see how close a fit has been obtained. A new improved parameter value can then be estimated and the whole process repeated. This procedure continues until the 'best' parameter value is obtained where the estimated trip pattern is very similar to the actual trip pattern.

A transport model

In order to understand the working of the transport model more fully, consider an area in the northern part of Worcestershire, the three towns of Bewdley, Kidderminster and Stourport-on-Severn (figure 4.6). The three towns are nearly four miles from each other, with Kidderminster an industrial town, Bewdley a very pleasant, old-world market town by the river Severn, and Stourport a small light industrial centre which was developed as a canal town about two hundred years ago where the navigable River Severn was linked by canal to the industrial Midlands and North of England. Transport models are generally run on a very fine zoning system for an area using data collected from a special survey. In this example, and purely to describe the method of analysis, data are taken from the journey to work tables of the 1971 Census of Population. The journey from work to home trip

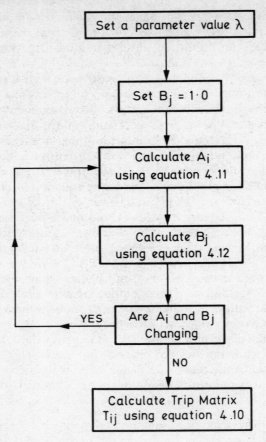

Figure 4.5   The iterative procedure for solving the doubly constrained model

matrix is given in table 4.10. Over 82% of those people working in the three towns also live in one of the three towns and this represents about 81% of the resident workers living in the area. The transport model will be used to try and describe this trip pattern, but any true operational model would have to take account of the trips across the boundary, about 18% of those employed in one of the three towns live outside the model area, and 19% of the employed residents work outside the model area. Table 4.10 gives the fixed origin totals O_i, the fixed destination totals D_j and the trip matrix T_{ij} against which to calibrate. The travel cost function used will be the exponential function

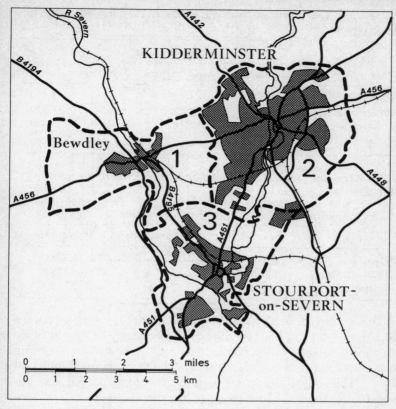

Figure 4.6   The north Worcestershire study region

$\exp(-\lambda c_{ij})$. The measure of travel cost will be the time taken to travel between the three centres assuming speeds of 20 mph on urban roads and 40 mph on other roads (table 4.11). There are problems in calculating the true time taken to travel from the zone to itself and it must be remembered that these are road travel times with no account taken of trip end movements, for example parking the car and walking to a destination within the town. This information provides an average travel time for the region of 4.957 minutes, which can again be used to find a good initial parameter in the travel cost function:

$$\text{initial parameter} = \frac{1.5}{\text{average travel time}} = \frac{1.5}{4.957} \simeq 0.3 \quad (4.13)$$

Table 4.10 The journey to work trip matrix for the north Worcestershire study region

Work zone	Residential zone			Totals
	Bewdley	Kidderminster	Stourport	
Bewdley	900	150	50	1,100
Kidderminster	1,370	17,770	2,180	21,320
Stourport	270	850	4,350	5,470
Totals	2,540	18,770	6,580	27,890

Table 4.11 The travel time (minutes) between zones in the north Worcestershire region

Work zone	Residential zone		
	Bewdley	Kidderminster	Stourport
Bewdley	1.0	8.7	8.775
Kidderminster	8.7	4.8	8.875
Stourport	8.775	8.875	2.1

The transport model can now be calculated using equations (4.10), (4.11) and (4.12) following the procedure outlined in figure 4.5 and previously described. Table 4.12 shows the balancing factors A_i and B_j at each iteration for the three towns. Setting all $B_j = 1.0$ and substituting into equation (4.11) gives initial A_i values which are then substituted back into equation (4.12) to give revised B_j values. This process is repeated until there are no changes in the A_i and B_j values between iterations. Table 4.12 shows that there are big changes in the values over the first six iterations, but then only fairly marginal changes until after about twenty iterations when the values have settled down. It might appear from the figures that the A_i values change less than the B_j values but this is because the results are given to six decimal places and the A_i values only have digits in the fourth and subsequent decimal places. In fact the theoretical basis of this procedure shows that it is the product of the two values, A_i multiplied by B_j, which is unique, and that the final values of A_i and B_j are somewhat arbitrary and could be affected by a constant coefficient. This example for north Worcestershire shows that only slight errors will be obtained by using the balancing factors after six to ten iterations and this will be the case even with a large trip matrix.

Table 4.12 Calculation of the balancing factors A_i and B_j using the iterative procedure

$\lambda = 0.3$	Bewdley		Kidderminster		Stourport	
Iteration	B_1	A_1	B_2	A_2	B_3	A_3
1	1.000000	0.000268	1.000000	0.000196	1.000000	0.000200
2	1.653681	0.000204	0.917560	0.000204	1.115707	0.000185
3	1.790205	0.000194	0.894834	0.000206	1.165848	0.000179
6	1.815834	0.000192	0.885618	0.000207	1.194541	0.000176
12	1.815839	0.000192	0.885281	0.000207	1.195838	0.000176
20	1.815839	0.000192	0.885280	0.000207	1.195840	0.000176

Table 4.13 The estimated journey to work trip matrix ($\lambda = 0.3$) for the north Worcestershire region

Work zone	Residential zone			
	Bewdley	Kidderminster	Stourport	Totals
Bewdley	722	258	120	1,100
Kidderminster	1,498	17,396	2,426	21,320
Stourport	320	1,116	4,034	5,470
Totals	2,540	18,770	6,580	27,890

The balancing factors obtained after twenty iterations are substituted into equation (4.10) to give the estimated journey from work to home trip matrix (table 4.13). Comparing this with the actual trip pattern of table 4.10 gives the calibration trip errors (table 4.14). It can be seen that although there is a close fit between the estimated and actual trip patterns, there is rather too much interaction over the region, with not enough employed persons living in their work zone. This is also shown by comparing the actual average travel time of 4.957 minutes against the model estimate of 5.1369 minutes. The higher average travel time indicates that the travel pattern in the model is overemphasizing interaction in the region.

The parameter value λ can be increased to reduce interaction in the area. As with the residential location model, only the closeness of the actual and estimated average travel time is used to test for goodness of fit. With a parameter of $\lambda = 0.35$, the estimated average travel time is 4.968 minutes which is very close to the actual value of 4.957 minutes. Automatic calibration procedures

Table 4.14 A comparison of the actual and estimated trip matrices (λ = 0.3) for the north Worcestershire region

Work zone	Residential zone			Totals
	Bewdley	Kidderminster	Stourport	
Bewdley	−178	+108	+70	0
Kidderminster	+128	−374	+246	0
Stourport	+50	+266	−316	0
Totals	0	0	0	0

Table 4.15 The estimated journey to work trip matrix (λ = 0.35) for the north Worcestershire region

Work zone	Residential zone			Totals
	Bewdley	Kidderminster	Stourport	
Bewdley	835	179	86	1,100
Kidderminster	1,435	17,768	2,117	21,320
Stourport	270	823	4,377	5,470
Totals	2,540	18,770	6,580	27,890

would give an even more refined parameter value λ when the average travel times are equal, but for our purposes the values are close enough with λ = 0.35, and the trip pattern is given in table 4.15. This provides a very close fit to the actual trip pattern, with only very small deviations from the actual situation (table 4.16). Such a close fit should not always be expected, for it must be remembered that it is far easier to obtain a good fit for a three zone model than for a 100 zone model. A single parameter λ is trying to reproduce the actual trip pattern and this becomes more difficult for a region with a large number of zones of small origin and destination zone totals.

At prediction, new activity totals are estimated for origin zones O_i and destination zones D_j and then using the calibrated parameter value λ = 0.35, the model is solved in the same iterative way, to show the future trip pattern. As explained earlier, in using the same parameter at prediction, it is being assumed that the trip behaviour which held at the base year will also hold at the future date. This is not completely satisfactory, but it does give a basis for prediction, since further predictions can be obtained by altering the parameter value to take account of expected changes in travel

Table 4.16 A comparison of the actual and estimated trip matrices (λ = 0.35) for the north Worcestershire region

| Work zone | Residential zone | | | Totals |
	Bewdley	Kidderminster	Stourport	
Bewdley	−65	+29	+36	0
Kidderminster	+65	−2	−63	0
Stourport	0	−27	+27	0
Totals	0	0	0	

behaviour and differences between the two sets of predictions observed.

This type of model has been used in transport planning since the 1960s. Previously the singly constrained model was used with a friction factor to ensure that destination zone totals were reproduced. Then in the 1960s the doubly constrained model was introduced which incorporated the friction factor within the model as a second balancing factor B_j.

Transport planning

Urban modelling within transportation planning follows a well developed and specialized procedure. Only a rather brief outline of this procedure will be presented here, but there are now several introductory books that can be consulted (e.g. Morlok 1978, Hutchinson 1974 and Bruton 1970). Almost all transportation studies begin by conducting a huge survey of the study region to obtain up to date base year information. To model the trip pattern, the area is divided into fine zones and the number of trips generated from each zone and the number of trips attracted to each zone is recorded. It is generally modelled at a highly disaggregated level for different types of travel mode, private, public and walking, and for different types of trip, home based trips, work trips, shopping trips, recreation trips, commercial trips, and other trips. For example, one analysis might involve journey by private transport from home to work and so the origin zone totals O_i would be the number of work trips by private transport generated from each residential zone, while destination zone totals D_j would be the number of home based work trips by private transport with destination in each work zone. The doubly constrained model would be calibrated for this type of trip, and then for all the other trip patterns, giving a series of different parameter values for different trip purposes. At prediction, the zone totals O_i and D_j are estimated outside the spatial interaction model using relationships obtained from base year data. These generally involve regression analysis or category analysis and use landuse characteristics and socio-economic characteristics to establish a relationship at the base year. They are then used at the prediction stage to determine the future level of activity in each zone by taking any changes into account. With these estimated future zone totals O_i and D_j, the interaction model produces the trip pattern T_{ij} at the future date. This procedure is followed for all the different types of trip pattern in the transport study. All the resultant trip patterns are then assigned to the road network to give the estimated flows on each of the road links. At prediction this will show where congestion might occur, and also allow the testing of alternative new road networks to see how well each alternative copes with the expected future traffic flows.

The doubly constrained spatial interaction transport model is therefore just one of a number of models in the transport planning process. To study the future transport needs of a region, there is firstly a model to estimate for different trip purposes, the number of trips generated from each fine zone and the number of trips attracted to each fine zone. Then for each of the trip purposes, the spatial interaction trip distribution model estimates the flow of trips between zones, which is followed by a modal split model to separate the trips into the different modes of travel: car, bus, train, motor cycle, bicycle and walking. A traffic assignment model then assigns trips on to links in the road network and on to public transport. Finally some evaluation procedure is used to compare alternative future strategies and to try and find a preferred road network and transport policy.

Many large-scale transportation studies have now been carried out all over the world. They were first developed in the USA in the 1950s with studies of Detroit, Chicago, Penn Jersey and New York, and continued throughout the 1960s for all the major conurbations and cities. The emphasis of the early studies was very much on traffic movements, particularly the future networks. Gradually the landuse function became an increasingly important aspect, although the studies still continued to take an insufficient number of alternative landuse patterns into account. This form of analysis was quickly taken up in Europe and in the 1960s and early 1970s most of the towns and cities of Europe and almost all the major capitals of the world underwent a transportation study. In Britain these were carried out in the 1960s firstly for London and the Manchester conurbation, quickly followed by studies of other conurbations like Glasgow, Birmingham, Liverpool, and towns like Worcester and Derby. A fairly typical British example was the SELNEC study (south-east Lancashire, north-east Cheshire) for Greater Manchester. An extensive survey was conducted in 1965 and 1966 and the full modelling procedure performed, with a number of alternative road networks and public transport systems compared through a largely economic evaluation in order to choose the best single transport plan. It was also typical in that it concentrated very much on traffic management with insufficient attention given to changes in landuse patterns in the future.

Transportation studies have become highly developed modelling exercises and the models have been well researched and widely applied. One criticism against the procedure is that it is applied like an engineering exercise for the purpose of designing a road network. Too much attention has been paid to technical detail and too little to considering the actual transport needs of the community in the study region. Also since landuse activities are very important in determining the level of traffic flows, a number of alternative future landuse patterns should be evaluated. In the past, transport studies have tended to consider just one future landuse scheme and the evaluation has been of alternative transport systems to best serve this landuse pattern. This is clearly an incorrect bias, for a much greater emphasis should be placed on the future distribution of landuse activities, which should then be analysed within an overall landuse transportation study. This is happening with some of the more recent studies such as those developed by Echenique (see Chapter 5) which have integrated a much expanded Garin–Lowry model with a transport model into a comprehensive landuse transportation modelling exercise.

All the other urban models covered in the book consider landuse explicitly within their structure and the emphasis in using them is on evaluating alternative distributions of activities. The technical process is not nearly so well developed as in transport planning, and the models are applied at a far more aggregate level. They are used in a much more general way as just one part of an overall planning project, whereas in transport studies the models have generally been the whole basis of the work. Also those models based on the gravity model, such as the retail shopping model, the residential location model and the Garin–Lowry model (see Chapter 5), deal with the movement of persons but at an aggregate level. The emphasis is on the effect of landuse changes, not the assignment of trips to links in a road network. It is also important to remember that the spatial distribution model applied in transport studies, suffers from all the same general assumptions and limitations as any other gravity based model and that the other models in the process, for trip generation and attraction, modal split and traffic assignment, also have their problems.

THE UNCONSTRAINED MODEL

The earliest applications of the gravity model used an unconstrained formulation in that neither the origin zone totals nor the destination zone totals were fixed. Newton's law of gravitation was adapted to study spatial interaction in the urban system, by postulating that the interaction between two cities varies directly with the size of the two cities and inversely with the square of the distance between them:

$$T_{ij} = G \frac{P_i P_j}{d_{ij}^2} \tag{4.14}$$

where

$$
\begin{aligned}
T_{ij} &= \text{the interaction between cities } i \text{ and } j \\
P_i, P_j &= \text{the size of population in cities } i, j \\
d_{ij} &= \text{the distance between cities } i \text{ and } j \\
G &= \text{a constant to be determined at calibration.}
\end{aligned}
$$

This early gravity model readily gives the Reilly breaking point set out earlier. For an intermediary point k on the breaking point between the cities i and j, then, there is an equal amount of interaction attracted to each city:

$$T_{ki} = T_{kj} \tag{4.15}$$

Using equation (4.14)

$$G \frac{P_k P_i}{d_{ki}^2} = G \frac{P_k P_j}{d_{kj}^2} \tag{4.16}$$

Therefore

$$\frac{P_i}{d_{ki}^2} = \frac{P_j}{d_{kj}^2} \tag{4.17}$$

which is identical to equation (3.6) used to determine the breaking point between two cities.

A more general formulation of the unconstrained gravity model can be obtained from equation (4.14):

$$T_{ij} = G O_i D_j d_{ij}^{-\gamma} \qquad (4.18)$$

where

T_{ij} = interaction between origin zone i and destination zone j
O_i = a measure of the level of demand generated at the origin zone i
D_j = a measure of the level of attraction at the destination zone j
d_{ij} = distance between origin zone i and destination zone j
γ = parameter on the distance function to be found at calibration
G = a constant to be determined at calibration.

In order to calibrate this model there must be some overall constraint on the total amount of interaction T that can take place in the region. The constant G is then the ratio of the total interaction T to the total interaction generated from the model:

$$G = \frac{T}{\sum_i \sum_j O_i D_j d_{ij}^{-\gamma}} \qquad (4.19)$$

The operational procedure for running this model is to calculate the interaction matrix T_{ij} of equation (4.18) without G in the equation, and then use G from equation (4.19) to scale down all the trips in order to satisfy the overall total interaction constraint. The different versions of the family of gravity models depends on whether the origin zone totals O_i and the destination zone totals D_j are fixed levels of activity, or merely indexes reflecting the nature of the zone. In the unconstrained model of equation (4.18) there are no fixed zone totals O_i and D_j, just an overall total level of interaction T. This model can be expanded into the singly constrained model where either the origin zone totals O_i are fixed (equation (4.2)) and the competition term or balancing factor A_i replaces the constant G, or the destination zone totals D_j are fixed (equation (4.4)) and B_j replaces G. The doubly constrained model (equation (4.10)) involves both competition terms or balancing factors A_i and B_j, since both origin zone totals O_i and destination zone totals D_j are fixed.

The original versions of the gravity model were applied to urban

99

systems as early as the middle of the nineteenth century (see Carrothers 1956), but it was Reilly who really expanded the use of the gravity model in his work on retailing. In the late 1950s and the early 1960s the singly constrained gravity model took over as the major form of model and this is still the formulation used in landuse planning studies, with most applications dealing with the case of fixed origin zone totals O_i. In transportation studies during the 1950s this model was further constrained on the destination zone totals but it was not until the 1960s that this procedure was fully incorporated within the gravity model and the doubly constrained model applied.

It is no surprise that the development and application of the gravity model mirrors the development and availability of computers. Reilly had to carry out his work by hand which is possible for calculating breaking points between two cities, but quite impossible for running a singly or doubly constrained model of any size. As computers became available and as computer core size increased, firstly the singly and then the doubly constrained versions of the gravity model were developed and became widely applied. The number of zones in the study areas increased and hierarchical spatial systems were developed. In the 1970s activities in the model began to be disaggregated and automatic procedures developed to speed up the calibration process. All these developments were only made possible by the rapid increase in computer size and general availability.

BEHAVIOURAL THEORY AND ENTROPY MAXIMIZATION

The formulation of the gravity model has sometimes been criticized because of its lack of any theoretical basis. The best attempt to develop an explanation and justification of the approach is in the work of Alan Wilson based on the entropy mazimization principle of statistical mechanics (Wilson 1967, 1970 and 1974). The concept of entropy can be most simply considered as a physical law which provides a macro-analytical description of the movement of gas particles under various conditions. Wilson draws the analogy between the movement of gas particles and the movement of individuals, for example the journey to work trip distribution and the retail shopping trip pattern. There are in fact many distributions that satisfy any given set of conditions, and entropy maximization determines the most probable distribution.

By varying the conditions set on the trip distribution, the whole family of gravity models can be derived.

Consider the doubly constrained transport model (equation (4.10)) where the distribution of trips T_{ij} is subject to three conditions:

$$\sum_j T_{ij} = O_i$$

$$\sum_i T_{ij} = D_j \qquad (4.20)$$

$$\sum_i \sum_j T_{ij} c_{ij} = C$$

The origin zone totals O_i and destination zone totals D_j are fixed levels of activity, and there is also an overall total travel cost C for the system, where c_{ij} is the cost of each trip between i and j. What is required is an assignment of trips, T_{ij}, that satisfies these constraints and entropy maximization provides a method for determining the most probable distribution of person movements T_{ij}. The entropy maximization procedure involves maximizing the function

$$Q = \frac{(\sum_i \sum_j T_{ij})!}{\prod_i \prod_j (T_{ij}!)} \qquad (4.21)$$

subject to the constraint equations (4.20). In fact it is more convenient to maximize the logarithm of equation (4.21) and Wilson has shown how this can be interpreted as the entropy of the system. By a process of mathematical manipulation using Lagrange's method of undetermined multipliers, the doubly constrained gravity model given in equations (4.10), (4.11), (4.12) can be derived, but with a negative exponential travel cost function.

The singly constrained model of equation (4.2) can be obtained in a similar way by specifying three constraints:

$$\sum_j T_{ij} = O_i$$

$$\sum_i \sum_j T_{ij} c_{ij} = C \qquad (4.22)$$

$$\sum_i \sum_j T_{ij} V_j = V$$

The activity generated from each origin zone O_i is fixed, there is an overall total travel cost C for the system, while the latter term represents a constraint on the total amount of benefit gained where V_j is the benefit of locating at j and V is the total benefit gained by all locations. A similar manipulation using the logarithm of equation (4.21) will produce the singly constrained model of equation (4.2) again with a negative exponential travel cost function.

This work by Wilson has provided a general statistical derivation of the gravity model, so much so that a gravity model is now generally called an entropy maximizing model. Not only has it provided a general framework to study the whole family of interaction gravity models, but it has also been extended to derive further models (Wilson 1970). By specifying different conditions, disaggregated models can be derived where employment might be disaggregated by occupation and industry, residential population by housing type or socio-economic group and retail expenditure by different types of goods. In a wider context models have been formulated to fit within a general accounting procedure using input–output analysis and linear programming techniques. The entropy maximizing procedure also shows the relationship between spatial interaction models and optimizing models as well as allowing new types of model to be formulated linking the two methods (see Chapter 7).

DISAGGREGATED SPATIAL INTERACTION MODELS

The models discussed so far deal with the location of activities at an aggregate level. They are coarse models that reflect a general location pattern over a region and distribute aggregate activities such as employment, population and retail expenditure. However, there will be different kinds of locational behaviour within this aggregate pattern, and to take this into account disaggregated models have been developed. To some extent the entropy maximizing approach to modelling has made this type of model construction easier. By postulating different constraints which refer to the disaggregation of activities, disaggregated models can be formulated.

Retail shopping models can be disaggregated by type of retail goods and hence by different type of shopping centre selling these goods, and by mode of travel to shopping centres. The Berkshire shopping model (Moseley 1977) described in the last chapter is classified into two commodity groups, durable and consumer goods, and two travel modes, private and public transport (figure

3.13). This fourway division, two commodity groups by two travel modes, can model the different shopping patterns involved. For example, people using public transport (which also includes walking) for convenience goods shopping, have a far shorter trip pattern than people using private transport for durable goods shopping. Rather than one general model for all types of goods by all travel modes, four linked gravity models are used with different parameter values to show the different shopping trip patterns.

In a residential location model, employment can be divided into different wage groups and housing into different house types based on price. A model of the Reading area (Cripps and Cater 1972, Batty 1976) classified the working population into three income groups: professional, white collar and blue collar. Housing types were classified by size and tenure into five groups: large and small owner-occupied houses, private rented in poor and good condition, and public rented accommodation. Prices were then derived to match this classification. The model also included a budget term which takes into account the differing prices of houses by location and balances against these the proportion of income available to different wage groups to spend on housing after travel costs have been deducted. Even more highly disaggregated residential location and retail distribution models have been developed for the city of Leeds (Wilson, Rees and Leigh 1978). The Garin–Lowry model which will be described in the next chapter and is basically two linked spatial interaction models, one for residential location and one for the location of services, has been extensively disaggregated and applied in many parts of the world. Wilson in his book (Wilson 1974) describes a general model of over 200 equations which involves an extensive disaggregation of activities.

There are good reasons for developing models that consider the different interaction patterns within a single activity and gain a better description of the real world. There are however considerable difficulties in applying a disaggregated model in a region. It leads to an enormous increase in data requirements which often involves mounting a huge survey of the study area. It can be quite difficult obtaining good reliable aggregate data, but highly disaggregated interaction data are an even greater problem. It is also more difficult to model the lower levels of interaction that take place between disaggregated activities rather than the larger levels of interaction at an aggregate level. Considerably more time is required to develop and operate the model, and computer storage requirements and computer runtimes are substantially increased. It is not surprising, therefore, that many disaggregated urban models have been developed as research exercises rather than in a practical planning situation. The comparison of the Lewisham and Berkshire shopping models in the last chapter discussed some of the problems involved in disaggregation and the dilemma facing practising planners on how much disaggregation to introduce into their urban models.

AN ASSESSMENT OF URBAN GRAVITY MODELS

Urban models are by definition a mathematical abstraction of the real world. They attempt to combine the most important characteristics of an urban system within a mathematical formulation to represent a simplification of a complex real world process. A whole family of spatial interaction models based on the gravity concept have been explained and their usefulness demonstrated. However, any modelling exercise is bound to have its limitations and operational problems (see Sayer 1976). This certainly need not invalidate the use of urban models. What it does mean is that any model builder must be very aware of the difficulties and develop, operate and evaluate the models with these problems very much in mind. A general overall assessment of modelling will take place in the last chapter of the book but it is worth considering at this point, some of the limitations of this type of urban model, and also methods for overcoming or minimizing the problems, which will help to explain why these models have been so widely applied.

(1) They are only partial models that simulate interaction for one activity or landuse, such as retail sales, residential location and transport. This implies that while one part of the urban system is being modelled all other parts are held constant. Clearly all parts of the urban system are interacting simultaneously. More general models have been developed, particularly the Garin–Lowry model and its extensions, and these are covered in the next chapter. However, the more general the model, the more complex the mathematical formulation, the greater the amount of data and the longer the time required to develop and operate the model. It is not surprising, therefore, that partial models have been popular, particularly the retail shopping model.

(2) There is still a lack of behavioural theory and causal explanation underlying the models. They were originally derived

through an analogy with a physical law, Newton's law of gravity, and now taking a social physics approach, entropy maximization has given the models a statistical explanation. However, they still describe the spatial interaction of activities within an urban system rather than explain the behavioural reasons for this pattern of location. A residential location model describes the locational pattern of employed persons about their workplace by assuming that they are attracted to an area by the quantity and quality of housing available, and deterred from living in an area by the cost of travel from work. This still ignores many factors affecting locational behaviour. On the other hand, the models do provide a good general description of spatial interaction over a region and have proved useful at prediction in providing information about likely future changes to parts of the system.

(3) They are static equilibrium models and simulate the urban system at one point in time, which is assumed to be in equilibrium. Obviously there are dynamic elements within all urban systems, but these models merely represent a cross section at one point in time and do not try to consider any of these dynamic elements. At prediction, input variables are determined and static equilibrium forecasts made for the future date. In doing this, it is being assumed that the aggregate behaviour that held at calibration will persist in the future. There are good reasons why this type of model has been so widely applied. Such models are relatively easy to formulate, data can be fairly easily obtained, certainly at an aggregate level, and they can be operated quite quickly. Attempts have been made to build dynamic models (Batty 1976) but the conceptual formulation of such models becomes enormously complex and the time series data required to operate them almost impossible to obtain.

(4) Singly constrained models are essentially demand models in that activities are allocated to destination zones without any reference to the level of supply in these zones. The supplies of housing, industry, shops and other services are generally not modelled but they can be considered through the application of constraints on development and by testing alternative development policies. Constraints can be applied by restricting the amount of activity allowed to locate in particular destination zones. This is useful at prediction when policy restrictions can be imposed on the region. In considering two of the alternative sites for a third London airport, discussed in the next chapter, for environmental reasons stringent restrictions were imposed on the amount of

residential development that would be allowed close to the new airport. Residential population was re-allocated to zones outside the flight path areas. Some of the more advanced general models, like the Echenique models also to be discussed in the next chapter, do incorporate additional supply models of the stock of developed land and urban buildings.

(5) The models were developed to consider activities at an aggregate level dealing with population, employment and retail activity. As previously explained, within each aggregate interaction matrix there are several different patterns and disaggregated models can be developed to take account of these differences, although there are problems of extra data, more complex models and increased computer time required in using these models.

(6) They deal with a closed region in that all interaction has to take place within the model area with no trips crossing the regional boundary. This condition is imposed through the balancing factor of the model formulation. It is important therefore to draw the boundary of the regions so that interaction across the boundary is minimized and therefore zones with large levels of activity should not be sited near the boundary. The introduction of external zones can partly overcome the problem where only the interaction between the region and the external zones is modelled. In the Berkshire shopping model, although central London is 20 miles outside the study area, it had to be included as an external zone since a small but significant amount of durable goods retail expenditure was spent there. In the Venice model described in Chapter 5 (figure 5.7), Padova and Treviso, while not included within the Venice region, have an influence on the area and so were included as external zones (figure 2.1).

(7) By retaining the calibrated parameter value on the distance function at prediction, it is being assumed that the behavioural trip pattern established at calibration will also hold at prediction. This is not very satisfactory for testing the impact of a large new development, such as a new hypermarket or a new motorway, since the effect of this new facility will almost certainly change the behavioural pattern. In fact most future changes in the location of activities, such as population, employment and shops, will alter the behavioural trip pattern, although these models are only trying to consider general aggregate behaviour. However, a predictive run with the calibrated parameter does give an initial forecast of the likely impact, although these will probably be minimum impact levels. The parameters can then be altered to try and take account

of changes in the behavioural pattern. In the shopping model described at the end of the last chapter the estimates obtained from running the model at prediction with the calibrated parameters were remarkably close to the results obtained from a shopping survey for the same date.

(8) There is a whole range of practical problems that are encountered when building an operational model, and some of these problems have been covered already. A region is divided into zones, but how large or how small should they be in order to describe trip behaviour in an accurate way? There are difficulties in measuring certain variables within the models, particularly the travel cost or distance between zones and the zonal attraction index. Data collection can cause problems, although aggregate models generally use published information, but for the more complex models extensive surveys are generally required. There are further problems in finding the best parameter values at calibration and great care has to be taken in interpreting model output at prediction. However, most of these practical problems will be encountered no matter what type of urban model is being developed, and all that can be done is to minimize the difficulties involved.

It can be seen that although there are problems in developing and using spatial interaction models to describe the urban system, there are very good reasons why they have been so widely applied. They can be developed quickly and cheaply, reproduce the base year situation quite accurately at calibration, and at prediction provide broad answers to alternative future strategies.

5 A general urban model: The Garin–Lowry model

The spatial interaction models considered in the last two chapters are partial models that simulate one part of the urban system. General models that attempt to describe several parts of the urban system and simulate the allocation and interaction between several landuse activities would clearly be more useful tools of analysis. However, they are obviously more difficult to construct because of the complex links and interactions between the various urban subsystems. General models can be formulated by coupling together partial gravity models, or by dealing with highly expanded and disaggregated linear or optimizing models. Alternatively, large hybrid models have been developed, particularly in North America, by combining a number of different forms of gravity, linear and optimizing model within an overall equation structure. This type of general model will be discussed in the last chapter after all the basic models have been introduced. As an example of a general model, the widely applied Garin–Lowry model which is based on the gravity concept will be described. This model combines through the economic base mechanism, a residential location model and a service location model which is similar to the retail shopping model. The model will be explained in some detail, and then it will be shown how its generality can be further improved and expanded by attaching additional submodels and by its integration within an overall landuse transportation model structure.

THE LOWRY MODEL

The Garin–Lowry model takes its name from Garin's reformulation of Lowry's model of metropolis (Garin 1966, Lowry 1964).

Lowry's original model was part of a study of the Pittsburgh region and consisted of a series of equations for deriving and allocating landuse activities. The logical structure of the model can be set out in twelve equations. Employment is split into basic and service or non-basic categories and it is assumed that other activities can be determined from a given level of basic employment. The equation system estimates total employment, population and service employment, and then the distribution of these activities is obtained using a further set of gravity-type functions. There is some disaggregation of the activities involved, together with maximum population density constraints and minimum non-basic employment constraints. Implied within the original Lowry formulation is some form of the economic base mechanism. Garin's reformulation of the model explicitly incorporates spatial interaction gravity models within the overall framework, and integrates these models within the economic base methodology.

In addition to Garin's reformulation of the Lowry model, there have been a number of models developed in North America that have followed the original structure of the Lowry model much more closely. These include the time-oriented metropolitan model (TOMM) also developed for the Pittsburgh region, the bay area simulation study (BASS) and the projective landuse model (PLUM) for the San Francisco Bay area, as well as other models of Santa Clara, Georgia, Hawaii and Vancouver (see Putman 1979 and Goldner 1971). These models have further disaggregated the activities, included additional constraints, and sometimes dealt with incremental changes in activities with these changes staggered over a longer time period. In order to make each model more realistic, a larger and more complex equation structure has been developed although this has meant that large amounts of detailed data are required. There have, therefore, been these two lines of development from the original Lowry model, by extending the original set of equations, and through Garin's reformulation of the model, and it is this latter model that will be considered for the rest of this chapter.

THE ECONOMIC BASE MECHANISM

In order to understand how the Garin–Lowry model is constructed it is useful to begin by considering the economic base mechanism for the region as a whole (figure 5.1). Economic base theory assumes that it is the basic employment sector of the economy that

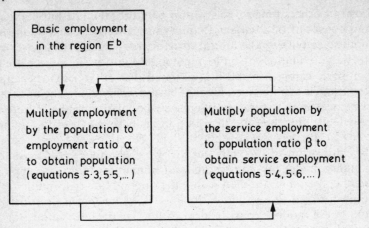

Figure 5.1   An outline of the economic base model

determines the level of service or local employment and population in the region. Total employment E is split between basic employment E^b and service (non-basic) employment E^s, and the procedure works through two multipliers, the population to employment ratio α and the service employment to population ratio β:

$$\alpha = \frac{\text{total population}}{\text{total employment}} \qquad (5.1)$$

$$\beta = \frac{\text{total service employment}}{\text{total population}} \qquad (5.2)$$

Service employment can be regarded as serving the local population and is therefore directed to the production of goods and services for the residents in the study area. Basic employment is the rest of the employment in the region, and is directed to the production of goods and services for elsewhere.

The general idea of the economic base method is that from a given input of basic employment, and working through the two multipliers α and β, the total population, total service employment and therefore total employment of the region can be determined, following an iterative procedure (figure 5.1). If each iteration number is shown between brackets ( ), then the population $P(1)$ generated from the initial level of basic employment E^b can be calculated by applying the population to employment ratio α:

$$P(1) = \alpha E^b \qquad (5.3)$$

Now this population needs to be serviced, and so local service employment $E^s(1)$, is generated by applying the service employment to population ratio β:

$$E^s(1) = \beta P(1)$$

Substituting equation (5.3) into this equation

$$E^s(1) = \alpha \beta E^b \qquad (5.4)$$

This service employment $E^s(1)$ will also generate population in the region in a similar way to the basic employment:

$$P(2) = \alpha E^s(1)$$

Substituting equation (5.4) into this equation

$$P(2) = \alpha^2 \beta E^b \qquad (5.5)$$

Again, this second iteration of population will need servicing, and so will generate local service employment $E^s(2)$:

$$E^s(2) = \beta P(2)$$

Substituting equation (5.5) into this equation

$$E^s(2) = \alpha^2 \beta^2 E^b \qquad (5.6)$$

This iterative procedure continues, with employment generating population which in turn generates employment and so on, although the level of service employment decreases at each iteration. For the region, total employment E can be calculated by summing the iterations of service employment and the initial basic employment:

$$E = E^b + E^s(1) + E^s(2) + E^s(3) + \ldots \qquad (5.7)$$

Substituting equations (5.4), (5.6), etc., into this equation

$$
\begin{aligned}
E &= E^b + \alpha \beta E^b + \alpha^2 \beta^2 E^b + \alpha^3 \beta^3 E^b + \ldots \\
&= E^b (1 + \alpha \beta + \alpha^2 \beta^2 + \alpha^3 \beta^3 + \ldots)
\end{aligned} \qquad (5.8)
$$

The function in α and β within the brackets is a geometric progression, and this summation can be expressed in a simple mathematical form:

$$E = \frac{E^b}{1 - \alpha \beta} = E^b (1 - \alpha \beta)^{-1} \qquad (5.9)$$

Similarly the total population of the region P can be calculated:

$$P = P(1) + P(2) + P(3) + \ldots \qquad (5.10)$$

111

Substituting equations (5.3), (5.5), etc., into equation (5.10), and again using the summation of a geometric progression:

$$P = \frac{\alpha E^b}{1 - \alpha\beta} = \alpha E^b (1 - \alpha\beta)^{-1} \qquad (5.11)$$

From this explanation of the economic base mechanism, it can be seen that from an initial input of basic employment and given the regional multipliers of population to employment ratio and service employment to population ratio, then the regional population, service employment and total employment levels can be determined. However, there are a number of difficulties in applying this technique (see Sayer 1976). In particular it is an oversimplification to assume that the growth or decline of a region is determined solely by the basic employment sector of the economy. There are several other determinants of growth, for example regional growth can be generated by an increase in the service employment sector. Critics of the technique also argue that although it might be possible to show an empirical relationship between basic employment, population and service employment, this could well be caused by other factors in the urban system affecting all three activities rather than there being a causal relationship between them. It is also totally a demand model and deals with an equilibrium situation. It therefore ignores the supply of labour and other activities, and allows no unemployment or labour shortages in the region. Also in using the model predictively, there are problems in making assumptions about how the multipliers α and β will change in the future. In addition there are considerable difficulties in making the division between basic and non-basic employment (see Massey 1973). Despite these criticisms the economic base model has been quite widely applied, largely because it does provide a technique for considering the principal activities of population and employment in a region. However, these difficulties must be borne in mind during its application.

THE GARIN–LOWRY MODEL

The Garin–Lowry model is essentially two gravity models, one for residential location and one for service location, coupled together through the economic base mechanism just outlined. As with the original Lowry model, it assumes that the settlement structure of a region can be described in terms of the three main components of the urban system, population and employment and the interaction between them, both in a spatial and a functional sense. When a region is divided into zones, the Garin–Lowry model follows along similar lines to the regional economic base model, except that it also considers the spatial distribution of the activities and the interaction between them. From an initial zonal distribution of basic employment, the level of population, service employment and total employment in each zone is determined, together with the journey from work to home trip matrix and a relative journey to service centre trip matrix. The structure of the model and the way that the two distribution gravity models are linked together is shown in figure 5.2. For a region divided into a number of zones, the initial input into the model is a distribution of basic employment E_i^b at the work zones. This employment is distributed to residential zones using a residential location model, similar to the gravity model described in the last chapter (equation (4.5)) and the singly constrained model (equation (4.2)):

$$T_{ij} = A_i E_i H_j \exp(-\lambda c_{ij}) \tag{5.12}$$

where

$$A_i = \left[\sum_j H_j \exp(-\lambda c_{ij}) \right]^{-1}$$

In this initial run $E_i = E_i^b$, the distribution of basic employment over the region, T_{ij} is the number of people working in zone i and living in zone j, H_j is the attraction index for zone j, for example the number of dwellings, c_{ij} is the cost of travel between zone i and zone j, and λ is a parameter on the distribution function to be determined at calibration. The number of employed residents in each zone, $T_j(1)$, can be determined by summing a column of the trip matrix $T_{ij}(1)$, where the number between the brackets shows that this is the first iteration of the model:

$$T_j(1) = \sum_i T_{ij}(1) \tag{5.13}$$

The population P_j generated by this employment can be obtained by multiplying the number of employed residents in each zone T_j by the population to employment ratio α:

$$P_j(1) = \alpha T_j(1) \tag{5.14}$$

This population now needs servicing, and will therefore generate service employment at service centres. So the population is

113

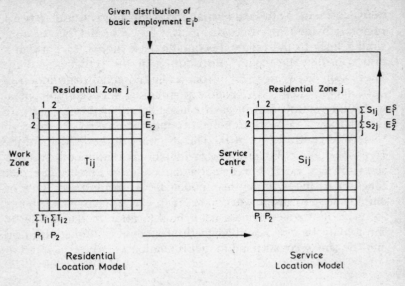

Figure 5.2 The structure of the Garin–Lowry model

distributed from the residential zones to the service centres by using another singly constrained gravity model, but this time a destination constrained model (equation (4.4)). It is in fact very similar to the origin constrained retail shopping model (equation (4.3)), except that the model now deals with all service activities not just retail trade, and so population is not converted to consumer expenditure:

$$S_{ij} = B_j \, P_j \, F_i \exp(\, \mu c_{ij}) \qquad (5.15)$$

where

$$B_j = \left[\sum_i F_i \exp(-\mu c_{ij}) \right]^{-1}$$

Here P_j is the distribution of population generated from the previous input of employment (equation (5.14)), S_{ij} is the flow of people from residential zone j to service centre i, F_i is the attraction index for service centre zone i, for example the service floorspace, c_{ij} is the travel cost between zone i and j, and μ is a parameter on the distribution function to be determined at calibration. The number of people using each service centre S_i can be determined by summing a row of the person trip matrix S_{ij}:

$$S_i(1) = \sum_j S_{ij}(1) \qquad (5.16)$$

The amount of service employment required to serve the number of people travelling to each zone $E_i^s(1)$ can be determined by multiplying by the service employment to population ratio β:

$$E_i^s(1) = \beta S_i(1) \qquad (5.17)$$

This service employment is now at its place of work in the service centres, and the full procedure can be taken into the second iteration. Service employment can now be distributed to zones of residence using the residential location model (equation (5.12)); the employed residents in each zone converted to population by multiplying by the population to employment ratio α(equation (5.14)); the resultant population distributed to use the facilities in the service centres using the service location model (equation (5.15)); and the number of people using each service centre converted into service employment by the service employment to population ratio β(equation (5.17)). This provides input into the third iteration of the model. The whole iterative procedure can be continually repeated until an equilibrium state is reached.

The output from the model will be a set of results at each iteration, which will have to be summed to give total activities by zone and the interaction between zones. Again using a number between brackets to represent the iteration number, the population by zone P_j is obtained by summing the population from equation (5.14) at each iteration:

$$P_j = P_j(1) + P_j(2) + P_j(3) + \ldots \qquad (5.18)$$

Similarly total service employment in each zone E_i^s is obtained by summing the service employment from equation (5.17) at each iteration:

$$E_i^s = E_i^s(1) + E_i^s(2) + E_i^s(3) + \ldots \qquad (5.19)$$

Total employment, E_i, is then the sum of basic and service employment for each zone:

$$E_i = E_i^b + E_i^s \qquad (5.20)$$

The journey to work trip matrix T_{ij} is obtained by summing the trip matrices from each iteration:

$$T_{ij} = T_{ij}(1) + T_{ij}(2) + T_{ij}(3) + \ldots \qquad (5.21)$$

115

The matrix of person trip movements to service centres, S_{ij}, is obtained in a similar way:

$$S_{ij} = S_{ij}(1) + S_{ij}(2) + S_{ij}(3) + \ldots \qquad (5.22)$$

The journey from work to home trip matrix, T_{ij}, is fairly straightforward and shows the number of employed persons travelling from each work zone to each residential zone. Since people generally travel to work each weekday, this matrix can be considered as the evening work to home daily person trip pattern. The morning trip pattern will be the reverse flow T_{ji}, the daily person movements from home to work. The service distribution matrix S_{ij} is more difficult to understand because it is only a relative trip matrix. It shows where the residents of each zone want their services located. For example, if the number of person movements in the service trip matrix S_{ij} between a residential zone and two service centres, shows values of 200 and 100, then it means that twice as many trips will be made to the first zone than to the second zone, and, therefore, twice as much service employment will be required to serve them, which of course does not allow for economies of scale. It does not show how often these trips will be made, each day or each week or any frequency. Also all the 300 residents will travel to each service centre, but they will travel twice as often to the first zone as to the second zone. It does, however, show the relative volume of service trips between residential zones and service centres, which can only be converted into person trips using other travel behaviour data.

When building an operational Garin–Lowry model it is not really necessary to go through a very large number of iterations until the increments of population and service employment reach zero. In practice after about six iterations only very small amounts of population and service employment are being generated. In order to save a considerable amount of computer time, it is better to break into the iterative procedure and approximate the distribution of the remaining activity. It was shown in the description of the economic base mechanism that the total population of the region (equation (5.11)), and the total employment for the region (equation (5.9)) could be calculated from a given input of basic employment E^b and the regional multipliers α and β. Break into the procedure after the residential location model has determined the zonal population at the fifth iteration. Sum the total population generated at each iteration within the model and compare it with the regional total, in order to find the amount of population still to be distributed. Do not change the fifth iteration zonal population totals that were output from the residential location model, but scale up the population totals that are going to be input into the service location model, so that all the remaining population will be distributed to service centres. The remaining service employment at the service centres will be determined, which will be used in the residential location model to determine the final journey from work to home trip distribution and the final iteration of zonal population. The results obtained from this shortened procedure will be extremely close to those obtained from the full procedure, and this will be shown in the small example to follow.

The Garin–Lowry Model can alternatively be presented in quite a compact form using matrix algebra notation (Garin 1966, Batty 1976), and it can be computed in this form using matrix operations.

A Garin–Lowry model of north-east Lancashire

To look at the procedure involved in the Garin–Lowry model, consider a small example in north-east Lancashire (figure 5.3). The three towns of Burnley, Nelson and Colne are situated in a valley at the edge of the Pennine Hills and developed as textile towns in the nineteenth century, but now have a far more mixed industrial structure. It is difficult to make a three zone model self-contained, and there is in fact a significant amount of interaction with towns to the west of Burnley which would have to be taken into account if an operational model was being developed. The actual calculations in the residential location and service distribution models will not be presented because they are similar to the residential location model and shopping model previously described. It is the iterative procedure and the method of linking the two models that is new and therefore being presented.

Data for these towns are taken from the Population Census Reports, and the population and total employment are shown in table 5.1. This information, together with the journey to work trip matrix is fairly straightforward information to collect. More difficult is the division of employment into basic and service employment, but using the British Standard Industrial Classification, the primary and manufacturing sectors 1 to 17 were classified as basic employment and the service sectors 18 to 24 as service

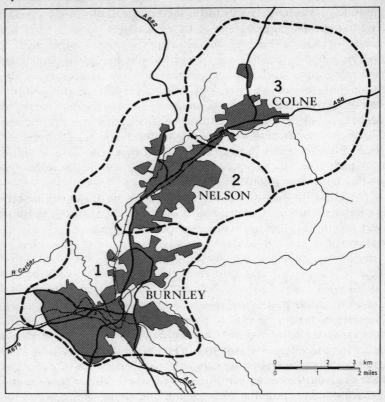

Figure 5.3   The north-east Lancashire study region

employment. An operational study would need a far more refined definition than the one used here (see Massey 1973). With this information the two multipliers, the population to employment ratio α (equation (5.1)) and the service employment to population ratio β (equation (5.2)), can be calculated giving $\alpha = 2.07925$ and $\beta = 0.18886$. Another problem is finding suitable attraction indexes for the two distribution models. Here the number of dwellings in each town, weighted by an environmental factor, was used in the residential location model, while retail floorspace was used as a proxy for all service activity in the service location model. The travel cost matrix was calculated as in previous examples, in terms of an overall travel time, assuming different speeds on urban and rural roads. The person trip movement pattern to service centres is generally only available if a special

Table 5.1 Population and employment data for the north-east Lancashire region

	Population	Total employment	Basic employment	Service employment
Burnley	76,960	40,240	22,820	17,420
Nelson	42,250	18,160	12,220	5,940
Colne	20,100	8,600	5,650	2,950
Totals	139,310	67,000	40,690	26,310

survey has been conducted in the study region. If this information is not available, all that can be done is to see if the trip pattern looks 'reasonable', while giving satisfactory zone totals in terms of service employment.

With this information the model was then run a number of times, gradually changing the parameters until a reasonably close fit was obtained with $\lambda = 0.35$ in the residential location model (equation (5.12)) and $\mu = 0.25$ in the service distribution model (equation (5.15)). This indicates that people travel further to use services than they do for their journey to work. The main output from the model is shown in tables 5.2 and 5.3 and figure 5.4. The level of population and service employment allocated to the three towns at each iteration (figure 5.4) shows how there is a rapid decrease in the quantities to be allocated after the first few iterations. The first iteration of population is the result of the distribution of basic employment to zones of residence which is then multiplied by the population to employment ratio α to give population in each zone. This population, fed through the service distribution model, and then multiplied by the service employment

Table 5.2 The estimated journey from work to home trip matrix and zonal population for the north-east Lancashire region

Work zone (origin)	Residential zone (destination)			
	Burnley	Nelson	Colne	Totals
Burnley	36,755	3,005	186	39,946
Nelson	530	15,791	2,040	18,361
Colne	32	2,018	6,643	8,693
Totals	37,317	20,814	8,869	67,000
Population	77,591	43,278	18,441	139,310

Table 5.3 The estimated person movements from residential zones to service centres and zonal service employment for the north-east Lancashire region

Service centre zone (destination)	Residential zone (origin)			Totals	Service employment
	Burnley	Nelson	Colne		
Burnley	75,312	13,562	1,808	90,682	17,126
Nelson	2,045	24,868	5,603	32,516	6,141
Colne	236	4,847	11,029	16,112	3,043
Totals	77,593	43,277	18,440	139,310	26,310

to population ratio β, generates the first iteration of service employment. This then leads into the second iteration and so on. The figure shows that 94% of the activity is distributed on the first three iterations, and 99.64% on the first six iterations. To break into the iterative procedure and allocate all the remaining activity during the sixth iteration as previously described, means that only 0.36% of the activity is being allocated in this way. Most of this will be distributed to the correct zones and therefore the errors involved will be negligible.

The final journey from work to home trip pattern, which is the summation of the trip patterns at each iteration (equation (5.21)), is shown in table 5.2. It shows the distribution of all workers to their zone of residence, and the summation of a column of the matrix gives the total number of employed residents in each town, which when multiplied by the regional population to employment ratio α gives the estimated population in each town. The equivalent trip matrix showing the person movements from residence zones to service centres, which is again the summation of the trip patterns at each iteration (equation (5.22)), is shown in table 5.3. The population allocated to each zone is distributed to service centres, and the summation of a row of the matrix gives the number of people supporting each centre, which is then multiplied by the service employment to population ratio β to give the service employment required in each town. This example has been used principally to explain the modelling procedure, but it can be seen from the tables that quite a reasonably close fit has been obtained for population and service employment in each of the towns (tables 5.1, 5.2 and 5.3).

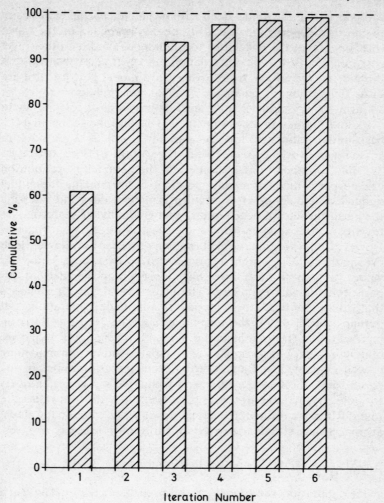

Figure 5.4 The cumulative percentage of regional population and service employment allocated at each iteration

CALIBRATING THE MODEL

The Garin–Lowry model is calibrated at a base year, very often a census year, in a similar way to the partial models previously described, where the output from the model is compared with the actual base year information. Here though the situation is more complex in that the model deals with two linked partial models and there are two parameter values to be determined, λ on the travel cost function of the residential location model and μ on the travel cost function of the service location model. It can be shown that the best calibration statistics to measure model performance are those derived by the technique of maximum likelihood, which for a Garin–Lowry model are the average travel costs for journey to work and journey to service centres. It can also be shown that the best initial estimates for the parameter values λ and μ are 1.5/average work trip cost and 1.5/average service trip cost. Starting from these initial estimates of the parameters, calibration can be performed on a trial and error basis, running the model under a whole series of different parameter values and assessing the performance after each run, so that gradually the search moves towards what appears to be the best level of performance. However, some automatic calibration methods are available which use mathematical search techniques to find the best parameter values, and these procedures have considerably speeded up this part of the modelling process. There are several search techniques that could be used to perform an automatic calibration, but perhaps the fastest is the technique based on Newton–Raphson type methods. The mathematics behind this search technique are quite complex, but its application to spatial interaction modelling is well explained in Batty (1976). From initial estimates of the parameters, the Newton–Raphson technique searches iteratively for improved parameter values until eventually the best values are found when the estimated average travel cost is equal to the actual average travel cost for journey to work and journey to services.

PREDICTING WITH THE MODEL

After calibration the model can be used predictively. The usual procedure is to make best estimates of the variables within the model for some future data; best estimates of the basic employment distribution E_i^b, the residential attraction indexes H_j, the service attraction indexes F_i, the travel cost matrix c_{ij}, and the multipliers α and β. A predictive run of the model using the calibration parameter values for λ and μ would provide the most likely population and employment distribution for the area at the future date. However, the variables within the model can be altered further in order to test the impact of major changes in the region and to simulate the outcome of public policy alternatives:

(1) To simulate economic policy alternatives with regard to employment, alter the distribution of basic employment E_i^b.

(2) To simulate residential policy alternatives alter the location of new residential development H_j, and apply capacity constraints to certain zones.

(3) To simulate service centre policy alternative, the location of new services F_i can be altered and capacity constraints applied to certain centres.

(4) To simulate constrained planning policies, particularly environmental policies, then alter the constraints on the amount of population and service employment allowed in particular zones.

(5) To simulate transport policy alternatives modify the transportation network by changing the travel cost matrix c_{ij}.

(6) To simulate changes in accessibility in the region which might result from a change in transport policy, alter the parameters λ and μ on the travel cost functions.

(7) To simulate the effect of changes in female employment rates and the effect of a change in the overall level of service provision then change the multipliers α and β.

This type of model can therefore be used, not only to gain a fuller understanding of the planning problems of the area, but also to estimate the consequences of certain planning policies. For example, the model of the Venice region to be described later, considers the effect of a series of alternative transport, employment and residential policies on the historical centre.

Constraints on the allocation of activities to zones

Any future allocation of population and employment could well be subject to constraints on the capacity of zones to accommodate the growth. The amount of land available for urban development will be determined either by the crude physical capacity of the zone or by planning policies, which might relate to safeguarding areas of high agricultural value or environmental considerations. Maximum and minimum capacity constraints can be imposed on the level of population and the level of service employment allowed in any zone. After each run of the model, zones can be tested to determine if the new allocation is within the capacity limits. In the gravity model, the constraints procedure modifies the attraction index in the equation. For example, the attraction index in the residential location model is H_j and if for zone j the estimated population is above the maximum allowed, then a coefficient W_j will be applied, with $W_j < 1.0$, to give the new attraction index $W_j H_j$. This new attraction index will be lower than the original value, and hence when the model is rerun, fewer workers will be attracted to residential zone j and the population reduced to a level nearer the constrained value. The value of W_j could be set as the ratio of the maximum constrained population over the estimated population of zone j, but because of the iterative nature of the model, and since the redistribution might result in other zones exceeding their capacities, it can take several runs of the model to reach an equilibrium that satisfies all the locational constraints. However, there are some fast automatic constraint procedures that can be applied to the model. Probably the best is the polynomial-structural algorithm which moves quickly to an equilibrium situation when all the capacity constraints are satisfied (see Batty *et al.* 1974). A good example of how constraints have been applied to Garin–Lowry models will be described shortly in looking at the urbanization effects of a proposed new airport for London, with new residential development severely restricted near the airport site.

OPERATIONAL GARIN–LOWRY MODELS

The earliest versions of the Garin–Lowry model were developed in the late 1960s particularly in Britain, and then during the 1970s its application spread rapidly with operational models being developed in many parts of the world. In Britain models were developed for local authority areas such as Bedfordshire (Cripps and Foot 1969) and Cheshire (Barras *et al.* 1971), at the town scale for Reading, Cambridge and Stevenage (Echenique, Crowther and Lindsay 1969) and for larger regions, as for example in the Nottinghamshire–Derbyshire Subregional Study (Batty 1970, 1976), and to investigate the effect of building a new town in central Lancashire (Batty 1969, 1976). Considerable expansion of the model took place during the 1970s with, for example, a disaggregation of landuse activities, the inclusion of further submodels and an integration of the model within a more comprehensive landuse transportation model structure. This last development was particularly the work of Echenique and the model has been applied in many parts of the world, but especially in South America, Europe and the Middle East (Echenique and

Williams 1979). Other versions of the Garin–Lowry model have been developed in European countries, India, Australia, Nigeria (Ayeni 1979) and also for Moscow (Posokhin *et al.* 1980). There have been a number of applications in North America, for example, Toronto, Baltimore, Dallas–Fort Worth (Turner 1975) and Los Angeles (Richardson and Gordon 1979), although it is the alternative development from the Lowry model which extended the original equation structure that has proved more popular. Some of the developments to the basic Garin–Lowry model will be covered later, but to demonstrate how it can be applied in practice, two operational models will now be described in some detail. Firstly a model to consider the impact, in terms of urbanization of the location of a third London airport (Cripps and Foot 1970), and secondly a model of the Venice region to study the effectiveness of alternative future planning policies on the historical centre of Venice (Piasentin, Costa and Foot 1978).

The urbanization effects of a third London airport

The introduction of a major airport in any area will mean the rapid introduction of a large number of basic jobs and a consequent increase in population due to the inflow of workers and dependent families. This in turn will lead to an increase in service employment and also extra basic employment due to the attraction of firms into the area through the opening of the airport. The Commission on the Third London Airport estimated that the basic employment at a four lane runway airport by 1996 would be about 65,000 employees while an additional net increase of nearly 18,000 basic jobs could be expected due to the opening of the airport. This in turn would generate an extra 42,500 service employment and lead to an overall population increase of about 314,000 residents. This would obviously have an enormous effect on the urban activities of any area, resulting in major new development, particularly residential development, road improvements, shopping centres and the provision of other services.

The Garin-Lowry model, which is well able to consider just these sorts of relationships in the urban system, was calibrated for 1966 and the forecasts made for 1996, by which time an airport could be fully developed and operational. The region likely to be affected by an airport at Thurleigh or Cublington is centred on the County of Bedfordshire, but also includes parts of Buckinghamsire, Northamptonshire, Huntingdonshire and Hertfordshire.

Forecasts were performed, firstly dealing with the expected growth of the area without an airport and, secondly, with the addition of an airport at Thurleigh and alternatively at Cublington. There is expected to be considerable growth in this area without any airport, with basic employment and consequently service employment and population roughly doubling between 1966 and 1996, a third of this activity being located in the new city of Milton Keynes, and the rest located largely around existing major urban areas. This region is expected, therefore, to undergo considerable expansion between 1966 and 1996 even without an airport. An airport would then add an extra population of almost a third of a million residents to the region.

Studying the impact of the airport sited at Thurleigh involved both an unconstrained and constrained allocation of urban activities. Firstly, the model estimated the demand for residential and service locations and for travel between home and work and home and service centres, unconstrained by planning policies. Figure 5.5 shows the unconstrained allocation of population which tends to show a concentration of people in zones fairly close to the airport site. Constraints on urban development were then applied, particularly around the airport where nuisance from noise increases the nearer one lives to the airport. New development was, therefore, excluded from all areas likely to have a noise number index (NNI) of above 40 once the airport had been developed, since noise levels above this cause too much disturbance. Other local physical constraints included areas of high agricultural value, high landscape value, mineral-bearing land and areas affected by air pollution from the Bedfordshire brickfields. Figure 5.5 also shows the constrained allocation of population together with the 30, 35 and 40 NNI isopleths around the new airport at Thurleigh. This constrained allocation shows that there is now no population growth within the area affected by noise, and new development is far more concentrated in three main urban areas.

The effect of satisfying these constraints, of course, is to lengthen the journey to work. The average distance to work for those employed at the new airport is now about 15 km (9.5 mile), whereas the unconstrained average distance was about 11.5 km (7.2 mile). Figure 5.6 shows a comparison of the locational behaviour of workers at Thurleigh and Cublington airports for the unconstrained and constrained situations, together with behaviour of workers at Heathrow, with the curves showing the cumulative percentage of workers locating over increasing travel times away

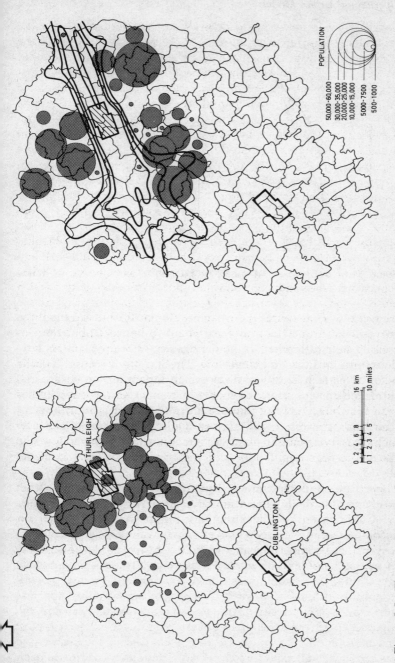

Figure 5.5   The unconstrained and constrained allocation of net change in population 1996 due to the location of an airport at Thurleigh

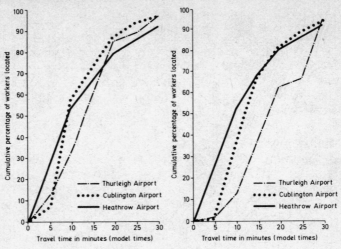

Figure 5.6 Journey from work to home for an unconstrained and constrained allocation

from the workplace. There is a close similarity between the three curves when no planning constraints are imposed, but there is considerable difference in the constrained allocation, particularly between Thurleigh and Heathrow. This is entirely the result of the planned pattern of urban development separating workplace and residence and consequently higher journey to work costs, together with very large flows of interurban traffic on the journey to work from major areas to the airport. Output from the model also includes service employment distribution which largely follows the distribution of population, and the trip pattern from home to service centres.

Here just one constrained situation for an airport at Thurleigh has been described, while a similar form of analysis was performed for Cublington. It is clear that several alternative strategies for accommodating the new development could have been put forward and compared using the Garin–Lowry model. There are, of course, problems in applying this type of urban model to an area, but the model does provide a picture of the general urbanization effects of the location of an airport supplying information on activity totals and spatial interaction over the region. It is obvious that a new airport is going to have considerable impact on what is at present a fairly rural area, and the urban model provides an idea of the extent of this impact.

Modelling the Venice urban system

This study (Piasentin, Costa and Foot 1978) examines the problem of Venice in the context of the whole Venetian urban system (see figure 2.1) and uses urban modelling techniques to consider the effectiveness of alternative planning policies for the area (see figure 5.7).

The problems of Venice are now well known with the historical centre fighting for survival. There is the physical condition of the city where the frequent floods and the air and water pollution are ruining the environment of the lagoon and the historical centre so making residence and any kind of activity difficult. At the same time the flight of population towards the mainland is considerably altering the socio-economic structure of the city. There has been an enormous decrease in the population of the island of Venice (zone 14), from 192,000 in 1951 to 107,000 in 1976, with a big movement to Mestre (zone 19) and Marghera (zone 20) from 1950 up to the mid-1960s; since then the movement has been to areas further inland. The social structure of the city has changed, with a rapidly increasing proportion of professional and high income workers living in Venice and a consequent decrease in blue-collar workers and their families. Over two thirds of the employment of the subregion is concentrated in Venice, Mestre and Marghera, and there are large flows of workers travelling from the other parts of the area to work in these centres, with over 17,000 commuting to Venice (zone 14) each day.

Venice is clearly part of a larger urban system (figures 2.1 and 5.7), therefore any consideration of the future socio-economic development of Venice has to refer to this larger dynamic unit. Whatever is happening to Venice cannot be divorced from the rest of the urban area and vice versa. The socio-economic relationships observed in the Venetian area can be successfully formalized within the Garin–Lowry model. The model was calibrated for 1971 and the input information was fairly standard except that the residential attraction index was a composite function including the quantity of housing, house price and the mean time to the main employment centres. House price is important because it varies considerably over the area, with prices in Venice two and a half times as high as those in the outer area. The mean time to the main employment centres can be considered more of a proxy for various other factors which have a positive influence on residential attraction, such as the type of housing available, the distinction of

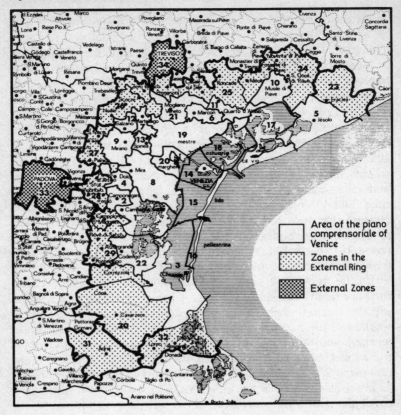

Figure 5.7   The zoning system for the Venice study region

residents according to social conditions and the opportunity of obtaining a supplementary income.

A series of predictive runs of the model were then performed to study a variety of alternative transport, employment and residential policies for the area. Firstly, a transport policy that reduced travel time from all areas to Venice (zone 14) by ten minutes, would have the effect of furthering the population shift away from Venice, and to a lesser extent Mestre (zone 19) and Marghera (zone 20), to areas further inland. These outer areas become more attractive as residential areas to workers in the main employment centres of the island of Venice, Mestre and Marghera. So, other things remaining equal, especially house prices, this policy would provide a further incentive to residents to leave Venice and lead to an increase in urban sprawl within the surrounding area. A second transport policy, that caused an increase of 20% in transport costs over the whole area, would reduce the whole commuting propensity in the system and make residents concentrate as far as possible near their workplaces, and the nearby service centres. Areas with a high level of employment like Venice would attract a great many more inhabitants and areas that are typically dormitory residential would lose population. This would therefore put further pressure on the residential capacity of Venice and cause an additional increase in house prices.

Since some of the problems of Venice are caused by the petrochemical industries at Marghera and Mestre, two alternative employment policies for the future were tested. Firstly, an expansion of these industries leading to 10,000 extra employment jobs on the lagoon, south of Marghera in the commune of Mira (zone 8). The results show a very strong pressure for residential development in Mira (zone 8), Mirano (zone 9) and Dolo (zone 4). Venice is not really influenced, but would naturally feel the environmental effects. Secondly, an employment policy to reduce industrial activity close to Venice involving the decentralization of 10,000 basic jobs from Marghera (zone 20) to Codevigo (zone 22) on the lagoon much further south. The effect would be to cause a movement of population away from Mestre and Marghera and towards the south of the study area. Venice would hardly be affected at all by this process of redistribution in terms of either population or service employment redistribution. However, the high pressure for residential development in the area near Codevigo and the large decrease in population in Mestre and Marghera, seems to pose serious doubts about the practicability of such a policy.

One residential policy simulation was performed to look at the effect of increasing the residential capacity of Venice by the restoration of old underutilized houses and the transfer of some accommodation to residential use. The results indicate that the increase in housing capacity would not generate a large enough increase in population. It would seem that any policy to increase the residential capacity of Venice is very closely connected to the control of house prices.

Here then the Venetian urban system was studied as a system of employment and residential relationships in order to estimate the effects of certain planning policies on Venice. Any number of predictions can be performed, but those described above reveal three main aspects of the residential equilibrium of Venice: a low sensitivity to the amount of employment at Marghera (zone 20); a high sensitivity to any modifications in transport costs; and a high sensitivity to house prices.

FURTHER DEVELOPMENTS TO THE GARIN—LOWRY MODEL

Early applications of the Garin—Lowry model tended to be aggregate landuse studies, looking at the distributions of population and employment and the interaction between them. Later developments have involved expanding this basic model by the disaggregation of activities, by the inclusion of additional activities often in the form of extra submodels, by the inclusion of evaluation procedures, and by combining into a more integrated structure the landuse planning and transportation planning aspects of a study. To explain these developments, two models will be described: the urban system model developed by Voorhees and associates, and the landuse transportation models developed by Echenique and his colleagues at Cambridge.

The urban systems model

The urban systems model (Turner 1975) shows how the basic Garin—Lowry model can be further developed to include a series of submodels which provide considerable information in the evaluation of alternative strategies. It has been applied to the Dallas—Fort Worth region in Texas as well as to a number of other areas, and considers four topics of particular interest at evaluation: transportation, urban and economic development, social equity, and the environment and energy. Firstly a more elaborate transport system is constructed. Movement between zones is expressed as generalized cost rather than time or distance, and there is an additional trip matrix to account for the trips made from work to use services. Different levels of highway and transit provision are then tested and the total transport costs compared. Secondly, dealing with the allocation of new development, a constraints procedure is included, similar to that already discussed, but this can be modified and zonal constraints overriden if the pressures for development become too great. To test the efficiency of the siting of the new development, a further submodel determines the cost of providing public utilities for the various alternative schemes, and also sees how well the urban development fits in with the proposed transport system. Thirdly, another submodel looks at the accessibility of different socio-economic groups to the various urban activities, jobs, dwellings and the recreational, cultural, social and medical facilities. Accessibility is measured as the number of opportunities available within specified ranges of generalized travel cost. Different planning policies provide rather different levels of opportunity for the various socio-economic groups, and in evaluating the policies an attempt can be made towards some greater form of social equity. Fourthly, a submodel deals with the level of atmospheric pollution and energy consumption resulting from the alternative transport systems. It can be seen that these refinements to the basic model provide a great deal of additional information that can be extremely useful in comparing and evaluating alternative planning policies for a region.

The Echenique models

Marcial Echenique and his partners, starting from a basic Garin–Lowry model framework, have gradually developed during the 1970s a comprehensive land-use transportation model (Geraldes, Echenique and Williams 1978, Echenique and Williams 1979). This development has occurred during the application of the model to a number of cities around the world: Santiago in Chile, Caracas in Venezuela, São Paulo in Brazil, Tehran in Iran, Bilbao in Spain, São Paulo in Brazil for a second time and Buenos Aires in Argentina. It has already been noted that a gravity model is basically a demand model determining the level of activity in each zone. From the beginning, Echenique included an urban stock model dealing with the allocation of floorspace, in order to simulate the supply side of the urban land market. It also meant that the activities in the model were converted to landuse, measured in terms of floorspace. This has now been expanded to deal with differential costs of location, rents per unit of land and the provision of public services. The Garin–Lowry framework has also been expanded to include theoretical elements from Alonso's economic theory of urban location. When applying the model, the demand and supply of land in each zone has to be in balance, which is achieved by repeatedly rerunning the model and relocating activities until an equilibrium solution is reached. This landuse model is then linked with a regional allocation model and a detailed transport model. The regional model deals with the country as a whole and takes account of expected future trends and policies in order to estimate future levels of employment, population and real income for the particular city being studied. The transport model takes the person flow distributions from the landuse model, converts them into trip distributions by means of a set of trip rates, and then in a fairly conventional way, assigns these trips to the network, taking account of traffic congestion and capacity constraints. These three models are all integrated through time and at prediction, output from the models at a previous time period is used as input information at the next time period. Throughout the modelling procedure, activities and landuses are dealt with at a disaggregated level. The Tehran model for example uses four employment categories, eight residential income groups and four modes of travel. Thus it can be seen that Echenique has developed a highly comprehensive landuse transportation model which is capable of reproducing the main interactions between urban development and transport. Output from the model can be used to evaluate a wide range of policy options by comparing the different schemes in terms of economic efficiency, the distribution costs and benefits and environmental impact.

Applying the Garin–Lowry model

This section has shown how it is possible to expand the Garin–Lowry model into a highly comprehensive planning model. However, with disaggregated activities and a large number of zones, special surveys will have to be undertaken to collect the base year information which overall will lead to high development costs over quite a long time period. On the other hand, the basic Garin–Lowry model, using published and other available information at an aggregate level, can be developed very quickly and very cheaply. Between these two extremes, there are of course varying degrees of sophistication and in studying an area, the type of model developed will depend completely on each particular situation. Why is the model being developed? What form of analysis is required? How comprehensive a model is required? How much disaggregation of the activities is needed? How much time can be spent on model development? How much money is available for developing the model? These are the sort of questions that have to be answered before deciding on the type of model to be built and these answers will probably be different for a small local authority compared with a large national city. A small local authority might develop a fairly cheap, straightforward, rather aggregate model whereas a national city is much more likely to develop a large comprehensive landuse transportation model.

AN ASSESSMENT OF THE GARIN–LOWRY MODEL

The Garin–Lowry model has been widely applied with operational models developed in many parts of the world. It does however have its problems and limitations, just like any mathematical representation of a real world urban system (see Sayer 1976). Most of the limitations that were discussed in relation to the spatial interaction gravity models in the last chapter will also be true for the Garin—Lowry model, since its distribution functions are also gravity models. It is a static equilibrium model although recursive predictions can be made in the future. The model is concerned with empirically observed relationships and does not attempt to explain the social, economic and spatial relationships determining the trip pattern. It is basically a demand model, although the supply of certain activities can be brought into the model, usually in the form of constraints to development or as an additional stock model, and this has been incorporated into a number of operational versions of the model. When the calibrated parameter values are retained at prediction, it is being assumed that the behavioural distribution pattern remains unchanged, when in fact changes in such things as the level of car ownership, public transport and new roads are continually altering the pattern. However, this does give an initial estimate at prediction and the parameters can be altered to try and consider likely effects of any changes in this pattern as indeed can the location of new housing and employment. There are also the usual operational problems of zoning, data collection and calibration, but these apply to the development of any urban model.

There are in addition certain problems associated just with the Garin–Lowry model. Its formulation incorporates the economic base mechanism and a number of problems concerning this theory have already been discussed. These include in particular the problem of assuming that all growth in a region is a result of changes in the basic employment distribution, the difficulty of making the division between basic and service employment, and the fact that it is totally a demand model. It has also been mentioned previously that within the model there are no economies to scale in the growth of service centres, with all centres growing in proportion to the number of trips made to each centre.

In reality, larger centres probably attract a more than proportional number of trips, and although it complicates the model, there is no reason why the model should not take this into account. All the multipliers and ratios used in the model are regional values whereas there will be a variation over the region. Again this could be included in the model, but at the expense of a more complex model. Basic employment is determined outside the Garin–Lowry model and then fed in as an input variable. In fact there is no reason why basic employment should not be determined internally as a submodel within the system being modelled. However, it is treated as an exogenous variable because it is felt that so many divergent factors influence the level and distribution of basic employment over a region, that it is preferable to treat it in a separate analysis and modelling exercise.

Some of these problems can be overcome but at the expense of greatly complicating the model structure. The problem that then arises is that parts of the model become quite sophisticated, while other parts retain their original simplicity, such as the gravity model which is a general aggregate distribution model with a single parameter to distribute activities over the region. How far should activities be disaggregated and other parts of the model expanded while at the same time retaining the simple distribution models? It could be argued that a simple model, developed quickly and cheaply, will provide sufficiently reliable output. Alternatively it could be argued that any new development to the model that improves its representation of the real world should be incorporated.

These problems have led some critics to reject the use of the Garin–Lowry model (Sayer 1976, Lee 1973). However, despite these difficulties there are good reasons for its popularity and widespread application. It is conceptually a better model than the original Lowry model, but the main advantage is that it is manageable in terms of technique and cost. Data requirements are fairly light, and if used intelligently it can provide valuable information on future alternative policies for a region. There have been considerable developments to the model in the 1970s, particularly in terms of calibration and constraints procedures, disaggregation of activities, the inclusion of additional submodels and its integration into a full landuse transportation model. It is, therefore, highly flexible in its use, since it can be used at an aggregate level and run quickly and cheaply as in the Venice model, or a far more complex form of the model can be applied within a very large and costly landuse transportation study, as in Bilbao and São Paulo.

6 Linear urban models

An alternative method of modelling the urban system is to develop a model based on linear regression and econometric techniques. The model deals with the zonal distribution of landuse activities over a region by deriving a set of linear equations, each of the form

$$Y_i = b_0 + b_1 X_{1i} + b_2 X_{2i} + \ldots \tag{6.1}$$

Here X_{1i}, X_{2i}, . . . are the independent variables that explain and are thought to cause the variations in the zonal distribution of the dependent variable Y_i in a region of n zones with $i = 1$ to n in equation (6.1). These variables are socio-economic and landuse activities, with information collected for each zone in the region. Generally population and employment are used as the dependent variable Y_i, either at an aggregate level or more usually in a disaggregated form. Other dependent variables might be retail floorspace, the amount of residential development or the numbers attending recreational sites. These linear models have generally been developed for variables representing change over a given time period, rather than the total level of activity at one point in time. The independent variables X_{1i}, X_{2i}, . . . are chosen because they are thought to have an influence on the dependent variable and will explain the zonal variation over the region. These might include the level of accessibility to population and employment, land area, the level of employment and population at a previous time period, and the availability of public utilities. Using zonal data on all the variables Y_i, X_{1i}, X_{2i}, . . . the coefficients b_0, b_1, b_2, . . . are derived at calibration using the least squares regression procedure to give the 'best' linear relationship. It can be seen that the linear model is only an allocation model in that land use activities are allocated to zones, and it does not model the spatial

137

interaction between these activities. This can only be obtained by developing a further model and using the output from the linear regression model as input into a spatial interaction gravity model. This is very different from the Garin–Lowry model considered in the last chapter which both allocates activities to zones and determines the interaction between these activities over the region. The linear regression model has been used very little in Britain where the gravity model has been much preferred. However, in the USA there have been a large number of linear models developed since the mid-1960s, and these will be discussed later.

LINEAR REGRESSION

Regression analysis is such a widely used technique that only an outline of the procedure and the calculations will be given here. There are now a very large number of introductory statistics books, several specifically written for planners, geographers and social scientists (e.g. Baxter 1976, Silk 1979 and Yeomans 1968) and any of these will contain a chapter explaining the theory of regression and the calculations involved in determining the equations. There are also a number of books that deal only with regression techniques (e.g. Chatterjee and Price 1977) and these can be consulted if a more detailed explanation is required. Also every computer has a software regression package so that obtaining the calculated equations is now very easy. The vitally important point that is stressed in this chapter is the interpretation of the regression equations and their use in the urban modelling process.

Simple linear regression

Consider firstly the situation of one independent variable X_{1i} and a regression equation of the form

$$Y_i = b_0 + b_1 X_{1i} \tag{6.2}$$

Data are collected on the variables Y_i and X_{1i}, for a series of observations which for spatial data is a set of zones, and the basic idea is to find the 'best' average straight line to represent the relationship between the variables. To explain this further, the Isle of Wight in southern England (figure 6.1) has been divided into an eight zone region and data collected on population and employment for 1971 for each zone (table 6.1). Since the Isle of Wight is only linked to the mainland by boat, it forms a fairly closed urban

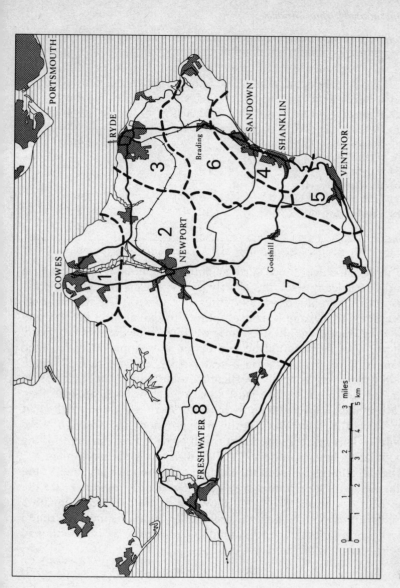

Figure 6.1 The Isle of Wight study region

Table 6.1 Population and employment for the Isle of Wight

Zone		1971 population	1971 employment
(1) Cowes	(C)	18,910	8,640
(2) Newport	(N)	22,309	10,850
(3) Ryde	(R)	23,204	7,620
(4) Sandown– Shanklin	(S)	15,890	4,960
(5) Ventnor	(V)	6,931	2,070
(6) Brading	(B)	6,502	1,690
(7) Godshill	(G)	5,406	1,410
(8) Freshwater	(F)	10,347	2,860
Totals		109,499	40,100

system. However, it is also an important holiday centre and a retirement centre for the elderly, which means that the employment to population activity rates are lower than the national average. The example is used purely to explain the process and any real model would need at least thirty zones, preferably many more. This information on population and employment for each zone can be presented on a scatter diagram (figure 6.2) where population (Y_i) is on the vertical axis and employment (X_{1i}) is on the horizontal axis. The least squares regression procedure then determines the coefficients b_0 and b_1 of equation (6.2) that produce the best average linear regression line through these points. This regression equation will provide best estimates of the population in each zone $\hat{Y}_i$ for the given levels of employment X_{1i}. The differences between the actual population in each zone Y_i and the estimated population from the regression equation $\hat{Y}_i$ are the vertical deviations $(Y_i - \hat{Y}_i)$ shown in figure 6.2. Since equation (6.2) represents the general regression equation, then for zone i with employment X_{1i}, the estimated population $\hat{Y}_i$ can be obtained by substituting X_{1i} into this equation:

$$\hat{Y}_i = b_0 + b_1 X_{1i} \tag{6.3}$$

The best average straight line through the observed points of figure 6.2 must ensure that the sum of the vertical deviations about the regression line are equal to zero, i.e.

$$\sum_i (Y_i - \hat{Y}_i) = 0 \tag{6.4}$$

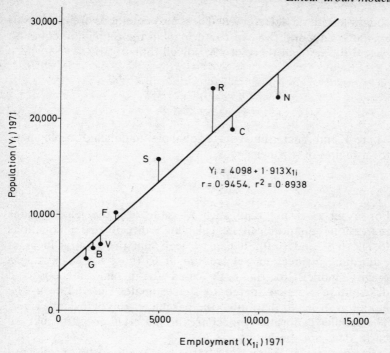

Figure 6.2 The scatter diagram and regression line for population against employment

However, the least squares regression procedure involves minimizing the sum of the squared deviations between the actual and estimated populations:

$$\text{minimize} \sum_i (Y_i - \hat{Y}_i)^2 \qquad (6.5)$$

By substituting for $\hat{Y}_i$ (equation (6.3)) into equation (6.5), this minimization can be reformulated in terms of available data and the coefficients b_0 and b_1:

$$\text{minimize} \sum_i [Y_i - (b_0 + b_1 X_{1i})]^2 \qquad (6.6)$$

This equation can be minimized using differential calculus. By performing a partial differentiation with respect to b_0 while holding b_1 constant, and setting the equation equal to zero, and then similarly with respect to b_1 holding b_0 constant, two normal

141

equations can be determined. These two equations are in terms of available data and the two coefficients in the regression equation b_0 and b_1, and can therefore be solved for b_1 and b_0:

$$b_1 = \frac{\sum_i (Y_i - \overline{Y})(X_{1i} - \overline{X}_1)}{\sum_i (X_{1i} - \overline{X}_1)^2} \tag{6.7}$$

$$b_0 = \overline{Y} - b_1\overline{X}_1 \tag{6.8}$$

where $\overline{Y}$ and $\overline{X}_1$ are the average zonal population and employment for a region of n zones:

$$\overline{Y} = \frac{\sum_i Y_i}{n} \text{ and } \overline{X}_1 = \frac{\sum_i X_{1i}}{n} \tag{6.9}$$

For a set of zonal data such as table 6.1, the least squares regression equation can be calculated directly from equations (6.7), (6.8) and (6.9). It can be seen that the general ideas of calibrating a linear model are similar to those for calculating a gravity model, for in both cases the actual and observed distributions are compared to the estimates derived from the model in order to determine the parameter or coefficient values. The detailed calibration procedures are different of course, but the basic ideas are similar.

For the Isle of Wight data (table 6.1) the following results are obtained from equations (6.7), (6.8) and (6.9):

$$\begin{aligned} b_1 &= 1.9131 & b_0 &= 4098 \\ \overline{Y} &= 13687.4 & \overline{X}_1 &= 5012.5 \end{aligned} \tag{6.10}$$

The least squares regression model (equation (6.2)) has now been calculated:

$$Y_i = 4098 + 1.9131 \, X_{1i} \tag{6.11}$$

where

$$Y_i = \text{population } X_{1i} = \text{employment}$$

The regression line is plotted on the graph (figure 6.2). By substituting employment (X_{1i}) into the regression equation (6.11), the estimated population ($\hat{Y}_i$) from this general relationship can be calculated for each zone (column 3 in table 6.2). For example at Cowes (zone 1), with an employment of $X_{11} = 8640$, the regression population estimate $\hat{Y}_1$ will be

$$\begin{aligned} \hat{Y}_1 &= 4098 + (1.9131)(8640) \\ &= 4098 + 16{,}529 = 20{,}627 \end{aligned} \tag{6.12}$$

142

Table 6.2 A comparison of the observed and estimated zonal population totals for the Isle of Wight

Zone i	1971 employment X_{1i}	1971 observed population, Y_i	1971 estimated population, $\hat{Y}_i$	Residual, $Y_i - \hat{Y}_i$
(1) Cowes	8,640	18,910	20,627	−1,717
(2) Newport	10,850	22,309	24,855	−2,546
(3) Ryde	7,620	23,204	18,676	4,528
(4) Sandown– Shanklin	4,960	15,890	13,587	2,303
(5) Ventnor	2,070	6,931	8,058	−1,127
(6) Brading	1,690	6,502	7,331	−829
(7) Godshill	1,410	5,406	6,796	−1,390
(8) Freshwater	2,860	10,347	9,569	778
Totals	40,100	109,499	109,499	0

The difference between the observed population Y_i and estimated population on the regression line $\hat{Y}_i$ for each zone i, is the residual deviation (column 4 in table 6.2), that is the variation in population that cannot be explained by the variation in employment in each zone. These residuals are, of course, the vertical deviations from each observed point Y_i to the regression line $\hat{Y}_i$ in figure 6.2. For Cowes (zone 1) the observed population Y_1 is 18,910, the estimated population $\hat{Y}_1$ is 20,627 and, therefore, the residual $(Y_1 - \hat{Y}_1)$ is −1717. The sum of the residuals for all zones is equal to zero which confirms equation (6.4) and shows that equation (6.11) represents the best average straight line through the points. It can also be shown that the sum of the squared residuals is equal to 39,731,552 which is the minimum possible value for any straight line on the graph. This confirms that the least squares regression equation has been calculated since equation (6.5) has been satisfied.

The graph (figure 6.2) and regression equation (6.11) show there is the general relationship that the larger the employment in each zone the larger the population, but the level of population cannot be completely explained in this way. In any urban socio-economic system, a perfect linear relationship cannot be expected since there will always be other factors that have not been taken into account. Here for example, the zone furthest from the regression line is Ryde, but this is partly explained by the fact that each day 500 people travel to the mainland to work and this has not been taken into account. Another factor is that there are different proportions of retired people within the population in the different zones over the island.

The strength of the relationship between population Y_i and employment X_{1i} can be measured by the product moment correlation coefficient r. If there is a perfect linear relationship between the two variables and every observed point lies on the regression line then $r = 1.0$ for a positive relationship or $r = -1.0$ for a negative relationship. If there is a complete scatter of points on the scatter diagram then $r = 0.0$ and there is no relationship at all between the variables. The equation for calculating the product moment correlation coefficient between two variables Y_i and X_{1i} is in terms of available data:

$$r = \frac{\sum_i (Y_i - \overline{Y})(X_{1i} - \overline{X}_1)}{\sqrt{[\sum_i (X_{1i} - \overline{X}_1)^2]}\sqrt{[\sum_i (Y_i - \overline{Y})^2]}} \qquad (6.13)$$

For the Isle of Wight $r = 0.9454$, which indicates a strong positive relationship between population Y_i and employment X_{1i}. A related and very important measure of association is the coefficient of determination r^2 which is the squared product moment correlation coefficient. This measures how far the zonal variations in the dependent variable Y_i population, can be explained by the zonal variations in the independent variable X_{1i} employment. For Isle of Wight data (table 2.1), $r^2 = (0.9454)^2 = 0.8938$. This can be interpreted in percentage terms by multiplying by 100 and indicates that 89.38% of the variation in zonal population Y_i can be explained by variations in zonal employment X_{1i}. Since the maximum value of r^2 is 1.0, giving a total variation to be explained of 100%, there is still 10.62% of the variation in zonal population to be explained by other factors not included in this regression equation.

It is very important to recognize that the product moment correlation coefficient, the coefficient of determination and the least squares regression equation represent a statistical relationship. The two sets of figures from table 6.1 have been fed into equations (6.7), (6.8), (6.9) and (6.13) to provide the results set out above, but this does not prove that there is a causal relationship between the two variables Y_i and X_{1i}, merely a statistical relationship. It is for the model builder to decide if this represents a meaningful relationship. In this example, since the region is divided into such large zones it is not unreasonable to expect a high relationship between the level of employment in each zone and the level of population. If the region had been divided into much smaller zones this might not be so clear since there could be a spatial separation between employment and population. It is vitally important therefore that only independent variables that can reasonably be thought to express some relationship with the dependent variable should be included in the regression. A linear model has to be judged by the reasonableness of its variables as well as its fit to empirical data. It is not sufficient just to obtain a high r^2 value, the model must represent a causal relationship. It is important, therefore, to study the regression coefficients carefully to see if they fit in with known ideas and theories. There are a number of examples in books and articles where a very high r^2 value has been obtained from variables that are totally unrelated. Probably the most common form of mistake is in assuming that a direct relationship exists between two variables when in fact both are changing in response to a third variable, and there is no link between the first two variables. It must also be remembered that linear regression deals with straight line relationships and although some methods do exist for including non-linear relationships by transforming variables and by using polynomial equations, they have very rarely been included in linear urban models. Considerable thought therefore has to be given in deciding on the independent variables to include within a regression model.

This procedure of finding the best linear relationship between the variables using the least squares regression technique is the calibration process. In a gravity model, the parameters on the distance functions are determined at calibration for some base year and similarly here the coefficients in the regression model are determined at some base year. In using both models at prediction, the variables on the right-hand side of the equation have to be updated and input into the relationship in order to determine the variable on the left-hand side of the equation. The regression model, just like the gravity model, assumes that the relationship between the variables that was found at calibration, will also persist at prediction.

In order to estimate zonal population at 1981 and 1991 from the Isle of Wight regression model, zonal employment at these two dates has to be estimated and input into equation (6.11). This is not altogether very satisfactory and so almost all studies using this type of model have dealt with the incremental change of activities over a given time period, generally a five- or ten-year period. This

145

Table 6.3 Population and employment changes 1961 to 1971 for the Isle of Wight

Zone i	Population change 1961–71, ΔPOP_i	Employment change 1961–71, $\Delta EMPL_i$	Population 1961, $POP61_i$	Population growth rate 1961–71
(1) Cowes	1,918	770	16,992	1.113
(2) Newport	2,830	680	19,479	1.145
(3) Ryde	3,359	650	19,845	1.170
(4) Sandown–Shanklin	1,504	210	14,386	1.105
(5) Ventnor	496	30	6,435	1.077
(6) Brading	1,338	150	5,164	1.259
(7) Godshill	992	280	4,414	1.225
(8) Freshwater	1,310	190	9,037	1.145
Totals	13,747	2,960	95,752	1.144

of course means that reliable data for at least two dates are required which can often be a problem. For the Isle of Wight, data on population and employment in each zone were collected for 1961 and 1971 (table 6.3) to provide the change over the ten year time period. Using ΔPOP_i to represent the change in population and $\Delta EMPL_i$ to represent the change in employment, the regression equation was calculated with $Y_i = \Delta POP_i$ as the dependent variable and $X_{1i} = \Delta EMPL_i$ as the independent variable to look at the relationship between the zonal changes over the ten years:

$$\Delta POP_i = 698.5 + 2.76 \, \Delta EMPL_i$$

$$r = 0.822 \tag{6.14}$$

$$r^2 = 0.676$$

These results and the scatter diagram (figure 6.3) show that although there is a general positive relationship with the zones showing a larger employment increase also experiencing a larger population increase, the points are rather scattered about the regression line. The coefficient of determination r^2 shows that 67.6% of the variation in the zonal population change can be accounted for by variations in zonal employment changes. Again, this is only a statistical relationship and the user has to decide if it is a meaningful relationship.

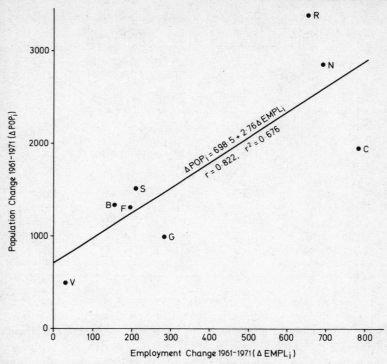

Figure 6.3 The scatter diagram and regression line for population change 1961–71 against employment change 1961–71

Alternatively it might be felt that population change is a function of the population in each zone at the base year. Using $Y_i = \Delta POP_i$ as the dependent variable and $X_{1i} = POP61_i$ the population at the base year 1961 as the dependent variable, produced the following equation:

$$\Delta POP_i = 169.9 + 0.1294\ POP61_i$$
$$r = 0.8777 \tag{6.15}$$
$$r^2 = 0.7704$$

Again there is a general positive relationship (figure 6.4) between the variables with the largest increases in population occurring in the zones with the largest base year population. This scatter diagram (figure 6.4) also shows that the zones that were urban centres in 1961, zones 1 to 5, show a strong positive relationship. Indeed a regression with just these five observations provides a

147

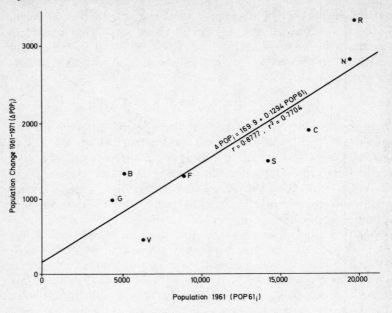

Figure 6.4 The scatter diagram and regression line for population change 1961–71 against employment 1961

coefficient of determination of $r^2 = 0.892$ which indicates that 89.2% of the variation in population change can be accounted for by the variation in zone population at the base year 1961. The other three zones (6, 7 and 8) are larger rural areas and these have experienced a proportionately greater increase in population over the ten years. This can also be seen by looking at the last column of table 6.3 which shows the growth rate on each zone.

Multiple regression

So far only linear models with one independent variable have been considered, but it would obviously be far better to include several independent variables using multiple regression analysis. The modelling procedure is similar with data collected on a number of variables for the n zones in a region ($i = 1$ to n), which is used to determine the coefficients in a multiple regression equation:

$$Y_i = b_0 + b_1 X_{1i} + b_2 X_{2i} + b_3 X_{3i} + \ldots \qquad (6.16)$$

Here the zonal variations in a series of independent variables X_{1i}, X_{2i}, X_{3i}, . . . are being used to explain the zonal variation in one dependent variable Y_i. Using the same data for the Isle of Wight (table 6.3), consider the regression model that tries to explain variations in the population change 1961–71 by two independent variables, the population at the base year 1961 and the employment change 1961–71:

$$\Delta POP_i = b_0 + b_1 \, POP61_i + b_2 \Delta EMPL_i \qquad (6.17)$$

With multiple regression it is no longer possible to graph the full information and the calculation of the coefficients b_0, b_1, b_2 becomes more difficult using a hand calculator, although it is very straightforward on a computer and every computer has a software regression package. The basic ideas of multiple regression are identical to those outlined earlier for a simple regression equation, to minimize the sum of the squared deviations between the actual population change 1961–71 and the estimated population change 1961–71 over all the zones. Applying differential calculus again to determine this minimization will produce three normal equations which can be solved to give values for b_0, b_1 and b_2. Multiple regression equations with any number of independent variables X_{1i}, X_{2i}, X_{3i}, . . . are determined in a similar way with the normal equations solved by matrix algebra to give the regression coefficients b_0, b_1, b_2, b_3, ... A multiple correlation coefficient r and coefficient of determination r^2 can also be calculated.

The linear model of equation (6.17) can be calculated for the Isle of Wight:

$$\Delta POP_i = 238.74 + 0.0933 \, POP61_i + 0.9819 \, \Delta EMPL_i$$
$$r = 0.8923 \qquad (6.18)$$
$$r^2 = 0.7962$$

By including two independent variables, population at 1961 and the change in employment, the overall level of explanation of the variation in population change 1961–71 has increased, so that the coefficient of determination is now $r^2 = 0.7962$. It is important at this stage of the analysis to study the spatial pattern of the residuals from the regression equation, firstly to discover if there are problems of autocorrelation which will be explained shortly, and secondly to assist in searching for additional variables that could usefully be included in the regression. In fact any number of other variables which are thought to have an influence on changes in population could be included as independent variables, such as measures of accessibility to employment and population.

This multiple regression equation is the calibration result. If it is used to predict population changes 1971 to 1981, then the 1971 population (X_{1i}) and an estimate of the employment change 1971 to 1981 (X_{2i}) have to be input into the equation. Therefore only variables that can be determined and estimated outside the model at the prediction stage can be used as independent variables in this type of model. However, this problem can be overcome by setting up a series of simultaneous equations and this will be dealt with shortly.

The activities in the Isle of Wight model are all at an aggregate level, but all operational linear models have been developed with disaggregated activities. The empiric model (Hill 1965) developed for the Boston region separated population into two and employment into three categories while the 131 zone model of the north-eastern corridor of the USA (Putman 1970) split population into four groups and employment into four categories of basic employment and six of non-basic employment. One equation is then formulated to determine each category of population and employment using a whole range of independent variables.

Testing the significance of variables within the regression equation

One important aspect of the calibration of a multiple regression equation model is in determining the significant independent variables, that is the variables that are important in explaining the zonal variation in the dependent variables. The tests of significance are usually performed on sample data to determine the probability of a non-zero b coefficient occurring through sampling. For example, in equation (6.2), if the coefficient b_1 is equal to zero, then the variable X_{1i} has no influence on the variations in the dependent variable Y_i. However, a non-zero value for b_1 might have occurred because sample data were used, and so tests of significance are performed on the coefficient to consider this. For a linear model containing several independent variables such as equation (6.16), the non-significant variables are gradually eliminated from the regression equation. However, the information used in the linear urban models is not sample data, it is the full information for each zone in a region at different points in time. In this case tests of significance are not used to see if the b coefficients differ significantly from zero, but rather to determine the important variables within the regression model, and also to highlight problems when independent variables are interrelated.

During this significance testing it is also important to check that the assumptions underlying regression analysis have not been violated, looking particularly at the residuals and this will be explained shortly.

To test the significance of each independent variable, firstly calculate the standard error of the b coefficient and secondly calculate a 't' value, which is the coefficient divided by its standard error (SE(b)):

$$t_v = \frac{b}{\text{SE}(b)} \tag{6.19}$$

where v is the number of degrees of freedom. This information will always be provided by a regression computer package, but for a more detailed description of this form of analysis consult the statistic books already referenced. The calculated value of t can be compared to the t distribution tables with $v = n - q - 1$ degrees of freedom where n is the number of observations and q is the number of independent variables in the regression equation. If the calculated value of t is greater than the theoretical value in the tables at the 5% probability level, then the variable is regarded as having a significant influence in explaining variations in the dependent variable. If it is lower than the theoretical value of t then it is regarded as a non-significant variable. Consider equation (6.15) where the calculated t value is placed in brackets under the b coefficient:

$$\Delta POP_i = 169.9 + 0.1294\ POP61_i \tag{6.20}$$
$$(4.487)$$
$$r^2 = 0.7704$$

The theoretical value of t at the 5% level is $t_6 = 2.45$ and since the calculated value of $t = 4.487$ is greater than this value, then $POP61_i$ is regarded as a significant variable. This indicates that there is a significant statistical relationship between zonal changes in population 1961–71 and the zonal population level at 1961. For the multiple regression model of equation (6.18), the t values are included to form equation (6.21):

$$\Delta POP_i = 238.74 + 0.0933\ POP61_i$$
$$(1.72)$$
$$+ 0.9819\ \Delta EMPL_i \tag{6.21}$$
$$(0.795)$$
$$r^2 = 0.7962$$

The theoretical value of t is $t_5 = 2.57$ and since both the calculated t values of 1.72 and 0.795 are below this level, neither of the variables is significant. Also there has only been a marginal increase in the level of explanation in ΔPOP_i from 77.04% in equation (6.20) to 79.62% in equation (6.21). This is caused by the fairly strong relationship between the two independent variables in the model, for the coefficient of determination between $POP61_i$ and $\Delta EMPL_i$ is $r^2 = 0.70$. One of the basic assumptions of regression analysis is being violated, i.e. that independent variables are not interrelated, so that instead of both variables explaining different parts of the zonal variation in population change, they are both attempting to explain the same variation. If two independent variables are highly correlated, then it is best to include in the final model the one that contributes most to the overall r^2 value. In this case $POP61_i$ should be retained and then possibly other independent variables, such as a measure of accessibility, added into the multiple regression model. The reasons for retaining $POP61_i$ are firstly because it has a higher simple coefficient of determination against ΔPOP_i than does $\Delta EMPL_i$ with $r^2 = 0.7704$ in equation (6.20) compared with $r^2 = 0.676$ in equation (6.14), and secondly because its calculated t value in equation (6.20) is larger. However, if a variable is not significant but is not highly correlated with any other variable, then it can be included or excluded from the final model depending on whether the information will be readily available at prediction.

These tests of significance are, therefore, used in a regression model in two ways. Firstly to detect problems of correlated independent variables, when in order to satisfy regression assumptions, the least significant of the variables is omitted from the equation. Secondly to give the model builder the option of eliminating non-significant variables that add little to the overall level of explanation at calibration, which would reduce the amount of data required for prediction, although if data on non-significant variables are available it does no harm to include them in the final model. The regression equations will be computed several times before a satisfactory final linear model is developed. In the model of the north-east corridor of the USA (Putman 1970), the tests of significance on the independent variables relating to employment indicated that only one of the accessibility measures could be included in each equation because they were so highly interrelated, although some other non-significant variables were retained in the model.

The theoretical assumptions of linear regression

Regression analysis is a highly developed statistical technique and there is a set of basic assumptions related to its use (see Johnston 1978). Firstly, it is being assumed that a linear relationship exists between the dependent variable and the set of independent variables. There are certain transformations that can possibly be applied to the variables and non-linear relationships estimated, although it does become difficult to explain their meaning once they have been estimated. Secondly, the independent variables X_{1i}, X_{2i}, X_{3i}, . . . should not be interrelated; they should be independent and uncorrelated. However, with any set of socio-economic variables collected by zone over a region, there is almost certain to be some correlation amongst the independent variables, a problem known as multicollinearity. This will be indicated by the significance testing and if two highly correlated variables are considered for an equation, then the least significant one can be omitted from the final model as described for equation (6.21). Thirdly, the residuals from a regression equation should be uncorrelated with any of the variables in the equation, and importantly for urban modelling, independent and randomly distributed spatially. Any violation of this latter assumption on the residuals is called autocorrelation, and this can be tested. Spatial autocorrelation occurs when there is a clustering of positive or negative residuals over a region. Extra variables should be included to overcome these problems. In addition, if tests of significance are performed on the equations then the residuals should also be normally distributed. All linear regression models should be analysed to see how far the assumptions are satisfied because this will indicate whether the model has been wrongly formulated. The analysis will often indicate the next stage in the construction of the model, such as variables to omit, extra variables to include, or even maybe a transformation of other variables.

Unlike the gravity model where there are no statistical assumptions, a linear urban model based on regression analysis is faced with a stringent set of assumptions. With the type of socio-economic data used in urban modelling studies, there are often problems in satisfying these assumptions. During a study it is possible to minimize the errors but sometimes difficult to eliminate them completely. However, this does not invalidate the model. Regression analysis provides a readily available, robust technique for deriving a set of linear equations for determining the allocation of landuse activities. It should be judged on how well it performs at calibration and prediction, not on the problems of satisfying every assumption perfectly.

THE PROCEDURE FOR DEVELOPING A LINEAR URBAN MODEL

The linear regression models dealt with so far have been single equations looking at the zonal variation in one activity, whereas all operational linear urban models have developed a series of equations to consider the allocation of several disaggregated activities. The empiric model of the Boston region contained five equations and located two categories of population, white collar and blue collar, and three categories of employment, manufacturing, retail and other, while the model of the north-eastern seaboard of the USA contained twenty-four equations. There are two ways of developing a series of equations to form a linear urban model, either using ordinary regression equations or a simultaneous set of equations. The ordinary regression method applies multiple regression to each of the equations in order to derive the coefficients. Most linear urban models however have developed a simultaneous set of equations which provides a more realistic model, but leads to a more complicated estimation process, very much in the field of econometrics.

To study these two modelling procedures, consider a set of data on population and employment collected for all the n zones in a region at two points in time, t and $t + 1$, which would probably be five or ten years apart. If a distinction is made between basic and service employment, and if accessibility indexes which will be described later are derived, then a total of eight variables can be used in the model:

ΔPOP_i = change in population of zone i from time t to $t + 1$

$\Delta SERV_i$ = change in service employment of zone i from time t to $t + 1$

$\Delta BASIC_i$ = change in basic employment of zone i from time t to $t + 1$

POP_i = population of zone i at time t

$SERV_i$ = service employment of zone i at time t

$BASIC_i$ = basic employment of zone i at time t

$ACCPOP_i$ = accessibility to population index for zone i at time t

$ACCEMP_i$ = accessibility to employment index for zone i at time t

A model can now be developed to try and explain the zonal variation of changes in population and service employment over the region from time t to $t + 1$, ΔPOP_i and $\Delta SERV_i$ respectively. Most operational models have also tried to determine changes in basic (or manufacturing) employment within the model, but here it is being assumed that basic employment changes are so highly influenced by external factors that they are best estimated outside the model, as happens with the Garin–Lowry model.

The ordinary regression model can now be developed by postulating one multiple regression equation for each dependent variable. The independent variables included in each equation are the ones thought to have an influence in explaining variations in the dependent variable:

$$\Delta POP_i = a_0 + a_1\ \Delta BASIC_i + a_2\ POP_i + a_3\ SERV_i$$
$$+ a_4\ BASIC_i + a_5\ ACCEMP_i \qquad (6.22)$$

$$\Delta SERV_i = b_0 + b_1\ \Delta BASIC_i + b_2\ POP_i + b_3\ SERV_i$$
$$+ b_4\ ACCPOP_i \qquad (6.23)$$

The procedure for developing this model is identical to the method already described with the coefficients a_0 to a_5 and b_0 to b_4 in the equations estimated separately using the multiple regression procedure. During the calibration process, tests of significance are performed and the regression assumptions checked, before a final model is derived. At prediction the independent variables in each equation are updated and predictions made about the zonal allocation of population and service employment over the next time period.

A simultaneous regression system can also be developed to try and explain the zonal variation of changes in population and service employment from time t to $t + 1$:

$$\Delta POP_i = a_0 + a_1\ \Delta SERV_i + a_2\ \Delta BASIC_i + a_3\ POP_i$$
$$+ a_4\ SERV_i + a_5\ BASIC_i + a_6\ ACCEMP_i \quad (6.24)$$

$$\Delta SERV_i = b_0 + b_1\ \Delta POP_i + b_2\ \Delta BASIC_i + b_3\ POP_i$$
$$+ b_4\ SERV_i + b_5\ ACCPOP_i \qquad (6.25)$$

This is a simultaneous system of equations because change in population (ΔPOP_i) and change in service employment ($\Delta SERV_i$) are dependent variables in one equation and independent variables in the other equation. In equation (6.24) it is being postulated that zonal population changes are explained by changes in service employment and other independent variables, while in equation (6.25) that zonal service employment changes are

155

explained by changes in population and other independent variables. With this type of equation system, these two variables are called endogenous variables, while all the other six variables, only on the right-hand sides of the equations, are termed exogenous variables. At prediction only exogenous variables are input into the model, while all endogenous variables are determined within the model.

This system of equations cannot be solved adequately by ordinary multiple regression because it leads to biased estimates of the coefficients in the equations, and also because these equations could not be used at prediction. There are however several methods of estimating the coefficients in a set of simultaneous equations, here a_0 to a_6 and b_0 to b_5, the most popular being the two stage least squares method. Computer packages are readily available to perform this type of computation, particularly packages dealing with econometric techniques. Put very simply, the first stage of the technique is to calculate the reduced form estimates for population and service employment change from multiple regression equations expressing each as a function of all the exogenous variables. The second stage entails using these reduced form estimates as the explanatory variables on the right-hand sides of the simultaneous system in equations (6.24) and (6.25), and performing multiple regression on the equations to determine the coefficients a_0 to a_6 and b_0 to b_5. At prediction, the coefficients of the reduced form equations and the coefficients of the simultaneous equations (6.24) and (6.25) will be used in the same two stage procedure to give predictions of population and service employment changes over some future time period. Equation systems of this type can always be solved, but occasionally there may be problems of identification.

It must be remembered that a regression analysis represents a statistical relationship and that it is up to the user to decide how far this set of equations represents the urban system. The selection and formulation of the variables is therefore critical in the development of a linear model. In the simultaneous regression model above, the exogenous variables selected for each equation are those thought relevant to the endogenous variables from the total set of variables available. Any other variable likely to effect variations in population and service employment changes could have usefully been included, if the data were available. These might have included variables representing landuse constraints, the provision of public utilities, restrictions on the density of development or the provision of recreation. It is entirely up to the model builder to decide on the variables to be included in the system of equations and for this reason it will take several applications of the regression computer program before deciding on a final model. Almost all operational models have dealt with the zonal variation of activities over a given time period, but this can be represented either as the actual zone changes in the activities, the method used here, or as the zonal share of the total regional change in the activities. It is difficult to know which is more correct and both methods have been used in practice. The results at calibration will be similar but the prediction of changes over some future time period will be marginally different.

A LINEAR URBAN MODEL OF CENTRAL BERKSHIRE

A linear urban model based on the simultaneous regression equations described above (equations (6.24) and (6.25)), can now be developed for a twenty-three zone study region in central Berkshire (figure 6.5). The region consists of Reading (zones 1 to 6), Wokingham (zone 15) and Henley (zone 22), together with the surrounding suburban and rural area. A region of twenty-three zones is still rather too small, but it can be used to explain the procedure.

Unless very expensive surveys are to be conducted, information is only available at census years, which in Britain means 1961, 1966, 1971 and 1981. In this study, data on the zonal distribution of population and employment were collected for 1961 and 1966 in order to calibrate the model on the changes between the two dates. This might seem quite old data, but it does allow the model to be used predictively and the results checked against known future data in order to test its effectiveness. The division of employment into basic and service was similar to that used in the Garin–Lowry model, with sections 1 to 17 of the British Standard Industrial Classification treated as basic, and sections 18 to 24 as service. The collection of reliable data for two points in time can prove difficult but it is vital for a model dealing with changes over time.

This provides information for six of the eight variables, the other two being accessibility indexes. Here accessibility measures for each zone the level of opportunity for employment in the region and the level of opportunity to residential areas in the region.

157

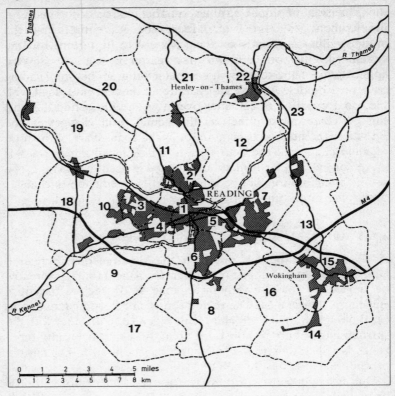

Figure 6.5   The central Berkshire study region

There are in fact several possible measures of accessibility, but the one used here is based on the gravity concept:

$$\text{ACC}_i = \sum_j D_j \exp(-\lambda c_{ij}) \qquad (6.26)$$

In this equation ACC_i is the accessibility index for zone i, D_j is the population or employment in zone j, c_{ij} is the measure of travel cost between zones i and j, here travel time, and λ is a parameter, for this data estimated as 0.2. A zone that contains a high level of employment within the zone and in nearby zones will reveal a high accessibility to employment index. Remote zones in the region will have a low accessibility to employment index. These indexes are calculated for both employment and population which is a measure of the residential opportunity in the region.

The calibration process involves running the regression model a number of times, testing for the significance of the variables, checking that the regression assumptions have not been violated and interpreting the meaning of the regression coefficients. The simultaneous regression model of equations (6.24) and (6.25) produced the following result, with the calculated t values placed under the coefficients, and REDΔPOP$_i$ and REDΔSERV$_i$ denoting the reduced form of the variables gained from the first stage of the two stage regression procedure:

$$\Delta POP_i = 2514.51 + 27.702 \; RED\Delta SERV_i - 15.415 \; \Delta BASIC_i$$
$$\quad\quad\quad (0.973) \quad\quad\quad\quad (0.952)$$
$$+ \; 0.129 \; POP_i - 5.830 \; SERV_i$$
$$(1.344) \quad\quad (1.109)$$
$$+ \; 2.822 \; BASIC_i - 0.073 \; ACCEMP_i \quad\quad (6.27)$$
$$(1.529) \quad\quad\quad (0.503)$$
$$r = 0.856 \quad\quad r^2 = 0.733$$

$$\Delta SERV_i = 80.611 - 0.037 \; RED\Delta POP_i + 0.555 \; \Delta BASIC_i$$
$$\quad\quad (3.663) \quad\quad\quad\quad (12.614)$$
$$- \; 0.0003 \; POP_i + 0.153 \; SERV_i$$
$$(0.083) \quad\quad\quad (38.25)$$
$$+ \; 0.0045 \; ACCPOP_i \quad\quad\quad\quad\quad (6.28)$$
$$(2.647)$$
$$r = 0.999 \quad\quad r^2 = 0.998$$

To test the level of significance of the variables, the theoretical t value at the 5% level for equation (6.27) is $t = 2.114$ and for equation (6.28) it is $t = 2.106$. It can be seen that many of the variables in both equations are not significant, and this can largely be explained by the interrelationships between some of the variables which are shown up in the correlation matrix (table 6.4). By inspection of this matrix and the level of significance of the coefficients, accessibility to employment (ACCEMP$_i$) was removed from equation (6.27) and population at 1961 (POP$_i$) from equation (6.28), because of their high correlation with other variables in the equation. When the model was recomputed, service employment at 1961 (SERV$_i$) in equation (6.27) was still not significant and, therefore, removed. The removal of these three variables lead to an increased level of significance of the other variables and on recomputation, this produced a simultane-

Table 6.4 The correlation matrix between variables in the simultaneous regression model of the central Berkshire region

	POP_i	$SERV_i$	$BASIC_i$	ΔPOP_i	$\Delta SERV_i$	$\Delta BASIC_i$	$ACCPOP_i$
$SERV_i$	0.6722						
$BASIC_i$	0.7284	0.9028					
ΔPOP_i	0.1892	-0.3478	-0.0167				
$\Delta SERV_i$	0.7042	0.9885	0.9113	-0.3026			
$\Delta BASIC_i$	0.5747	0.4634	0.6423	0.2719	0.5801		
$ACCPOP_i$	0.8455	0.5413	0.5331	0.1559	0.5697	0.3929	
$ACCEMP_i$	0.8063	0.5342	0.4937	0.0859	0.5609	0.3613	0.9821

ous regression model containing only significant variables:

$$\Delta POP_i = 44.745 - 3.844\ RED\Delta SERV_i + 2.372\ \Delta BASIC_i$$
$$(5.547) \qquad\qquad (2.174)$$
$$+ 0.144\ POP_i + 0.924\ BASIC_i \qquad\qquad (6.29)$$
$$(2.571) \qquad\quad (2.897)$$
$$r = 0.837 \qquad r^2 = 0.700$$

$$\Delta SERV_i = -80.099 - 0.037\ RED\Delta POP_i + 0.555\ \Delta BASIC_i$$
$$(4.625) \qquad\qquad (12.907)$$
$$+ 0.152\ SERV_i + 0.0044\ ACCPOP_i \qquad (6.30)$$
$$(50.667) \qquad\quad (3.508)$$
$$r = 0.999 \qquad r^2 = 0.998$$

It can be seen that service employment change $\Delta SERV_i$ is almost perfectly reproduced by the model but population change ΔPOP_i rather poorly. The overall r^2 values have been reduced only slightly by removing the non-significant variables from the model. Also this latter model satisfies the regression assumptions relating to the independence of the exogenous variables far better. These r^2 values relate to changes over the five year period, but if they are added to the level of population and service employment at the base year 1961, then the correlation between the actual value and the regression estimate of the variables for 1966 is 0.979 for population and rounded to 1.00 for service employment. This might seem an odd way of presenting results because most of the high correlation is due to the common 1961 population and service employment values, but this is the way in which results from operational models are generally presented.

The main problem with the model is the negative coefficients which in equation (6.29) suggest that as service employment increases in a zone so population decreases, and similarly in equation (6.30), as population increases in a zone so service employment decreases. This is caused by the nature of the data, and the fact that changes in population and service employment are dominated by zone 1 the Reading central shopping area. Over this five year period considerable redevelopment took place with older substandard inner residential areas being cleared and replaced by an expanded shopping area and multistorey offices. Zone 1 experienced a large decrease in population and a large increase in service employment, which was very different from the changes in all other zones where there was generally a moderate increase in both population and service employment. This domination of the change variables by zone 1 accounts for the strange signs on the coefficients which make sense for zone 1 but not for the other zones. With just the exogenous variables available here, the regression model cannot cope with this situation and other variables relating to redevelopment must be included to improve the explanation and provide more 'reasonable' coefficients. The model builder has to think very carefully about the variables to be included in a linear regression model and also perform considerable analysis and interpretation at calibration.

This calibrated regression model can now be used to predict forward to 1971, 1976, 1981, 1986 and 1991. With this set of variables, all the data except for basic employment changes are readily available either from collected information or from predictions at a previous time period. Basic employment changes for each zone have to be estimated outside the model and several alternative sets of estimates can be used, just as in the Garin–Lowry model. The assumption implicit in retaining the coefficients of the regression equation for prediction is that the relationship that gave 'best' estimates over the base time period, will continue in the future. In this model, although good estimates were obtained at calibration, the problem of the negative coefficients in the equations will obviously affect the model's ability to predict. The model would need refining and additional variables included in order to obtain reliable predictions.

An ordinary regression model could alternatively have been developed for the central Berkshire region. Indeed at calibration, this model estimates changes equally as well as the simultaneous regression model, and at prediction provides just as good results. However, there are still problems with negative coefficients and theoretically the simultaneous system of equations does seem more logical.

A GENERALIZED FORM OF THE LINEAR MODEL

It is probably best at this point to try and express the various models in a more compact mathematical form. They are not being altered in any way, merely presented more conveniently.

The multiple regression equation of equation (6.16) is reproduced in equation (6.31), with Y_i the dependent variable, X_{1i}, $X_{2i}, \ldots$ the independent variables, and b_0, b_1, $b_2, \ldots$ the regression coefficients:

$$Y_i = b_0 + b_1X_{1i} + b_2X_{2i} + \ldots \qquad (6.31)$$

If the model region is divided into n zones, and there are q independent variables, then equation (6.31) can be expressed as

$$Y_i = b_0 + \sum_{h=1}^{q} b_hX_{hi} \qquad (6.32)$$

Subscript h represents the number of the independent variable and i the zone number.

A system of ordinary regression equations such as equations (6.22) and (6.23), but with p dependent variables, and hence p equations, and with q independent variables, can be presented as

$$Y_{ki} = b_0 + \sum_{h=1}^{q} b_hX_{hi} \quad \text{for } k = 1 \text{ to } p \qquad (6.33)$$

The subscript k represents the number of the dependent variable, while h again represents the number of the independent variable, and i the zone number. The b coefficients will of course be different in each of the p equations and not all of the q independent variables need be included in each of the equations.

For a system of simultaneous equations, such as those set out in equations (6.24) and (6.25), and in the central Berkshire example, a distinction has to be made between the endogenous variables Y_{ki} and the exogenous variables X_{hi}. With p endogenous variables and q exogenous variables the system of equations can be presented as

$$Y_{ki} = b_0 + \sum_{\substack{g=1 \\ g \neq k}}^{p} a_gY_{gi} + \sum_{h=1}^{q} b_hX_{hi} \quad \text{for } k = 1 \text{ to } p \quad (6.34)$$

The subscript k represents the number of the endogenous variable in an equation, and g the other endogenous variables, while h represents the number of the exogenous variables and i the zone number. The a and b coefficients will be different for each of the p equations and again not all of the $q + p$ variables need be included in each of the equations.

OPERATIONAL LINEAR URBAN MODELS

The model developed for central Berkshire is a much simplified version of a linear model. Operational models contain many more endogenous and exogenous variables, and deal with a larger region. The original empiric model, developed in the mid-1960s, consisted of five simultaneous equations and since then many larger versions of the model have been developed, for example by Putman (1970) with a system of twenty-four equations, although not all are simultaneous. Later models have taken econometric techniques even further (see Putman 1979). This type of urban modelling has been quite widely applied in the USA but in Britain there are few examples, and none in a practical planning situation. To look at the nature of these operational linear models, the empiric model will be studied in some detail, followed by a description of some of its more elaborate successors, looking at the Putman example in particular.

The empiric model

The first large-scale linear urban model to be developed was the empiric model for the Greater Boston region in the USA (Hill 1965, Hill, Brand and Hansen 1965). The region was initially divided into twenty-nine very large zones (figure 6.6), with the city of Boston as only three zones. The model was designed to allocate population and employment to the zones in the region following a similar procedure to the one used in the central Berkshire example. Here though, population and employment were dealt with at a more disaggregated level, there were many more exogenous variables involved in the equations, and the variables measured the proportion of the regional total of each activity that was located in each zone.

A general model was developed with a system of five simultaneous equations to represent five endogenous variables. There were two equations for population, white collar and blue collar, and three equations for employment: retail and wholesale, manufacturing, and other employment. Alternative versions of the model were then developed and tested using different combinations from a total of twenty-two exogenous variables. A group of twelve variables was included in all five equations for each of the model alternatives. These variables related firstly to landuse densities for residential population, manufacturing employment and non-

Figure 6.6   The Greater Boston study region

manufacturing employment, and secondly to accessibility by car to urban activities of population and employment. There was also a group of ten variables which were sometimes included within the five equations; these variables related to accessibility by all forms of transport to population and employment, and to the provision of water supply and sewage disposal. As well as developing this model, a very full analysis of the region was performed, which is an essential preliminary to any modelling work. An analysis was performed of the interrelationships between growth of population and employment and a whole series of variables; an investigation was made into the changes and trends over the ten year base period 1950 to 1960; and factor analysis techniques were used to look for groups of locational activities.

Data were collected for 1950 and 1960 in order to model the

changes over the ten year period. These variables were expressed as the zonal share of the total regional change, rather than the actual change for each zone. The calibrated results were quite close for all versions of the model and it was then used to predict recursively in ten year intervals up to the year 2000, using output from one time period as input into the next run of the model. However, the model only estimates the changes in the zonal share of the regional total for a particular activity. In order to obtain an absolute value for each zone at some future date, this has to be multiplied by a regional total which is determined outside the model. Further alternative forms of the model were developed, and additional forecasts made with these existing models, to test the validity and sensitivity of the predictions. The results from the different models containing different numbers of exogenous variables were compared, the number of zones in the region enlarged to 123 and then eventually 626 traffic zones, and the length of forecasting period varied to twenty years and forty years. Finally the model was used in conjunction with a traffic model to look at alternative landuse transport plans for the region.

Further developments to the linear model

Since the development of the empiric model for the Greater Boston region, there have been over a dozen applications to city regions in North America. These include models of Atlanta, Denver, Seattle, Puget Sound, Minneapolis–St Paul and Washington DC in the USA and Winnipeg and Toronto in Canada. In Britain, however, this type of model has not proved at all popular and has really only been applied to north-west England (Masser, Coleman and Wynn 1971) and central Berkshire. All these operational models used a simultaneous equations structure, with population and employment separated into several categories as the endogenous variables, expressed in terms of change in regional share over a certain time period. The exogenous variables in the equations differed by study but were generally similar to those used in the original empiric model. So despite some criticism of the technique, linear models have been widely applied in North America, and for a detailed discussion of operational linear models see Putman (1979). To show how a linear urban model can be extended to form a very large operational model, one example from the USA will now be described.

A model of the north-east corridor region of the USA

The north-east corridor model (Putman 1970) is a complex linear model which was used to help in the evaluation of alternative transport policies. This is a large region stretching from Boston in the north, through New York and Philadelphia, to Washington in the south. It was divided into 131 districts or zones, and data were collected for 1960 and 1965. The structure of the model incorporates aspects of economic base theory, input, output and accessibility and involves a total of twenty-four equations, some of which are simultaneous equations, while others are ordinary regression equations. Employment was disaggregated into ten sectors, four of basic employment and six of non-basic employment, and one equation was developed for each sector. Population was treated as a total figure for each zone and a set of four equations dealt with the population total, births, deaths and migration. The equations in the population sector and the non-basic employment sector form a set of simultaneous equations. In addition, two other sectors of the economy were considered, personal incomes and landuse. A system of six multiple regression equations to represent six income levels estimated the total income generated from each employment zone, using employment as the independent variables. A further four equations dealt with the total assumed value of land and the level of industrial, commercial and residential landuse in each zone. It can be seen that this model deals with five main sectors of activity (basic employment, non-basic employment, population, personal incomes and landuse) and the equation structure involves both simultaneous and ordinary regression equations. The independent and exogenous variables in the equations include measures of accessibility, activities at a previous point in time, activity sector totals, land area, and also previously calculated variables.

The model was calibrated for the allocation of activities at one point in time (1965), although later work by Putman dealt with changes over a five year time period. The solution to this system of equations is taken in three stages. To begin with the four basic employment equations are solved to provide zonal forecasts. Secondly, making use of the basic employment forecasts, the set of ten simultaneous equations covering non-basic employment and population is solved in the way described for central Berkshire, to provide forecasts for these two sectors. Thirdly, using the results of the first two stages, the remaining ten equations are solved to provide forecasts for personal incomes and then forecasts of landuse and land value. In the model Putman had difficulty with one zone, Manhattan in New York, which did not conform to the general pattern of the region. This also happened in the central Berkshire model and it is an inherent problem of regression models, i.e. when one important observation acts differently from the others. However, after calibration to 1965 information, the model was used predictively to test several alternative transport policies for the region, such as a reduction in freight costs and passenger transport costs.

Stochastic linear models

One further extension is to develop a linear simulation model by linking the allocation of activities from multiple regression equations with a Monte Carlo simulation procedure. This type of model is very much associated with Chapin at the University of North Carolina, USA and it has not really been used in a practical planning situation. To explain the procedure, consider the study undertaken to look at the residential development around two reservoirs in North Carolina (Burby, Donelly and Weiss 1971). The model is intended to try and forecast in which areas new residential development will take place in the region over the next ten or twenty years. The area was divided into small grid squares and information collected on residential development between 1960 and 1970. A multiple regression equation similar to equation (6.1) was developed to determine the factors influencing residential development. The dependent variable related to the number of homes built in each grid square, and the independent variables related to other variables thought to influence this development, including the area left for development, accessibility to the shoreline, road distance to the nearest town, and accessibility to employment. This is identical to the development of an ordinary linear regression model, and the equation could have been used as a deterministic model to allocate new residential development.

However, the differences are at the next stage when the best equation at calibration was used to construct an attraction index for each grid square. The relative values of this index were then used to calculate the probability of development taking place in each grid square. A cumulative distribution of the probabilities was calculated and cumulative integer values assigned to each grid square, depending on its probability of development. The Monte Carlo simulation procedure then generates integer random numbers which allocates units of new residential development to appropriate grid squares. For instance, if it was estimated that 1000 homes will be developed in the next ten years, then 1000 random numbers can be generated in order to allocate each home to a grid square, which overall will provide a prediction of the distribution of residential development in the region. So this second stage of the model process means that new development is being allocated on a random probabilistic basis in order to try and simulate the actual decisions of potential residents where choice considerations operate. Predictions were made recursively at ten year intervals using new development allocated in the previous period to change the data on the independent variables and hence the probabilities for the next projection period.

This model is an interesting extension of the linear model, but it only simulates a small part of the housing market, looking at consumers' choice of new housing, and taking no account of many other factors such as the price mechanism, speculative building and redevelopment. Also for a large amount of development, the results from this probabilistic model will be very similar to those obtained directly from the regression equations.

AN ASSESSMENT OF LINEAR URBAN MODELS

Linear regression offers an alternative way of modelling the urban system, dealing with the allocation of activities to zones in a region. In developing a linear model however, a number of theoretical and operational problems will be encountered:

(1) Regression deals only with linear relationships and a low coefficient of determination (r^2) indicates a poor linear relationship between variables. However, many of the relationships within the urban system may be non-linear in form, and although there are occasions when certain variables can be transformed to produce a linear relationship, these can become difficult to interpret.

(2) Regression is a statistical technique with a set of basic assumptions. In dealing with spatial data there are continual problems of multicollinearity where the independent or exogenous variables are interrelated, and autocorrelation where the residuals are correlated, not normally distributed and spatially clustered. These problems can be minimized but it is difficult to eliminate them altogether.

(3) The models allocate activities to zones, but do not deal with interaction between zones. To gain this information, the zonal activity totals output from a linear model have to be run through a spatial interaction model, usually a doubly constrained transport model.

(4) Since most regression models deal with incremental changes over time, accurate data are required for at least two points in time; these data are usually very difficult to obtain. Inaccurate data for one of the dates can make nonsense of the incremental change data used in the model, which by their nature will be of relatively small magnitudes. Hopefully these data problems will improve.

(5) A linear model performs well if the allocation of activities between zones in a region conforms to a fairly general pattern, but the coefficients in the equation can be highly sensitive to individual zones in the region, particularly if they involve large changes in activities. A single zone caused considerable problems in two of the models discussed in this chapter: Manhattan in the north-east corridor model, and central Reading in the central Berkshire model.

(6) When the calibrated coefficients in the equations are retained at prediction, then the relationships between the variables that were found at calibration are assumed to hold in the future. Again this is not unreasonable in a region that conforms to a general growth pattern, both at calibration and in the future, but in a region of fluctuating zonal changes, rather unrealistic predictions can be produced.

On the other hand there are certainly a number of advantages in using this type of urban model:

(1) Regression is a highly developed statistical technique and has been widely applied in many fields of study. There is considerable literature that can be consulted on ordinary regression and simultaneous regression, particularly texts on econometric techniques which are largely the application of regression techniques to the working of the economy to test certain economic theories.

(2) Regression is a flexible technique, and any number of variables can be included in the model and their significance tested. A gravity model contains a fixed set of variables but with regression, the model builder can include any number of variables thought to influence the allocation of the activities.

(3) Many operational linear models have been developed and

these indicate that at calibration the model can reproduce the changes in the base period quite satisfactorily if the regional allocation of the activities conforms to a fairly general pattern. Problems arise in a region which has a few dominant zones that do not conform, such as central Reading and Manhattan in the examples previously discussed.

(4) Computer packages of ordinary regression and simultaneous regression are readily available on any computer, so that no special computer programs have to be developed and calculation of the model is very straightforward.

(5) The computer time taken to run a linear model is extremely short, with each run taking only a few seconds, even for a region with a large number of zones. The importance of this point in the development of a model will be determined by the availability of computer time and the method of payment for that time.

A linear model is therefore a robust, highly flexible model that is relatively easy to develop and operate, and performs well at calibration. A large number of operational linear models were developed in the late 1960s and 1970s and a detailed description of the principles for building spatial urban and regional econometric models is contained in Paelinck and Klaassen (1979).

A COMPARISON OF THE LINEAR MODEL WITH THE GARIN—LOWRY MODEL

Both the linear model and the Garin–Lowry model have been extensively applied and a comparison of their relative merits can now be undertaken. Two studies that have empirically tested the performance of the two models, work by Putman in the USA (US Department of Transportation 1976) and a study of central Berkshire in Britain (Foot 1974), have tended to indicate a preference for the gravity based urban model. However, it is useful to compare the characteristics of the two models in order to try and discover the reasons for one model being preferred to the other in a particular study:

(1) The linear model uses a well known, well documented and widely applied statistical technique with readily available computer programs that can be used on any computer. The Garin–Lowry model, however, is rather more difficult to develop, since it is not so widely documented and there are fewer computer packages available (Foot 1978).

(2) The Garin–Lowry model allocates activities to zones and

also determines the interaction between zones over the region, but the linear model only allocates activities to zones and if the interaction between zones is required, then it has to be determined in a later gravity based model. This gives the Garin–Lowry model a decided advantage.

(3) The data requirements of the linear model are generally rather more exhaustive than the Garin–Lowry model, although very much depends on the scale of the model being developed. If aggregate data for one base date are collected, then more variables are required within a linear model than are included in the Garin–Lowry model. However, an expanded Garin–Lowry model will require highly disaggregated data, but generally for one point in time. Linear models on the other hand are very often developed to model incremental changes over a time period, and in this case highly reliable data for two points in time are required.

(4) There are really no statistical assumptions underlying a Garin–Lowry model, but there are a set of statistical assumptions underlying the linear model which should be tested during calibration to check that the model has not been wrongly formulated.

(5) There is considerable flexibility open to the model builder in determining the variables to include within a linear model, but the Garin–Lowry model has a fixed relationship, although the activities can be disaggregated.

(6) A linear model can be highly sensitive to problems in the zoning system where certain zones do not conform to the general pattern of change in the region. The Garin–Lowry model copes with these problems rather better.

(7) One advantage of the linear model is that it is fast and inexpensive to operate in terms of computer time. The Garin–Lowry model is considerably more expensive but it does provide the extra information on the activity interaction between zones.

(8) During the 1970s the Garin–Lowry model was extensively researched and applied, dealing with automatic calibration procedures, automatic constraints procedures, the disaggregation of activities, the addition of further submodels, and its integration into a general landuse transport model. The application of linear models was also considerably extended, particularly in North America, with a further disaggregation of activities and the development of more comprehensive models, together with its integration within larger hybrid models which contain certain elements of several types of model linked by a set of accounting equations.

It can be seen that these two models have their strengths and limitations. Which model to develop for a particular study region will depend on a number of factors, such as the reason for developing the model and the type of questions posed, the nature of the region and the importance of the activity interaction patterns, data availability and the budget allocation for new survey work, the level to which the activities need to be disaggregated and the degree of comprehensiveness required, the time allowed for the modelling exercise and the role of the model within the overall project, and also very importantly the personal preference of the model builder (see Pack and Pack 1977).

7 Optimizing models

All the models considered so far describe and predict the location of activities to small areas and the interaction between these areas. Optimizing models, however, try to perform a similar function but at the same time reach an optimal solution. There are obviously many alternative location patterns that new development could take in a region over the next ten years. Optimizing models can consider these alternatives and determine the optimal pattern of new development subject to certain constraints. It is highly informative to know what policies could be followed so that, for example, a certain level of new residential development could be achieved but at the lowest possible cost, or in order to minimize the overall cost of transport from residential zones to service centres. It does not necessarily mean that these policies will be followed, because there will be many other factors not included in the optimizing model that have to be taken into account, but it does give something to which all other policies can be compared (see Laidlaw 1972).

Mathematical programming, and in particular linear programming, is used to find the optimal solution, and there are many books that can be consulted for a detailed account of the methods, either operational research books (e.g. Taffler 1979, Nagel and Neef 1976) or books just on linear programming (e.g. Laidlaw 1972, Thie 1979, Trustrum 1978). The optimizing procedure involves choosing an objective function equation that has to be optimized subject to a series of constraints. The objective function might be to find the allocation of new activities in order to minimize the overall cost of development in the region, or to minimize the overall cost of travel to work, or to maximize the social benefit which could be measured in several ways. The constraint equations show the restrictions to development in the zones and the region and these could include the maximum and minimum levels of development allowed in each zone for the different activities, environmental constraints on development, constraints on the provision of public utilities, constraints on the mix of different activities, such as industrial and residential development allowed in each zone, and constraints on the level of interaction allowed between certain zones. It can be seen that optimizing models require considerable detailed data, particularly cost data, which can be difficult to obtain. Mathematical programming has been used to study a wider set of planning problems than the other models considered in the book. As well as the allocation of landuse activities and transport, it has been used to study such problems as waste disposal, water resource management, and the provision and siting of hospitals and schools. Some of these examples will be described later, but a good account of the application of mathematical programming in socio-economic and environmental studies is contained in Greenberg (1978). Three models will be developed in order to explain the optimizing procedure for a landuse allocation interaction model. Firstly, a model minimizing the cost of development; secondly, a model minimizing the cost of travel; and thirdly, a model to determine the optimal allocation when both the development costs and the travel costs are minimized. A number of operational models will be described and the usefulness of optimizing models assessed.

OPTIMIZING THE ALLOCATION OF ACTIVITIES

In order to find the optimal allocation of new development in a region of n zones, the following objective function could be proposed:

$$\text{minimize } Z = \sum_{k=1}^{m} \sum_{j=1}^{n} v_{kj} X_{kj} \qquad (7.1)$$

where subscript k refers to the activity when there are a total of m activities and subscript j refers to the zone number, and therefore v_{kj} is the cost of developing one unit of activity type k in zone j, and X_{kj} is the number of units of activity type k to be developed in zone j. The activities could be new residential development and new industrial development, which might be disaggregated into different types of residential and industrial development. A whole series of constraint equations could be formulated to reflect any restrictions to development, but in order to gain an understanding of the linear programming technique, a very simple example will be presented.

An optimizing model of York

Consider the town of York in northern England (figure 7.1) with a population of about 105,000. A large proportion of the employed residents of York, about 86%, also work in York, but there is also a large flow of workers from surrounding residential areas to work in York. Neglecting any problem with administrative boundaries, assume that it was decided to expand the residential area of York by providing new residential development on the east of the city. Rather than divide the whole city into zones, consider just the two zones in figure 7.1 for new development and then the problem can be solved graphically. A total of 1200 new houses is required while in zone 1 a maximum of 500 houses can be built and in zone 2 a maximum of 1000 houses. Consider that a mix of different types of houses is to be developed and the cost of developing housing in zone 1 is £30,000 per house and in zone 2 £35,000 per house because the land is more expensive, and it costs more to provide a sewerage system. The council and builders wish to minimize the cost of development while providing the 1200 new houses. This is a simple example and the answer is quite obvious, but it will show the ideas behind optimizing models.

The objective function will be similar to equation (7.1) with one activity, residential development ($m = 1$), and two zones ($n = 2$):

$$\text{minimize } Z = v_{11}X_{11} + v_{12}X_{12} \qquad (7.2)$$

where

v_{11} = cost of new housing in zone 1 = £30,000 per unit
v_{12} = cost of new housing in zone 2 = £35,000 per unit

and

X_{11} = amount of new housing in zone 1
X_{12} = amount of new housing in zone 2

The object of linear programming is to determine the amount of new housing in zone 1 (X_{11}) and the amount of new housing in zone 2 (X_{12}) in order to minimize the equation (7.3):

$$\text{minimize } Z = 30,000X_{11} + 35,000X_{12} \qquad (7.3)$$

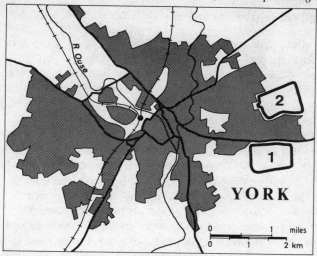

Figure 7.1 The York study region

Obviously the minimum cost of development is to spend no money and build no houses, but there are certain restrictions that have been set out above and can now be formulated in a set of contraint equations:

(1) A maximum of 500 new houses can be developed in zone 1, i.e.

$$X_{11} \leqslant 500 \qquad (7.4)$$

(2) A maximum of 1000 new houses can be developed in zone 2, i.e.

$$X_{12} \leqslant 1000 \qquad (7.5)$$

(3) A total of 1200 new houses must be built in zone 1 and zone 2, i.e.

$$X_{11} + X_{12} = 1200 \qquad (7.6)$$

(4) Two other constraints also apply which specify that negative values for X_{kj} in the final solution are not allowed, i.e.

$$X_{11} \geqslant 0 \qquad (7.7)$$
$$X_{12} \geqslant 0 \qquad (7.8)$$

This simple example has been formulated as a linear programming problem. It is called linear programming because all the equations are of linear form. Other types of programming are available when the equations are non-linear, but these are more difficult to solve.

177

A graphical solution

Since there are only two zones with one activity this linear programming problem can be solved graphically (figure 7.2). The amount of new residential development in zone 1 is plotted along the horizontal axis and the amount of new residential development in zone 2 along the vertical axis. The three constraint equations can then be drawn on the diagram (figure 7.2). The line $X_{11} = 500$ can be drawn which shows the limit of new development in zone 1. Any point to the left of this line is a feasible solution but any point to the right of this line cannot occur, otherwise more than 500 houses are being developed in zone 1. Similarly the line $X_{12} = 1000$ shows the limit of development in zone 2 with all points below this line a feasible solution, and all points above this line not allowed. The third constraint which postulates that 1200 houses must be built can now be drawn, and the optimal solution must lie on this line. Any point in the area OABRCD would provide a feasible solution for the first two constraint equations (equations (7.4) and (7.5)), but the other constraint equation (equation 7.6)) shows that the solution must lie on the line BC because this satisfies all three constraints.

The problem now is to determine what point on the line BC will optimize the objective function equation (7.3) and minimize the overall cost of development. This can be solved graphically by assuming some overall cost of development, say £55 million, which is substituted into the objective function to form equation (7.9) and then drawn on the graph:

$$55,000,000 = 30,000\ X_{11} + 35,000\ X_{12} \qquad (7.9)$$

Any other line parallel to this line provides a solution, and the first point reached as this line moves from the origin point O towards the feasible solution will be the optimum. This is the point B where $X_{11} = 500$ and $X_{12} = 700$. These values are substituted into the objective function (equation (7.3)) to calculate the overall minimum cost of development:

$$
\begin{aligned}
Z &= (30,000)\ (500) + (35,000)\ (700) \\
&= £39,500,000
\end{aligned}
\qquad (7.10)
$$

The cheapest solution would therefore be to develop the maximum number of 500 houses in zone 1 and then develop the

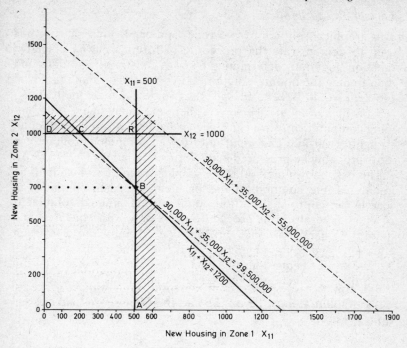

Figure 7.2 Graphical solution to determine the minimum cost of development for York

remaining 700 in zone 2. The point C on the graph where $X_{11} = 200$ and $X_{12} = 1000$ would also be a perfectly feasible solution, in that it satisfies all the constraint equations, but it is not the optimal solution. It would cost £41,000,000 to develop 200 houses in zone 1 and 1000 homes in zone 2 which is £1½ million more than the optimal solution set out above (equation (7.10)). This optimal solution was fairly obvious from the start, but for a large number of zones, with several different types of residential and industrial activities, and with a large number of constraint equations showing restrictions to development, then the solution would be far from obvious and the technique can provide useful information about the optimal allocation.

The simplex technique

This graphical solution of two zones and one landuse activity was used to demonstrate the procedure of formulating an objective function equation, determining a set of constraint equations and then finding the optimal solution. Anything larger than this trivial problem would have to be solved by some algebraic method and run on the computer. However, there are many linear programming computer software packages available that can be used quite straightforwardly. The input data to the computer program can most probably be presented in the form of equations (7.3) to (7.8).

The best known method is the simplex technique which finds an initial feasible solution to the problem and then continues to search for improved solutions until a final optimal solution is reached. The algebraic procedure deals only with equalities and therefore slack variables are introduced into the constraint equations that contain inequalities. By introducing slack variables X_{s1} and X_{s2} into equations (7.4) and (7.5), each with a zero cost in the objective function, a revised set of equations can be formed:

$$\text{minimize } Z = 30,000X_{11} + 35,000X_{12} + 0X_{s1} + 0X_{s2} \quad (7.11)$$

subject to

$$X_{11} + X_{s1} = 500 \quad (7.12)$$

$$X_{12} + X_{s2} = 1000 \quad (7.13)$$

$$X_{11} + X_{12} = 1200 \quad (7.14)$$

$$X_{11}, X_{12}, X_{s1}, X_{s2} \geqslant 0 \quad (7.15)$$

The slack variables show the spare capacity within each constraint equation, and in this example X_{s1} and X_{s2} will show the amount of unused capacity for new development in zones 1 and 2. The simplex technique will find an initial solution, for example point C on figure 7.2, and then search for improvements until point B is reached which is the optimal solution. A computer program of the simplex technique would provide the following results:

$$X_{11} = 500 \qquad X_{12} = 700$$

$$X_{s1} = 0 \qquad X_{s2} = 300 \quad (7.16)$$

$$Z = £39,500,000$$

This is the same solution as that obtained by the graphical method (equation (7.10)), but here the slack variables also show the spare capacity for new housing in each zone. Zone 1 is fully developed and therefore the slack variables $X_{s1} = 0$, but since only part of zone 2 is developed, then slack variable $X_{s2} = 300$ which indicates the number of houses that could still be built in the zone. It is also highly informative to perform a sensitivity analysis and observe the effects on the optimal solution that arise from changing the capacity for development in the zones and from changing the cost of development in each zone.

The graphical solution, and now the simplex technique, show the procedure involved in applying an optimizing model using linear programming: determining the objective function equation, formulating a set of constraint equations and running the model on the computer to obtain results that show the optimal allocation of new development.

The dual problem

All linear programming problems can be reformulated as dual problems involving the same data but with new variables. There will be as many variables in the dual problem as there are constraints in the original or primal problem, other than non-negative constraints. If the primal problem involved minimizing its objective function, then the dual will involve maximizing its objective function, and similarly if the primal is a maximization problem then the dual will be a minimization problem. However, the optimal value from the dual objective function will always be equal to the result obtained from the primal objective function. Since each new variable in the dual problem refers to a constraint equation in the primal, then certain useful information about the constraints can be obtained from solving the dual, as will be shown for the York example. This is only the very briefest of outlines involving the dual problem and for more detail see books on linear programming already referenced.

The linear programming problem for York to minimize the cost of new development (equations (7.3) to (7.8)) can be reformulated as a dual maximization problem involving the same data, and the overall optimal values from the two objective functions will be equal to £39.5 million (equation (7.10)). The allocations in the dual solution will indicate the marginal value that can be gained by relaxing each of the constraints in the original problem. There are three constraints in the York example and the dual problem shows that if the first constraint (equation (7.4)) could be relaxed and more development take place in zone 1, this would lead to a saving of £5000 per house on the overall cost of development. It also shows that the second constraint (equation (7.5)) is not critical, with capacity for development in zone 2 still available. If the third constraint (equation (7.6)), which sets the total level of new housing development in the region, could be relaxed and less housing developed, this would lead to a saving of £35,000 per house since less development would be taking place in zone 2, down to a total regional development of 500 houses. In this example of York the results are rather obvious, but for a large number of zones with different types of development this will not be the case. So the results of the dual problem can be of interest in looking at the sensitivity of the optimal solution to changes in the constraint equations of the original problem.

Landuse plan design model

This type of linear programming model was proposed by Schlager for the landuse transportation study of south-east Wisconsin (Schlager 1965). The object of the landuse plan design model was to minimize the overall cost of developing certain landuse activities, particularly residential, industrial, recreational and agricultural development. In a region divided into small zones, the constraint equations relate to a regional demand for each of the landuse activities, constraints on the total amount of development that can take place in each zone, and in order to introduce certain design standards, constraints on the mix of different types of new development that can take place in each zone and between zones.

The linear programming formulation is similar to the York example, except that there are now n zones and m different activities. The objective function is the same as equation (7.1):

$$\text{minimize } Z = \sum_{k=1}^{m} \sum_{j=1}^{n} v_{kj} X_{kj} \qquad (7.17)$$

where v_{kj} is the cost of developing one square metre of activity k in zone j and X_{kj} is the number of square metres of activity k to be developed in zone j. The York example considered only two zones and one activity (equation (7.2)), with residential development measured in terms of housing units not square metres. In practice, residential development can be disaggregated into different types of housing.

This cost minimization takes place subject to a series of constraints. The first is

$$\sum_{k=1}^{m} X_{kj} \leq N_j \qquad (7.18)$$

This first constraint sets the limit N_j to all types of development that can be allowed in each zone j and is equivalent to equations (7.4) and (7.5) in the York example. The second constraint is

$$\sum_{j=1}^{n} \omega_k X_{kj} = M_k \qquad (7.19)$$

This second constraint sets out the total demand M_k in the region for landuse activity type k. The variable ω_k is a ratio coefficient which allows for the extra service supporting land requirements for each activity k such as roads, parks and open spaces. In the York example, the equivalent equation is (7.6), although there is no ω_k factor since it was assumed to be included within X_{kj} which was measured as the number of housing units in each zone j. The third and fourth constraints are

$$X_{kj} \leq GX_{gj} \qquad (7.20)$$
$$X_{kj} \leq GX_{gh} \qquad (7.21)$$

These two equations set out the restrictions on the mix of different landuses within each zone and between zones. In equation (7.20), G is the ratio of activity k that is allowed in zone j relative to activity g, while in equation (7.21), G is the ratio of activity k in zone j that is allowed relative to activity g in zone h. The fifth constraint is

$$X_{kj} \geq 0 \qquad (7.22)$$

This is the usual linear programming constraint that ensures that only non-negative zonal allocations are possible. Any number of other constraint equations could be constructed to reflect other design standards or further restrictions to development.

Schlager tested the model on a small area within the study region, a thirty zone model of Waukesha, and dealt with residential, industrial, agricultural and recreational development, but each at a disaggregated level. Although not all zones could accommodate every type of new development, there were still about 400 zonal activities X_{kj} in the objective function equation (equation (7.17)). Data requirements for even this small example are, therefore, enormous. About 400 zonal activity development costs v_{kj} had to be calculated, as well as a full landuse inventory of every zone, in order to determine the amount of land that could be developed in each zone for each of the activities. Then additional data were required about the total demand in the region for each landuse activity, and also the landuse relationships within each zone and between zones had to be derived from certain design standards. This quantity of data is extremely difficult to assemble, particularly development cost data, and yet this model is a relatively simple linear programming model which Schlager applied to only a small area.

The assumptions of linear programming

There are certain basic assumptions underlying the use of linear programming models, which can sometimes cause problems. The first assumption is that the objective function and the constraint equations are of a linear form. In the objective function for example (equations (7.1), (7.2), (7.3), (7.17)) this means that there is a constant development cost per square metre or per house, no matter how much development takes place in a zone. How far this assumption is realistic will depend upon the economies of scale that can be obtained from a large development, and on the way that fixed costs such as administration and machinery, can be spread over the new development.

Linear programming also assumes the use of continuous variables which means that the optimal solution can contain parts of a square metre. In some situations this might be quite reasonable but on other occasions it might be preferable to use discrete blocks of development for residential and industrial estates. The linear programming solution can always be rounded off to provide a discrete solution which should be close to, but not necessarily exactly the same as, the discrete optimal solution.

Theoretical properties of linear programming

There are certain general theoretical properties that apply to a linear programming problem. Firstly the optimal solution will be at the intersection of two or more of the constraint equations or axes. In the graphical solution to the York example (figure 7.2), the solution is at point B, the intersection of equation (7.6) and the limit of equation (7.4). The same principle will apply to larger linear programming problems that are solved by algebraic methods, particularly the simplex technique.

The second property of linear programming is that the number of positive values for the zonal allocation variables X_{kj} in the final solution cannot be greater than the number of constraint equations other than the non-negative constraints. If a model contains more constraint equations than variables, then all the variables can take on positive values, as in the York example where there are three constraint equations and two variables X_{11} and X_{12}, with the final solution containing positive values for the two variables. But if for example a model deals with ten activities in a region of thirty zones, giving a total of 300 zonal activities X_{kj}, and contains 100 constraint equations other than the non-negative constraints, then there will be at most 100 of the zonal activities X_{kj} with positive values. This can be restrictive, particularly in dealing with transport problems.

OPTIMIZING TRAVEL COST

Much of the data and many of the models considered so far in the book deal with the spatial interaction of activities within a region and this can also be formulated as a linear programming model. Consider the doubly constrained origin–destination journey to work trip matrix shown in figure 4.4. Using the same notation with T_{ij} representing the number of person trip movements from work zone i to residential zone j, O_i the number of employees working in zone i, and D_j the number of employed persons living in zone j, such that $\Sigma_i O_i = \Sigma_j D_j$. The linear programming model would involve finding the optimal distribution of person trip movements T_{ij}, in order to minimize the overall cost of travel to work in the region. If c_{ij} is the cost of travelling from work zone i to residential zone j, then the objective function can be formulated:

$$\text{minimize } Z = \sum_{i=1}^{n} \sum_{j=1}^{n} c_{ij} T_{ij} \qquad (7.23)$$

The constraints to this minimization are the origin and destination zone totals:

$$\sum_j T_{ij} = O_i \qquad (7.24)$$

$$\sum_i T_{ij} = D_j \qquad (7.25)$$

And with the sign constraint

$$T_{ij} \geqslant 0 \tag{7.26}$$

This type of linear programming problem is termed a transport problem and there are special routines for solving the equation set. Alternatively it could be solved using a conventional linear programming routine on any computer. The optimal solution which minimizes the overall travel cost in the system can be used in several different ways and is not necessarily meant as an ideal situation. For example it can be used to see how far the actual distribution differs from the optimal distribution or to compare a set of optimal solutions resulting from a series of alternative future planning strategies.

To understand this transportation problem more clearly, a three zone model will be formulated, firstly in algebraic form, and then with data for the Bideford area of north Devon. The available data includes origin zone totals O_i, destination zone totals D_j and travel costs or travel times between zones c_{ij}. This provides information for a linear programming model of the following form which will find the distribution of trips T_{ij} which minimizes the overall cost of travel in the region:

$$\text{minimize } Z = c_{11}T_{11} + c_{12}T_{12} + c_{13}T_{13} + c_{21}T_{21} + c_{22}T_{22}$$
$$+ c_{23}T_{23} + c_{31}T_{31} + c_{32}T_{32} + c_{33}T_{33} \tag{7.27}$$

Subject to

$$T_{11} + T_{12} + T_{13} = O_1$$
$$T_{21} + T_{22} + T_{23} = O_2$$
$$T_{31} + T_{32} + T_{33} = O_3$$
$$T_{11} + T_{21} + T_{31} = D_1 \tag{7.28}$$
$$T_{12} + T_{22} + T_{32} = D_2$$
$$T_{13} + T_{23} + T_{33} = D_3$$

and all $T_{ij} \geqslant 0$ for $i = 1$ to 3, $j = 1$ to 3. Although six constraint equations are presented, one of these is redundant because any one of the equations can be formed from the other five, since the row and column totals are known and equal with $\Sigma_i O_i = \Sigma_j D_j$. With actual data (for example table 7.1), if the first five equations are known, then the values in the last equation can be found by subtraction. There are therefore only five constraint equations other than the non-negative constraints, which means that because

Table 7.1 The journey to work trip matrix for the north Devon region

Work zone	Residential zone			Totals
	Bideford	*Northam*	*Instow*	*Totals*
Bideford	3530	1110	180	4820
Northam	440	1690	50	2180
Instow	150	60	190	400
Totals	4120	2860	420	7400

of the theoretical property outlined above, no more than five of the trip movements T_{ij} can be positive values. In general, for n zones and with a trip matrix of size n^2, then at most $2n-1$ cells in the matrix can have positive values. For a thirty zone region, therefore, with a 30×30 trip matrix of 900 cells, only fifty-nine positions can have positive flows. This can be a severe restriction on the use of this type of linear programming model, although very much depends on the type of problem being studied. There are, however, several ways of expanding the model and increasing the number of constraints, for example by introducing minimum and maximum destination constraints rather than absolute limits, but these extensions will be discussed later.

An optimizing model of north Devon

Consider a small example around Bideford in north Devon (figure 7.3). The whole area caters for the holiday trade, particularly Northam, but there are some small industries mainly associated with the sea. Bideford is also a market town at the bridging point over the River Torridge, and the Instow zone is quite rural away from the coast. It is a fairly self-contained area with a very large proportion of people living and working in the area. The journey to work trip matrix for the three zones is given in table 7.1 for 1971. Rather than using cost of travel between zones the travel time will be used. This information is given in table 7.2, and has been calculated in the usual way assuming 20 mph in urban areas and 40 mph on other main roads. The overall total travel time for journey to work from this data is 19,316 minutes with an average travel time of 2.61 minutes.

The purpose of the optimizing model is to find the optimal journey to work trip pattern T_{ij} in table 7.3 in order to minimize the overall travel time. Formulating this as a linear programming

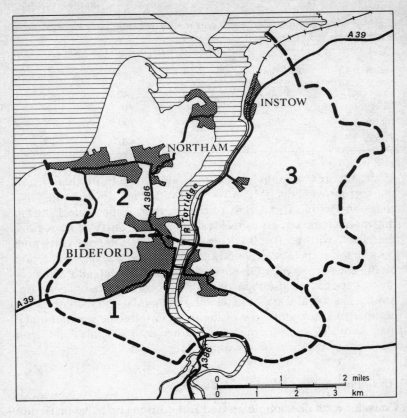

Figure 7.3   The north Devon study region

Table 7.2   The travel times (minutes) between zones for the north Devon region

Work zone	Residential zone		
	Bideford	*Northam*	*Instow*
Bideford	1.4	5.2	5.6
Northam	5.2	1.8	10.7
Instow	5.6	10.7	1.3

Table 7.3 The formulation of the transport problem for the north Devon region

Work zone	Residential zone			Totals
	Bideford	*Northam*	*Instow*	
Bideford	T_{11}	T_{12}	T_{13}	4820
Northam	T_{21}	T_{22}	T_{23}	2180
Instow	T_{31}	T_{32}	T_{33}	400
Totals	4120	2860	420	7400

problem involves substituting the data into the equation set (7.27) and (7.28) for c_{ij}, O_i and D_j:

$$\text{minimize } Z = 1.4T_{11} + 5.2T_{12} + 5.6T_{13} + 5.2T_{21} + 1.8T_{22}$$
$$+ 10.7T_{23} + 5.6T_{31} + 10.7T_{32} + 1.3T_{33} \quad (7.29)$$

Subject to

$$T_{11} + T_{12} + T_{13} = 4820$$
$$T_{21} + T_{22} + T_{23} = 2180$$
$$T_{31} + T_{32} + T_{33} = 400 \quad (7.30)$$
$$T_{11} + T_{21} + T_{31} = 4120$$
$$T_{12} + T_{22} + T_{32} = 2860$$

and T_{11}, T_{12}, T_{13}, T_{21}, T_{22}, T_{23}, T_{31}, T_{32}, $T_{33} \geq 0$. As previously stated, with only five constraint equations other than the non-negative constraints, then no more than five of the nine possible trip flows can take on positive values. This model can be solved by using the special transportation problem technique or by using a more general linear programming solution such as the simplex technique. Either method will provide the optimal solution shown in table 7.4 with $T_{11} = 4120$, $T_{12} = 680$, $T_{13} = 20$, $T_{22} = 2180$, $T_{33} = 400$ and the other four flows equal to zero. By substituting these values into the objective function equation (equation (7.29)), this gives a total travel time for journey to work of $Z = 13,860$ minutes and an average travel time of 1.87 minutes. This minimum travel time solution represents an overall reduction of 0.74 minutes from the actual average of 2.61 minutes and is achieved by allocating as many workers as possible to live and work in the same zone. This happens because with this type of data intrazonal travel times c_{ij} for $i = j$ are smaller than interzonal travel times c_{ij} (for $i \neq j$). Usually the number of trips T_{ij} for $i = j$ will equal the smaller of the

Table 7.4 The optimal journey to work pattern to minimize overall travel time in the north Devon region

Work zone	Residential zone			Totals
	Bideford	Northam	Instow	
Bideford	4120	680	20	4820
Northam	0	2180	0	2180
Instow	0	0	400	400
Totals	4120	2860	420	7400

row and column totals O_i and D_j. In table 7.4, $T_{11} = D_1 = 4120$, $T_{22} = O_2 = 2180$, $T_{33} = O_3 = 400$ and then the matrix is completed with smaller flows on the other interzonal routes.

These results do show the minimum travel time solution and can be compared to the actual situation. However, for journey to work trip movements, this information is not too useful on its own. People do not necessarily want to minimize their journey to work travel time but rather to maximize their net benefit. They are willing to incur an extra travel cost in order to travel further and live away from their work zone. There could be a number of reasons for this, for example to gain cheaper housing away from the main work areas, or to live in a more environmentally pleasing area. An objective function that simply tries to minimize travel cost is far too simple to represent the journey to work pattern. Location patterns are far more complex than the situation represented by this simple model and consequently it has been considerably extended in order to try and take other factors into account.

The application of linear programming transport models

Although the simple linear programming transport model is not sufficient on its own to determine journey to work patterns, it has been used quite successfully to consider a number of other locational and transport problems. In the field of education it has often been used to look at the allocation of children to schools. For example Yeates (1963) considered how students should be allocated to high schools in Grant County, Wisconsin. This was considered purely as a transportation problem with the distribution of students by small residential area O_i to be allocated to the thirteen high schools of size D_j. The optimal distribution T_{ij} that minimized travel time was used to draw up a catchment area for each school. A comparison of the actual with the optimal catchment areas showed that there was a high degree of similarity, but Yeates points out that since children attend school five days a week for about forty weeks in the year, even small deviations from the optimum can in fact be quite significant. There are of course problems in the analysis, particularly the fact that the residential distribution of the school population changes every year, but this method can also be useful in determining the best location of a new school from a series of proposed alternatives.

Catchment areas can also be derived for hospitals in a similar way although the needs of different sections of the population also have to be taken into account. In refuse collection, the trips made between residential areas and alternative refuse tips can be optimized, although generally a more refined model would be used. Similarly in water resource management, the distribution of water from a number of reservoirs to residential areas can be optimized. Other studies in North America have looked at the efficiency of the distribution between the points of supply and demand for the coal industry, the steel industry and the wheat and flour trade by comparing the optimal distribution with the actual situation. Another study in Britain (O'Sullivan 1972) set out the commodity flows between regions as a transportation problem, and since there were no intrazonal flows (T_{ij} for $i = j$) the model worked quite successfully.

Linear programming transport models have also been used to study broader problems. Waverman (1972) looked at national policy decision in North America in relation to the distribution of natural gas from gas fields to the whole of Canada and the USA. The optimal solution was compared to the actual situation where there are restrictions on the movement of gas between the two countries. He shows that this has led to a non-optimal pipeline network and a higher cost of natural gas than need have been the case. In another study, Hopkins (1972) used a similar model to look at the effect of transport costs on the USA furniture industry. It is a mobile, competitive industry and will respond to changes, particularly changes in transport costs. He tried to show how the changes in the location of the furniture industry over time was due to movements in response to transport costs as the industry as a whole attempted to move more towards an optimal location pattern.

Assumptions and extensions

All the linear programming assumptions that have already been discussed also apply to the transport model, but in addition it is assumed that the activity or product being distributed must be a homogeneous good such that each unit can be distributed from any origin to any destination. Many of the examples just described conform reasonably well to this situation, such as the distribution of water, natural gas and high school children. In order to study more homogeneous units in the journey to work pattern, workers could be disaggregated into different employment types and zonal residential capacities could be disaggregated into different house types, with the model run for the different combinations.

The model has proved a useful technique in dealing with the distribution and allocation of certain activities and products. The simple model can be expanded in several ways by introducing additional constraints, although this will turn it into a general linear programming model. In a journey to work model for example, with a predicted distribution of employment at some future date, then rather than use fixed residential capacities for each zone, minimum and maximum values could be used. Alternatively limits could be set on the flows allowed between certain zones, particularly the intrazonal T_{ij} for $i = j$ flows. However, for many trip distribution patterns, such as journey to work, it is probably better to devise a more general model by combining the transportation movements with other factors that effect the allocation and distribution of activities. They could all be included within an expanded objective function equation, which could be optimized subject to a number of capacity constraints, and one example of this type of model will now be described.

A GENERAL OPTIMIZING MODEL: TOPAZ

The two optimizing models described so far deal only with a part of the urban system, but by combining the two, a more general urban model can be developed which considers both the allocation of activities and the interaction between activities in the region. Probably the best known general model of this type is TOPAZ (technique for the optimal placement of activities in zones) which was developed by Brotchie and Sharpe at CSIRO in Australia and has been applied to several Australian cities (Brotchie and Sharpe 1975) and in the USA (Dickey and Najafi 1973).

For a region divided into n zones and considering the allocation of m types of landuse activity, the objective function of the model determines the allocation of activities X_{kj} which minimizes the overall combined cost of new development and travel cost:

$$\text{minimize } Z = \text{development cost} + \text{travel cost}$$

$$= \sum_{k=1}^{m} \sum_{j=1}^{n} v_{kj} X_{kj} + \sum_{i=1}^{n} \sum_{j=1}^{n} c_{ij} T_{ij} \qquad (7.31)$$

The development cost is identical to the first allocation model equation (7.1), with v_{kj} the cost of developing activity type k in zone j and X_{kj} the amount of activity k to be developed in zone j. The travel cost can be expressed initially in a similar form to the transportation problem equation (7.23), with c_{ij} the cost of travel between zone i and zone j and T_{ij} the number of daily trips between zone i and zone j. However, in order to gain a more realistic distribution of trips over the region, a singly or doubly constrained gravity model, as reported in Chapter 4, is used to determine trips T_{ij}. Consider the singly constrained gravity model of equation (4.2):

$$T_{ij} = \frac{O_i D_j \exp(-\lambda d_{ij})}{\sum_j D_j \exp(-\lambda d_{ij})} \qquad (7.32)$$

Here d_{ij} is the distance or travel time between zone i and zone j, and λ a parameter that can be found by calibrating base year information. In the optimizing model O_i represents the total daily trips generated from zone i for all landuse activities k, and D_j represents the total daily trips attracted to zone j for all landuse activities k:

$$O_i = \sum_k (X_{ki} + EX_{ki}) \, PR_k \qquad (7.33)$$

$$D_j = \sum_k (X_{kj} + EX_{kj}) \, AT_k \qquad (7.34)$$

where EX_{ki} and EX_{kj} are the existing levels of activity k in zone i and zone j, X_{ki} and X_{kj} are the amounts of new activity k allocated to zone i and zone j, PR_k is the daily trip generation rate for a unit of activity k and AT_k is the daily trip attraction rate for a unit of activity k.

Equation (7.32) can now be rewritten in the form in which T_{ij} is used in the overall objective function equation (7.31):

T_{ij} = trips generated from zone i
    × proportion of trips attracted to zone j

$$= \sum_k (X_{ki} + EX_{ki}) \, PR_k \frac{\sum_k (X_{kj} + EX_{kj}) \, AT_k \exp(-\lambda d_{ij})}{\sum_j \sum_k (X_{kj} + EX_{kj}) \, AT_k \exp(-\lambda d_{ij})}$$
$$(7.35)$$

This cost minimization takes place subject to certain constraints. The first is an equation that specifies the total amount of new development type k required in the region M_k and is similar to equations (7.6) and (7.19):

$$\sum_j X_{kj} = M_k \tag{7.36}$$

The second constraint is an equation that specifies the total area of land N_j which is available for all types of new development in zone j and is similar to equations (7.4), (7.5) and (7.18):

$$\sum_k X_{kj} = N_j \tag{7.37}$$

This equation is an equality because land which is not developed in the optimal solution is regarded as an activity. A third constraint equation equates the total land required for development with the total land which is available for development. The amount of land left undeveloped in each zone is therefore part of the solution:

$$\sum_k M_k = \sum_j N_j \tag{7.38}$$

There are also the usual sign constraints

$$X_{kj} \geq 0 \text{ for } k = 1 \text{ to } m, j = 1 \text{ to } n \tag{7.39}$$

All these constraint equations are linear, but since the gravity model is used to determine the trips between zones, where the activity to be allocated is in both the numerator and the denominator of equation (7.35), then the objective function is no longer a linear equation and the overall model no longer a linear programming problem. It is in fact a quadratic programming problem which is much more difficult to solve and although there are some solution techniques available, a faster alternative iterative method has been devised. This of course entails new computer programs specifically written to perform this procedure which can be a restraint on its use.

The model has been described in terms of minimizing the overall cost of development, but it has been used by Brotchie in terms of benefits less costs with the objective function being maximized to gain maximum overall benefit. These benefits and costs consider social, economic, aesthetic and ecological factors, but there are considerable problems in collecting these data and determining quantitative values. One difficulty with TOPAZ is in optimizing an objective function that involves adding two different types of costs together, the cost (or net benefit) of developing new activities in the zones of the region and the daily total cost (or net benefit) of all trips in the region. However, the model can be run several times and the different solutions compared in order to detect any problems. The model can also be further disaggregated, additional constraints formulated and extra submodels incorporated. These submodels can deal with the performance of the transport system looking at the mode of travel and assigning trips to the network, the level of pollution over the region, the cost of providing services, and the change in land values.

Operational TOPAZ models

TOPAZ has been quite widely applied in Australia and to a lesser extent in the USA. Sharpe, Brotchie and Ahern (1975) describe its application to Melbourne in Australia which has a projected increase in population from 2.4 million in 1970 to 4.5 million in the year 2000. It is planned that this expansion should be accommodated in eight corridors radiating from the present city (figure 7.4) and a TOPAZ model was used to try and evaluate the best pattern and sequence of urban development along these corridors. Two landuse activities, new residential and new industrial development, and two transport modes, private and public transport, were considered for a forty zone region. The optimization took place in terms of costs only for the three ten year time intervals between 1970 and 2000. Best estimates of input variables for these dates were obtained and the model run recursively for 1980, 1990 and 2000, to obtain a minimum cost development pattern by these dates and an overall optimal solution. This base solution (figure 7.4) showed strongest pressure for development in the Berwick corridor at the beginning of the time period followed by development in the northern corridors. A whole series of alternative solutions was generated by specifying additional constraints in order to test the sensitivity of the base solution to various corridor development proposals.

This work on Melbourne has been extended in a particularly interesting way (Sharpe 1980). TOPAZ has been used to determine the most efficient form of new development and transport movement in the city in order to minimize energy consumption. In Australia, road transport consumed 52% of the

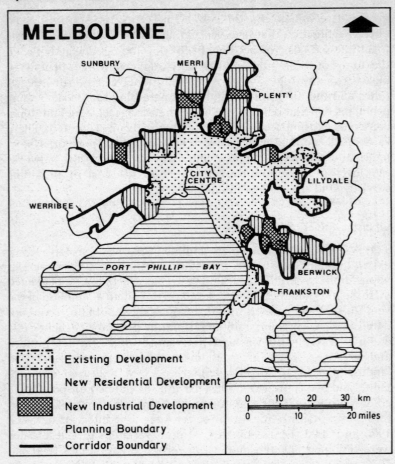

Figure 7.4 The TOPAZ base solution for Melbourne showing the allocation of residential and industrial activity 1970–2000

total oil-derived energy supplies in 1977, so that an analysis of urban transport and hence urban spatial structure is of vital importance in attempting to find ways of reducing energy consumption. A series of alternative planning strategies was tested by changing the variables in the model, such as development densities, infrastructure costs, private and public transport costs, zone constraints, traffic speeds, trip generation and vehicle occupancy rates. The 1977 energy situation was evaluated initially and then several different scenarios for the year 2000 were compared, both amongst themselves and with the 1977 situation. Of particular importance are firstly the situation if development and urban transport is allowed to proceed without any regard for energy conservation, and secondly the situation if an energy crisis is assumed to occur which would lead to severe restriction on energy consumption. This analysis indicated that savings of 40% could be achieved through changes such as increasing vehicle operating costs, increasing vehicle occupancy, higher density development, shorter trip behaviour and subcentre development within the urban area rather than fringe or satellite development. This application of TOPAZ shows how the model can be used to study highly relevant and topical questions, and since it is generally recognized that there could be an oil energy crisis in the 1980s and 1990s, this form of analysis could become increasingly important.

TOPAZ has also been used to investigate and evaluate future optimal patterns of development for Gosford–Wyong and Darwin, both in Australia (Brotchie and Sharpe 1975). The Gosford–Wyong area in New South Wales has a projected population growth from 100,000 to 500,000 between 1970 and 2000, and the model evaluated six different strategies for future urban development. In the Darwin study, alternative forms of expansion to the east of the town were evaluated. Here there was so little difference between the establishment costs for the forty-three zones that environmental factors were used instead to provide an environmental rating which was then costed and used to find the optimal development pattern.

In the USA Dickey and Najafi (1973) developed the model for a forty zone region of the New River Valley in south-west Virginia. A total of five types of landuse activities was involved: residential, commercial, industrial, recreational and public services. Using the best future estimates for variables, an optimal solution was determined showing the development pattern that minimized costs. Then an analysis was performed to test the sensitivity of this initial solution to changes in individual variables. Also a maximum cost solution was obtained together with minimum and maximum establishment cost solutions, in order to see how different were the best and worst solutions and development patterns. The local planners in the area thought the optimal solution very unlikely and that a more dispersed development was far more likely to occur. So further constraints were imposed and new solutions obtained.

TOPAZ is, therefore, a highly flexible general optimizing model that can provide economic and technical information on some of the social and environmental effects of development. There are, of course, problems in obtaining such detailed data, particularly cost data, but once they have been collected and future estimates derived for certain variables, then a whole series of alternative policies can be tested, more constraints can be added and their effect evaluated, and a series of sensitivity tests performed.

OTHER OPERATIONAL OPTIMIZING MODELS

Mathematical programming provides a flexible procedure for building urban models. The objective function can be optimized for any activity thought to be significant in determining landuse patterns, and any number of constraint equations can be imposed on the system. Consequently operational optimizing models are of many different forms since they have been formulated by people with different ideas on the principal planning variables involved in determining new location patterns, they have been developed to study different aspects of the urban system, and they are applied to areas with different planning problems. Models have been based on linear programming, the transport problem, quadratic programming and have also been included within larger hybrid models. They have been developed to minimize the cost of new development, the cost of transport and some more comprehensive overall total cost, or to maximize consumer benefit or consumer welfare. Some of the different sectors of the urban system that have been modelled include retailing, school and hospital catchment areas, industrial development, residential development and the housing market.

The Penn–Jersey regional growth model (Herbert and Stevens 1960) was one of the earliest optimizing models and attempted to simulate market conditions for residential location by basing its formulation on economic theory. The household housing budget, which is the amount of income that a household can spend on housing, is compared with the cost of housing in each zone for that household. This operation is performed for different groups of households and the optimal residential location pattern is obtained when the objective function of the model maximizes the net difference between housing budget and housing cost for all household groups, which of course gives maximum benefit over all households. The constraint equations ensure firstly, that the consumption of housing does not exceed the available supply, and secondly that all households are located to some housing. This original model has been extended by Harris (1972) and Wheaton (1974) to form a non-linear programming model. Transport costs are included in the objective function and the model also deals with non-residential land for development in the zones. This type of model has been developed for Hartford in Connecticut and Los Angeles, and by Senior and Wilson (1974) for the Leeds area in Britain.

In Europe there has been less emphasis on optimizing models compared with Australia and the USA. One of the few operational models developed in Britain was used to evaluate alternative strategies for the Tyne and Wear structure plan in north-east England in 1978. Dealing with residential and industrial development, a simple objective function was formulated to minimize the overall cost of development. All the various solutions were determined by formulating different constraint equations which related to land availability, resources available, planning standards and planners' preferred strategies. Also Coelho and Wilson (1976) have looked at the optimal location and size of shopping centres in Leeds through the maximization of consumers' welfare, with the optimizing procedure integrated with a spatial interaction model of shopping trip behaviour.

In Sweden an interesting optimizing model was developed for Stockholm (Lundqvist 1975, Karlqvist 1975) which was part of a long-term landuse transportation study of the region. The objective function contained two elements, firstly an interaction or transport cost indicator and secondly a weighted spatial congestion cost which measures the amount of activity in each zone. In minimizing the overall cost of development for the region and hence maximizing total welfare, these two elements are competing with each other within the same equation. To minimize interaction costs involves a high level of development in each zone and hence a high spatial congestion cost, and alternatively to minimize spatial congestion costs and have a dispersed development involves a high level of interaction cost. The main constraint equations set out an overall amount of development that was to take place in the next time period, together with maximum limits on the overall capital and labour resources available for carrying out this development. This quadratic programming model was solved using a heuristic tree searching procedure and run for three time periods between 1970 and 2000, but with particular interest in the years up to 1985. It was run in a hierarchical way dealing firstly with aggregate activities for twelve zones, and then disaggregated activities within each zone. A large number of alternative proposals were evaluated, which included a number of different transport systems, the impact of dispersed and concentrated development and attempts to determine efficient investment plans for Stockholm.

A number of other optimizing models have been developed by extending the landuse plan design model which was described earlier. In the original model (equations (7.17) to (7.22)) interaction between landuse activities could only be included as constraint equations within the linear programming formulation, such as new residential development only allowed within a certain distance from a secondary school. Later studies (see e.g. Hopkins 1977) have included activity interaction as a second factor within the objective function in a similar way to the TOPAZ model, and these will again form quadratic programming models.

The relationship between linear programming and a gravity model

One important theoretical development has shown that there is a direct link between the linear programming transportation problem and the doubly constrained gravity model. With the gravity model (equation (4.10)), the calibration procedure determines the parameter λ in the travel cost function $\exp(-\lambda c_{ij})$ in order to reproduce the actual trip pattern T_{ij}. However, it can be shown (Evans 1973) that as the parameter is varied to its limits of infinity, then when $\lambda = +\infty$ the minimum cost linear programming transport solution is reached, and the maximum cost solution is provided when $\lambda = -\infty$. This can be extended to show that any linear programming model can be seen as a limiting case of some entropy maximizing (gravity) model (see Chapter 4) in which some of the parameters tend to infinity. Alternatively, an entropy maximizing model can be considered a suboptimal solution of a linear programming model where the parameters have been obtained at calibration in order to reproduce the actual situation. Senior and Wilson (1974) extended this comparison to highly disaggregated residential location models for the Leeds area. The Herbert–Stevens regional growth model was expanded to include transport costs and competing landuse activities and was compared with the disaggregated entropy maximizing (gravity) model. Both models dealt with the same variables and it was shown theoretically and empirically that the programming model was a limiting case of the entropy model. They conclude that if the purpose of the study is to try and estimate the future distribution of landuse activities, then even with disaggregated zonal data, so much averaging goes on within the categories and within the zones, that trying to optimize the system is not really appropriate and that an entropy maximizing approach is better. However, optimizing models can usefully be used to study the urban system in other ways, and this point will be discussed shortly.

Interesting new models are now being developed that make use of this relationship between mathematical programming and entropy maximizing procedures. Methods have been developed by which maximum entropy formulations can be extended not only to satisfy the usual spatial interaction constraints (equations (4.20) and (4.22)), but also to satisfy some form of optimization, such as the maximization of consumer benefit. Models of this kind can be difficult to formulate, but the procedure has opened up new methods of constructing urban models. Coelho (1979) has developed a model for Santo André in Portugal which combines the mathematical programming and spatial interaction concepts by incorporating an entropy maximizing spatial interaction procedure within an overall social welfare optimization framework. It represents a form of cost–benefit analysis by considering the benefits accruing to consumers from accessibility and attractiveness, but within this optimization process, the more reliable entropy maximizing interaction procedure is used. The model generates an optimal landuse pattern for each alternative development strategy and provides estimates of the overall transport costs for work and service trips.

AN ASSESSMENT OF OPTIMIZING MODELS

The optimizing models described in this chapter have been applied in a number of different ways. Linear programming transport models have often been used to compare the actual distribution of an activity with some optimal distribution, as for example in studies of children attending schools and patients attending hospitals where a single factor such as travel time is being minimized. Differences are observed, and the model can also be used to locate new facilities. This simple type of application, dealing with a single objective variable can be quite successful, providing the assumptions underlying the model are fully understood.

However, the large-scale urban optimizing models which deal

with far more of the urban system cannot be used to estimate future patterns of development in a region in the way that the gravity models and regression models have been applied. As demonstrated in previous chapters, gravity and regression models are calibrated to an actual base year situation and then predictions made about future landuse pattern on the strength of this relationship. Optimizing models on the other hand are generally not calibrated but they determine the future development pattern that optimizes the objective function, subject to a set of constraints. The model does not, therefore, try to estimate the likely future landuse pattern, but it is used in a number of other important ways. It is very useful to know the development pattern that best satisfies certain objectives, such as minimizing overall cost or maximizing overall benefit for the region, subject to various restrictions, limitations and constraints. The model can be used to evaluate a set of alternative planning strategies. The results can be compared with each other, and to some overall optimal location pattern in order to test their efficiency and to see how far they satisfy the objectives of the planning study. In the Melbourne study, the broad consequences of several alternative corridor development strategies were compared, and then later work has looked at the optimal form of development and transport movement in terms of energy conservation. The Stockholm model compared a compact development and a dispersed development for the region, particularly in terms of investment. It is also informative to test the sensitivity of the results by varying certain variables and constraint equations. This procedure is clearly rather different from applying the gravity and regression models which attempt to estimate what will be the most likely future landuse pattern for a region. Optimizing models do, therefore, reveal different features from other urban models and are not applied in quite the same way.

There are, of course, a number of operational problems encountered in running optimizing models. Probably the biggest problem is in formulating the model, and in particular the objective function. As previously stated, mathematical programming provides a highly flexible procedure for urban modelling with the model builder determining the objective function and the constraint equations. However, this very flexibility can also be a problem in that it is often quite difficult to decide on the objective variables to be included, and it is in fact usually performed quite subjectively by the model builder. It is generally desirable to maximize the 'welfare' of the population within the region, but this is extremely difficult to quantify and, therefore, cost minimization is most often used. This cost minimization is generally confined to a small number of objective variables although there can still be data collection problems. Two of the most highly developed models, TOPAZ and the Stockholm model, only contain two elements in the objective functions. Other factors could have been included, but the problem arises that as more factors are included in the objective function, this increases the data requirements, the complexity of the model, and hence the difficulties in developing and operating the model.

Another difficulty is that data requirements are generally far greater for optimizing models than gravity based models, and in particular cost data are required. Much depends on the degree of disaggregation of the activities and the number of zones in the region but there can be considerable problems in obtaining this information. Highly diaggregated entropy maximizing (gravity) models do require large quantities of data, but there are simple gravity models that can be developed with very modest data requirements.

The main assumptions and theoretical properties of linear programming have already been covered. The assumption that the objective function and constraint equations are all linear can be overcome by using quadratic programming methods, such as TOPAZ and the Stockholm model, and even more complex mathematical programming methods are available. However, as the equations depart from linear functions, then the computation involved in solving the model increases considerably. Special algorithms were developed to solve the two operational models previously mentioned. Computational time on the computer is not particularly large, but linear programming packages are available on any computer, whereas more complex routines often have to be specially developed.

An optimizing model is also assumed to deal with continuous variables and although this is not usually the case, the optimal results can be rounded to discrete values to provide an optimal discrete solution or one very close to it, and this can be tested. Alternatively integer programming can be used which presents the results in discrete form. A further assumption that the objective variable to be distributed and located should be a homogeneous unit can generally be assumed to hold, although if there is a problem the activity can be disaggregated. For instance new development could be located as a single unit or it could be separated into residential and industrial development.

There are, therefore, several operational problems in developing an optimizing model, particularly in the formulation of the objective function and the collection of data. It has also been shown how the procedure of applying the model to a region is rather different from that followed by other urban models. Overall it can be concluded that under certain circumstances and to answer certain questions, an optimizing model can be highly informative. In addition, optimization provides a link between the different forms of urban model, as outlined above, and this might well be important in future theoretical developments in urban modelling.

8   Using urban models

The three main basic types of urban models based on gravity, linear and optimizing mathematics have now been introduced. Although every operational model is different in detail in order to fit in with the needs of each particular study, the majority of them follow these broad model types. A large number of operational models have been described and these show quite clearly the way the models have been applied in practice. There is though a further group of hybrid models which incorporate different aspects of the previous model types within an extensive equation structure. These hybrid models will now be discussed along with a general consideration of the way operational urban models can be most usefully applied. However, urban modelling is not without its critics (see e.g. Lee 1973, Sayer 1976, 1979) and this final chapter also considers these criticisms before drawing some general conclusions about the value of urban modelling.

HYBRID URBAN MODELS

Hybrid models have been developed largely in North America and have tended to be large comprehensive models which deal with highly disaggregated activities and simulate several sectors of the urban system. For example, population might be disaggregated by age group, occupation, and household formation, and employment by occupational requirements, with the model covering the location of industries and services, the housing market and residential location. There might also be further submodels dealing with retailing, the provision of public utilities such as schools and hospitals, and the transport network. Comprehensive models such as these can only be represented by a large set of equations which can include gravity, linear and optimizing mathematics as well as any relationships drawn from theoretical and empirical evidence. The data requirements are obviously enormous and the development of the models can take some considerable time, so that it is not surprising that they have tended to be rather expensive to develop.

Some of these hybrid models are extensions of the models already described in the book. The Echenique model described in Chapter 5, starting from a basic Garin–Lowry model has been considerably extended to form a large comprehensive landuse transportation model which is highly disaggregated and deals with both the demand and supply of activities (Echenique and Williams 1979). Many other hybrid models have been developed from the original Lowry model by extending the equation structure, and some of these were mentioned at the beginning of Chapter 5, for example the bay area simulation study (BASS) and the projective land use model (PLUM) (see Goldner 1971, Putman 1979). The BASS model uses linear regression models and entropy–gravity models together with a series of other equations in many of the submodels covering industrial location, the housing market, residential location and retail provision. The linear model developed by Putman (1970) and explained in Chapter 6 has been further extended and can now be regarded as a hybrid model. The TOPAZ model of Chapter 7, while essentially an optimizing model does include a spatial interaction function within the objective equation. Other models are being developed that link optimizing and entropy procedures (Coelho 1979).

There are other models that have been developed specifically as large-scale hybrid models involving any number of theoretical and empirical relationships and using any form of mathematics thought appropriate. They all take on a different form but two examples will show the nature of the models involved. The National Bureau of Economic Research (NBER) model simulates the housing market in large urban areas, but also deals with industrial location, the transport system and population changes (see Kain 1978). It has been applied to Detroit, Pittsburgh and Chicago and is partly dynamic in that it deals with changes over time and is never allowed to reach an equilibrium situation. The model consists of seventeen submodels to represent the three main sectors of housing demand, housing supply and the housing market. Some of these submodels are just accounting equations, others are linear econometric equations, while others involve linear programming and optimization. A second example is the New Haven model (see Birch *et al.* 1974) which is a general regional simulation model and tries to simulate the behaviour of the population in the region. The activities are highly disaggregated and the model involves a number of different forms of mathematics. It is a flexible model in that it can change its form to fit in with particular aspects of the urban system. The model can be developed as a large comprehensive model or for one sector such as retailing, but in this latter case the influence of other sectors on retailing will also be evaluated.

There are, therefore, a group of very large complex models that attempt to provide a much more detailed simulation of the urban system than the models considered earlier in the book. They do however have their drawbacks. The data requirements are enormous since the activities are so highly disaggregated and it can take considerable time and expense to develop models of this type. They do, however, extend the range of operational urban models available for urban analysis, from the very simple gravity models such as the retail shopping model through to these highly comprehensive hybrid models.

OPERATIONAL URBAN MODELS

Operational urban models are developed to gain an insight into the nature of the urban system, particularly the relationship between landuse activities, and then to predict the likely effects of certain future planning policies on the study region. Many examples have been described which look at the impact of large landuse changes or compare alternative future planning strategies and policies. Consider just two of the models from Chapter 5. Firstly the impact study of the effect of a new airport for London (Cripps and Foot 1970). Any new airport is bound to have an enormous impact on what is at present a fairly rural area and here the urban model provides an idea of the extent of this impact. Secondly the model of the Venice region (Piasentin, Costa and Foot 1978). The problems of the historical centre of Venice are well known but since it is just part of a large urban system, any study must involve the whole of this urban system. Urban modelling fits conveniently into this role, to provide information about the likely effects on the system resulting from a whole range of alternative planning policies.

The results from the models must be interpreted in an intelligent way. Since the models are still fairly coarse abstractions of real-world urban systems, they can only be used as a guide to the impact of various development strategies. They give a general indication of the likely consequences of certain actions and should not be accepted to the last unit of retail sales or to an individual trip movement. The models should be used as part of a larger overall analysis because there are obviously other factors, not included in the urban models, that have to be taken into account in formulating policies and making decisions. However, output from the urban models can provide a great deal of useful information to assist in this decision making process.

One way to test the ability of urban models to predict the future situation is to compare the results from some of the earlier models with what actually occurred. On the few occasions that this analysis has been performed the comparisons have been quite good. The analysis has been carried out on two retail shopping models. One example was described in Chapter 3, and looked at the impact of a new hypermarket. The results from an urban model were compared with the results obtained two and a half years later from a survey of customers using the hypermarket. The comparisons proved extremely close, except that the urban model could not deal with the very local effect on individual shops, although it did give an overall estimate of the local impact. In another shopping study, the predicted retail sales for 1971 contained in the Haydock study (McLoughlin, Foot and Nix 1966) were compared with the actual retail sales for 1971 (Foot 1979). Again there were quite reasonable fits between the two sales figures, apart from a few exceptions which could be explained by the assumption made in 1965 about the input data for 1971. For example, in two areas of north-west England new towns were proposed and so large increases in population, consumer expenditure and shopping facilities were included as input into the predictive runs of the model, but these proposals were later dropped. Also two other towns underwent major redevelopment of their town centres, and this was not taken into account sufficiently. Apart from these exceptions, the model predictions compared quite favourably with the actual retail sales for the shopping centres. So where this comparison has been attempted, the analysis has indicated a very reasonable fit between the output from the model at prediction and the actual results collected several years later.

All these results seem to indicate that urban models can provide a great deal of useful information. Now that computers are so readily available, the models can easily be developed and applied very quickly and cheaply. However, when using the models and interpreting the results it is important to be fully aware of the assumptions, limitations and problems that are involved.

ASSUMPTIONS, LIMITATIONS AND PROBLEMS OF APPLYING URBAN MODELS

A general assessment of the different urban models has been made at the end of each chapter after the models have been explained and operational models described. Several of the problems discussed are specific to certain models but it is worth considering again some of the more general problems associated with urban modelling.

It must always be remembered that urban models are a simplified mathematical representation of a part of the urban system. An equation or series of equations is designed to represent the workings of the real world and include what appear to be the most important variables or activities. The nature of each model is justified in relation to urban theory and through empirical evidence. However, there is still an insufficient knowledge and an inadequate theory of the complex workings of the urban system. Also it is obvious that many other factors and a number of market forces not included in the models will have an influence on the future pattern of development, and these must be considered in the final overall planning analysis.

All the urban models that have been used in a practical planning situation are static or comparative static equilibrium models that deal with a part of the urban system. There are good reasons why these types of models have been developed, for although they do obviously have their drawbacks, they are feasible and can actually be made operational. In reality, the urban system is clearly a dynamic constantly changing system. However, dynamic models quickly become highly complex even for one section of the urban system, while a model of the whole urban system is just too enormous and complicated to consider. Also, when these models are used predictively, and the calibrated parameters and coefficients are retained at prediction, it is being assumed that the interaction and location patterns that held at the calibration base data will persist in the future. This is obviously incorrect, particularly for impact studies, but it does give an initial forecast.

The parameters or coefficients can then be altered at prediction to try and adjust for changes in these patterns, such as a change in accessibility due to increased car ownership or a change in petrol prices.

There are also a number of practical problems that occur when building an operational model, and these were discussed in Chapter 2. There are problems in defining the study region and in deciding on the zoning system, which will vary with the type of study region. There is often a lack of suitable data. Even when data are available, there are problems in that the variables and activities often relate to different points in time and to different spatial units, and that often these spatial units do not represent sufficiently small areas. The availability of good data is always going to be a problem, although there is generally quite a lot of published information that can be collected and this can be supplemented by new surveys. All that can be done is to minimize these problems and then proceed with the model building exercise. One problem that has considerably improved is the availability of a computer on which to run the models. Now almost everyone has access to a fast computer sufficiently large to take a quite reasonably sized urban model.

It is important, therefore, that those using urban models are fully aware of all these problems. This does not invalidate their use, but means that they have to be interpreted in an intelligent way bearing these problems fully in mind. The models are analytical tools to help in looking at particular planning problems and to provide information on the most likely consequences resulting from certain planning actions. This will not solve urban problems, but taken in conjunction with information on other factors and other market forces at work within the urban system, they can help in determining preferred planning policies.

CRITICISMS OF URBAN MODELLING

It is not surprising in view of all these limitations that some strong criticisms are made about urban models (Lee 1973, Sayer 1976, 1979). Part of this criticism is a philosophical argument about scientific knowledge and the application of hard scientific methods to social science and policy science situations. There are, however, certain specific objections to the urban modelling approach to the investigation of urban problems (see Harris 1975).

Firstly it is felt that the models are far too simplistic. They do not include enough variables, deal with a static situation and rather than looking at the working of the urban system, merely represent some statistical relationship between activities from which predictions are then made. Instead the models should be dynamic, include far more variables and reflect the actual mechanics of the urban system. For example, in the residential location model of Chapter 4, the whole housing mechanism should be considered, not just a figure given for the number of houses in each zone. Some critics feel that the models provide so little extra knowledge on urban problems compared to the effort that goes into building the models that urban modelling is not a worthwhile exercise. These criticisms are valid up to a point, but in response it can be argued that simplicity is one of the strengths of urban models because it does mean they can be developed and operated. Of course, it would be better to build a dynamic model containing many more variables and dealing far more with the mechanisms at work in the urban system, but the whole model would soon become enormously complex and impossible to formulate. In a residential location model, the mechanism of the housing market dealing with developers, land values, building societies and many other variables, is such a complicated process that it is not yet fully understood and so it would be impossible to build it in as a small part of an urban model. The market mechanisms are also determined by world economic forces but just how can a detailed world economic model be included within a model of residential location or retail distribution for a small local region. The ideal urban model would certainly include all these different aspects of the urban system but the majority of models used at present are relatively simple because it means they can actually be developed and so provide information about the likely effect of future policies. Some of the larger, more comprehensive hybrid models do try and cover the urban system in far more detail, but these models are much more expensive and time consuming to develop, and they run into considerable data problems. They also begin to be criticized for being too complex and too difficult for planners to manage. Critics of the models have therefore turned from an attack on their simplicity to an assertion that they soon become too complicated.

Another criticism is that urban models are not useful tools of analysis because social behaviour cannot be represented in the form of mathematical equations and a far more flexible form of analysis is required. There is still considerable ignorance regarding how people respond to changes within the urban system and the models cannot really predict behaviour beyond the situation already observed. Also the interrelationships amongst the variables in the models are not fully specified. The world is just too complex to be described by general urban models and this whole approach to looking at urban problems is wrong. In reply to this criticism it can be argued that some form of urban analysis is going to be performed and that urban modelling, though far from perfect, is better than the alternative methods. There is some order or pattern in the urban system which urban models are trying to represent. They deal with patterns of mass behaviour and try to represent statistical regularities. Decisions are continuously being made about the form of new development and redevelopment and urban models can help in providing information to assist in making these decisions.

A further criticism relates to the nature of the models as static equilibrium models and particularly their use at prediction. The reality is an ever changing, dynamic world with continual political, social and technological changes and there is no way that urban models can be developed to predict the future situation. For example, a shopping model predicts the impact of a new hypermarket on the study region on the strength of the calibrated shopping pattern, when in fact in addition to all the other changes that will occur in the urban system, the development of the hypermarket will itself actually change the future shopping pattern. This problem of cause and effect is difficult to try and disentangle without developing a complex dynamic model, with all its additional problems. Static and comparative static models do, however, give an initial indication of the likely impact and then additional analysis can be performed to try and take other changes into account. The models can be run predictively under alternative assumptions about future technological changes and different political and social scenarios, and the results compared. This was just the form of analysis performed on the Venice region (Chapter 5) to study the effect of alternative future planning policies on the historical centre.

There are, therefore, a number of strong criticisms of urban modelling which some people think outweigh their usefulness. Other people, while bearing in mind their limitations, still think the models have a useful role to play within an overall urban analysis (see Batty 1979, Kain 1978, Harris 1979, Wilson 1978). One important point that must always be considered is that rather than just criticizing the models, they should also be compared with other alternative forms of urban analysis. The models might well be far from perfect, but they might also represent a better form of analysis of a particular planning problem than any of the alternative methods.

CONCLUSIONS

Urban modelling was introduced into the planning process as the systems approach to planning was being developed. The two complemented each other and led to a widespread interest in using models to help in the investigation of urban problems. They have been quite widely applied throughout the world and for a good account of their potential use see Batty (1979). At calibration the models test and refine theories and look for empirical relationships in order to gain an insight into the workings of the urban system. This provides a modelling structure for predicting the likely outcome of future planning policies which can assist in determining policy decisions for a region. A whole range of operational urban models is now available, from simple aggregate models to complex hybrid models, and the type of model to develop for a particular study region will depend on a number of factors such as the time and budget allocated to modelling, the level of detail required and how the model fits in with other forms of analysis. There are certainly limitations to the use of urban models in planning and so there is a continual need for further research and application (e.g. see Batty 1976, Wilson, Rees and Leigh 1978). Too much cannot be expected from these urban models for a perfect reproduction of the real-world situation is just not possible. However, by using existing data which can be supplemented by further survey work, a great deal of useful information can be produced from a modelling exercise. If this type of modelling is not to be used, then the alternative forms of urban analysis are probably poorer. Now that there is a general computer availability, particularly small desktop computers, urban models can be developed by almost any planning organization. The models can be built very cheaply and very easily at a fairly aggregate level, or they can be expanded and far more complex models developed with a corresponding increase in expenditure and time. In conclusion, it would appear that when analysing the urban system or looking at the consequences of planning policy decisions or development decisions then urban modelling can be a useful part of that analysis.

Bibliography

AYENI, B. (1979) *Concepts and Techniques in Urban Analysis*, London, Croom Helm.

BARRAS, R., BROADBENT, T.A., CORDEY-HAYES, M., MASSEY, D.B., ROBINSON, K. and WILLIS, J. (1971) 'An operational urban development model of Cheshire', *Environment and Planning*, 3, 115–234.

BATEY, P.W.J. and BREHENY, M.J. (1978) 'Methods in strategic planning: Part 1 A descriptive review; Part II A prescriptive review', *Town Planning Review*, 49, 259–73, 502–18.

BATTY, M. (1969) 'The impact of a new town', *Journal of Town Planning Institute*, 55, 428–35.

BATTY, M. (1970) 'An activity allocation model for the Nottinghamshire Derbyshire subregion', *Regional Studies*, 4, 307–32.

BATTY, M. (1975) 'In defence of urban modelling', *Journal of the Royal Town Planning Institute,* 61, 184–7.

BATTY, M. (1976) *Urban Modelling: Algorithms, Calibrations, Predictions*, Cambridge, Cambridge University Press.

BATTY, M. (1978) 'Urban models in the planning process', in Herbert, D.T. and Johnston, R.J. (eds) *Geography and the Urban Environment: Progress in Research and Applications*, vol. 1, Chichester, Wiley.

BATTY, M. (1979) 'Progress, success and failure in urban modelling', *Environment and Planning A*, 11, 863–78.

BATTY, M., BOURNE, R., CORMODE, P. and ANDERSON-NICHOLLS, P. (1974) 'Experiments in urban modelling for county structure planning: the Area 7 pilot model', *Environment and Planning A*, 6, 455–78.

BAXTER, M.J. and EWING, G.O. (1979) 'Calibration of production-constrained trip distribution models and the effect of intervening opportunities', *Journal of Regional Science*, 19, 319–30.

BAXTER, R.S. (1976) *Computer and Statistical Techniques for Planners*, London, Methuen.

BIRCH, D., ATKINSON, R., SANDSTRÖM, S. and STACK, L. (1974) *The New Haven Laboratory: A Test-bed for Planning*, Lexington, Ky, Lexington Books.

BROADBENT, T.A. (1971) 'A hierarchical interaction—allocation model for a two-level spatial system', *Regional Studies*, 5, 23–7.

BROTCHIE, J.F. and SHARPE, R. (1975) 'A general landuse allocation model: applications to Australian cities', in Baxter, R., Echenique, M. and Owers, J. (eds) *Urban Development Models*, Lancaster, Construction Press.

BRUTON, M.J. (1970) *Introduction to Transport Planning*, London, Hutchinson.

BURBY, R.J. DONELLY, T.G. and WEISS, S.F. (1971) *A Model for Simulating Residential Development in Reservoir Recreation Areas*, University of North Carolina, Water Resources Research Institute.

CARROTHERS, G.A.P. (1956) 'An historical review of the gravity and potential concepts of human interaction', *Journal of the American Institute of Planners*, 22, 94–102.

CASEY, H.J. (1955) 'The law of retail gravitation applied to traffic engineering', *Traffic Quarterly*, 9, 313–21.

CATANESE, A.J. (1972) *Scientific Methods of Urban Analysis*, London, Leonard Hill.

CHADWICK, G.F. (1971) *A Systems View of Planning*, Oxford, Pergamon Press.

CHAPIN, F.S. and KAISER, E.J. (1979) *Urban Land Use Planning*, Urbana, Ill., University of Illinois Press.

CHATTERJEE, S. and PRICE, B. (1977) *Regression Analysis by Example*, New York, Wiley.

COELHO, J.D. (1979) 'A locational-surplus maximization model of landuse plan design', in Breheny, M.J. (ed.) *Developments in Urban and Regional Analysis*, London, Pion.

COELHO, J.D. and WILSON, A.G. (1976) 'The optimum location and size of shopping centres', *Regional Studies*, 10, 413–21.

CRIPPS, E.L. and CATER, E.A. (1972) 'The empirical development of a disaggregated residential location model: some preliminary results', in Wilson, A.G. (ed.) *Patterns and Process in Urban and Regional Systems*, London, Pion.

CRIPPS, E.L. and FOOT, D.H.S. (1969) 'A landuse model for subregional planning', *Regional Studies*, 3, 243–68.

CRIPPS, E.L. and FOOT, D.H.S. (1970) 'The urbanisation effects of a Third London Airport', *Environment and Planning*, 2, 153–92.

DANIELS, P.W. and WARNES, A.M. (1980) *Movement in Cities: Spatial Perspectives of Urban Transport and Travel*, London, Methuen.

DAVIES, H.W.E., JACKSON, J.N. and ROBINSON, D.G. (1964) *Regional Shopping Centres in North West England*, Manchester, Department of Town and Country Planning, University of Manchester.

DICKEY, J.W. and NAJAFI, F.I. (1973) 'Regional landuse schemes generated by TOPAZ', *Regional Studies*, 7, 373–86.

DICKEY, J.W. and WATTS, T.M. (1978) *Analytic Techniques in Urban and Regional Planning*, New York, McGraw-Hill.

215

ECHENIQUE, M., CROWTHER, D. and LINDSAY, W. (1969) 'A spatial model of urban stock and activity', *Regional Studies*, 3, 281–312.

ECHENIQUE, M.H. and WILLIAMS, I.N. (1979) 'Developing theoretically based urban models for practical planning studies', in *The Application of Computers in Architecture, Building Design, and Urban Planning*, Berlin AMK, 365–76.

EVANS, S. (1973) 'A relationship between the gravity model for trip distribution and the transportation problem in linear programming', *Transportation Research*, 7, 39–62.

FOOT, D. (1974) 'A comparison of some landuse allocation/interaction models', *Geographical Papers*, 31, Department of Geography, University of Reading, Reading.

FOOT, D. (1978) 'Urban models I. A computer program for the Garin-Lowry model', *Geographical Papers*, 65, Department of Geography, University of Reading, Reading.

FOOT, D. (1979) 'Mathematical modelling in landuse planning', in Goodall, B. and Kirby, A. (eds) *Resources and Planning*, Oxford, Pergamon Press, 51–76.

FORRESTER, J.W. (1969) *Urban Dynamics*, Cambridge, Mass., MIT Press.

GARIN, R.A. (1966) 'A matrix formulation of the Lowry model for inter-metropolitan activity location', *Journal of the American Institute of Planners*, 32, 361–4.

GERALDES, P., ECHENIQUE, M.H. and WILLIAMS, I.N. (1978) 'A spatial economic model for Bilbao', in *Proceedings of the PTRC Summer Annual Meeting 1978* (F), London, Planning and Transport Research and Computation.

GILLIGAN, C.T., RAINFORD, P.M. and THORNE, A.R. (1974) 'The impact of out-of-town shopping', *European Journal of Marketing*, 8, 42–56.

GOLDNER, W. (1971) 'The Lowry model heritage', *Journal of the American Institute of Planners*, 37, 100–10.

GREENBERG, M.R. (1978) *Applied Linear Programming for the Socioeconomic and Environmental Sciences*, New York, Academic Press.

HALL, P. (1974) *Urban and Regional Planning*, London, Penguin.

HARRIS, B. (1968) 'Quantitative models in urban development: their role in metropolitan policy-making', in Perloff, H.S. and Wingo, L. (eds) *Issues in Urban Economics*, Baltimore, The Johns Hopkins Press.

HARRIS, B. (1972) 'A model of household locational preferences', in Funck, R. (ed.), *Recent Developments in Regional Science*, London, Pion.

HARRIS, B. (1975) 'Model building and rationality', in Baxter, R., Echenique, M. and Owers, J. (eds) *Urban Development Models*, Lancaster, Construction Press.

HARRIS, B. (1979) 'Computer aided urban planning: the state of the art', in *The Application of Computers in Architecture, Building Design and Urban Planning*, Berlin, AMK, 335–52.

HELLY, W. (1975) *Urban Systems Models*, New York, Academic Press.

HERBERT, J.D. and STEVENS, B.H. (1960) 'A model for the distribution of residential activity in urban area', *Journal of Regional Science*, 2, 21–36.

HILL, D.M. (1965) 'A growth allocation model for the Boston Region', *Journal of the American Institute of Planners*, 31, 111–20.

HILL, D.N., BRAND, D. and HANSEN, W.B. (1965) 'Prototype development of a statistical landuse prediction model for the Greater Boston Region', *Highway Research Record*, 114, 51–70.

HODDER, I. and ORTON, C. (1976) *Spatial Analysis in Archaeology*, Cambridge, Cambridge University Press.

HOPKINS, F.E. (1972) 'Transportation cost and industrial location: An analysis of the household furniture industry', *Journal of Regional Science*, 12, 261–77.

HOPKINS, L.D. (1977) 'Landuse plan design quadratic assignment and centre facility models', *Environment and Planning A*, 9, 625–42.

HUFF, D.L. (1963) 'A probabilistic analysis of shopping centre trade areas', *Land Economics*, 39, 81–90.

HUTCHINSON, B.G. (1974) *Principles of Urban Transport Systems Planning*, New York, McGraw-Hill.

JOHNSTON, R.J. (1978) *Multivariate Statistical Analysis in Geography*, London, Longman.

KAIN, J.F. (1978) 'The use of computer simulation models for policy analysis', *Urban Analysis*, 5, 175–89.

KARLQVIST, A. (1975) 'Models of Stockholm: ideas and experiences', in Baxter, R., Echenique, M. and Owers, J. (eds) *Urban Development Models*, Lancaster, Construction Press.

KRUECKEBERG, D.A. and SILVERS, A.L. (1974) *Urban Planning Analysis: Methods and Models*, New York, Wiley.

LAIDLAW, C.D. (1972) *Linear Programming for Urban Development*, New York, Praeger.

LAKSHMANAN, T.R. and HANSEN, W.G. (1965) 'A retail market potential model', *Journal of the American Institute of Planners*, 31, 95–108.

LEE, D.B. (1973) 'Requiem for large scale models', *Journal of the American Institute of Planners*, 39, 163–78.

LEWISHAM BOROUGH COUNCIL (1978) *Shopping in Lewisham: Shopping Model*, Planning Department, London Borough of Lewisham.

LOWRY, I.S. (1964) 'A model of metropolis', RM-4035-RC, RAND Corporation, Santa Monica, California.

LUNDQVIST, L. (1975) 'Transportation analysis and activity location in landuse planning with applications to the Stockholm Region', in Karlqvist, A., Lundqvist, L. and Snickars, F. (eds) *Dynamic Allocation of Urban Space*, Farnborough, Saxon House.

McLOUGHLIN, J.B. (1969) *Urban and Regional Planning: A Systems Approach*, London, Faber & Faber.

McLoughlin, J.B., Foot, D.H.S. and Nix, C.H. (1966) *Regional Shopping Centres in North West England: PART 2: A Retail Shopping Model*, Manchester, Department of Town and Country Planning, University of Manchester.

Mansfield, N.W. (1971) 'The estimation of benefits from recreational sites and the provision of a new recreational facility', *Regional Studies*, 5, 55–69.

Masser, I., Batey, P.W.J. and Brown, P.J.B. (1975) 'The design of zoning systems for interaction models', in Cripps, E.L. (ed.) *Regional Science: New Concepts and Old Problems*, London, Pion.

Masser, I., Coleman, A. and Wynn, R.F. (1971) 'Estimation of a growth allocation model for North West England', *Environment and Planning*, 3, 451–63.

Massey, D.B. (1973) 'The basic-service categorisation in planning', *Regional Studies*, 7, 1–15.

Morlok, E.K. (1978) *Introduction to Transportation Engineering and Planning*, New York, McGraw-Hill.

Moseley, J. (1977) *Shopping in Berkshire: The Shopping Model*, Reading, The Unit for Retail Planning Information.

Nagel, S.S. and Neef, M. (1976) *Operational Research Methods*, Beverly Hills, Sage.

Needham, B. (1977) *How Cities Work: An Introduction*, Oxford, Pergamon Press.

Openshaw, S. (1973) 'Insoluble problems in shopping model calibration when the trip pattern is not known', *Regional Studies*, 7, 367–71.

Openshaw, S. (1978) *Using Models in Planning: A Practical Guide*, Corbridge, Retail and Planning Associates.

Oppenheim, N. (1980) *Applied Models in Urban and Regional Analysis*, Englewood Cliffs, NJ, Prentice-Hall.

O'Sullivan, P. (1972) 'Linear programming as a forecasting device for interregional freight flows in Great Britain', *Regional Urban Economics*, 1, 383–96.

Pack, H. and Pack, J.R. (1977) 'The resurrection of the urban development model', *Policy Analysis*, 3, 407–27.

Paelinck, J.H.P. and Klaassen, L.H. (1979) *Spatial Econometrics*, Farnborough, Saxon House.

Piasentin, U., Costa, P. and Foot, D.H.S. (1978) 'The Venice problem: An approach by urban modelling', *Regional Studies*, 12, 579–602.

Posokhin, M.V., Gutnov, A.E., Popkov, I.S. and Shmul'ian, B.L. (1980) 'A systems model of the city and experiments in using it for a functional and spatial analysis of Moscow', *Environment and Planning B*, 7, 107–20.

Putman, S.H. (1970) 'Developing and testing an intraregional model', *Regional Studies*, 4, 473–90.

Putman, S.H. (1979) *Urban Residential Location Models*, Boston, Martinus Nijhoff.

REILLY, W.J. (1931) *The Law of Retail Gravitation*, New York, Knickerbocker.

RHIND, D. and HUDSON, R. (1980) *Land Use*, London, Methuen.

RICHARDSON, H.W. and GORDON, P. (1979) 'Economic and fiscal impacts of metropolitan decentralization: the Southern California case', *Environment and Planning A*, 11, 643–54.

ROBERTS, M. (1974) *An Introduction to Town Planning Techniques*, London, Hutchinson.

SAYER, R.A. (1976) 'A critique of urban modelling: from regional science to urban and regional political economy', *Progress in Planning*, 6(3), 187–254.

SAYER, R.A. (1979) 'Understanding urban models versus understanding cities', *Environment and Planning A*, 11, 853–62.

SCHLAGER, K.J. (1965) 'A landuse plan design model', *Journal of the American Institute of Planners*, 31, 103–11.

SENIOR, M. and WILSON, A.G. (1974) 'Explorations and syntheses of linear programming and spatial interaction models of residential location', *Geographical Analysis*, 6, 209–38.

SHARPE, R. (1980) 'Improving energy efficiency in community landuse transportation systems', *Environment and Planning A*, 12, 203–16.

SHARPE, R., BROTCHIE, J.F. and AHERN, P.A. (1975) 'Evaluation of alternative growth patterns for Melbourne', in Karlqvist, A., Lundqvist, L. and Snickars, F. (eds) *Dynamic Allocation of Urban Space*, Farnborough, Saxon House.

SILK, J. (1979) *Statistical Concepts in Geography*, London, Allen & Unwin.

TAFFLER, R. (1979) *Using Operational Research: A Practical Introduction*, Englewood Cliffs, NJ, Prentice-Hall.

THIE, P.R. (1979) *An Introduction to Linear Programming and Game Theory*, New York, Wiley.

TRUSTRUM, K. (1978) *Linear Programming*, London, Routledge & Kegan Paul.

TURNER, C.G. (1975) 'The design of urban growth models for strategic landuse transportation studies', *Regional Studies*, 9, 251–64.

US DEPARTMENT OF TRANSPORTATION (1976) '*Laboratory testing of predictive landuse models: some comparisons*', NSF-G1-38978, National Science Foundation, Washington, DC.

WAVERMAN, L. (1972) 'National policy and natural gas: the costs of a border', *Canadian Journal of Economics*, 5, 333–48.

WHEATON, W. (1974) 'Linear programming and location equilibrium: The Herbert Stevens model revisited', *Journal of Urban Economics*, 1, 278–87.

WILSON, A.G. (1967) 'A statistical theory of spatial distribution models', *Transportation Research*, 1, 253–69.

WILSON, A.G. (1970) *Entropy in Urban and Regional Modelling*, London, Pion.

WILSON, A.G. (1974) *Urban and Regional Models in Geography and Planning*, London, Wiley.

WILSON, A.G. (1978) Book review of Sayer (1976), *Environment and Planning A*, 10, 1085–6.

WILSON, A.G., REES, P.H. and LEIGH, C.M. (eds) (1978) *Models of Cities and Regions: Theoretical and Empirical Developments*, Chichester, Wiley.

YEATES, M. (1963) 'Hinterland delimitation: A distance minimization approach', *Professional Geographer*, 15, 7–10.

YEOMANS, K.A. (1968) *Statistics for the Social Scientist: I Introducing Statistics; II Applied Statistics*, London, Penguin.

Author index

Subject index

accessibility index, 154–5, 157–62, 167

activities: aggregate, 9, 13, 19, 25, 58, 60, 69, 81, 100, 102, 103, 105, 106, 107, 132, 134, 136, 137, 150, 154, 172, 176, 207, 213; disaggregation of, 9, 13, 19, 65, 67, 68, 87, 95, 102–4, 124, 132, 134, 136, 137, 150–4, 164, 165, 167, 172, 176, 183, 198, 203, 205–7, 211, 213; increments of, 145–50, 154–62, 165–6, 167, 170, 172

activity rate, 80–1, 110–12, 113–17, 118, 119–20, 123

aggregate activities, 9, 13, 19, 25, 207, 213; in linear models, 138, 139, 150, 156; in optimizing models, 176; in spatial interaction models, 25, 58, 60, 69, 81, 100, 102, 103, 105, 106, 107, 132, 134, 136

alternative plans: evaluation of, 5–6, 11–12, 30–1, 40, 59–60, 61–5, 70–2, 86, 96, 106, 122–3, 125–8, 130–1, 132, 134, 166, 190–1, 195–7, 200, 201, 202, 207, 212, 213; generation of, 5–6

archaeological models, 78

area under a curve, 43–4, 77

assessment of: linear models, 169–73; optimizing models, 201–4; spatial interaction models, 102–7, 171–3; urban models, 207–13

assignment of trips, 16, 26, 95–6, 98

assumptions, 30; gravity, 59, 65, 94, 105, 135, 153, 172; linear regression, 145, 153–4, 162, 169, 170, 172; optimizing, 184–5, 191–2, 203

Atlanta model, 166

attraction index: general, 73, 76, 78; residential, 79–80, 86, 113, 118, 123, 124, 129; service centre, 114, 118, 122, 123; shopping centre, 42–4, 46, 47, 59, 60, 73, 76

attractiveness: of residential zones, 79–80, 129; of shopping centres, 32–7, 41, 42–7, 63, 76

average trip length, 26–7, 28, 83–5, 91–3, 122

balancing factors, 74, 78, 79, 89, 92–3, 95, 113, 114

Baltimore models, 7, 60

basic employment, 109–12, 113–16, 117, 119, 123, 125, 131, 154–6, 157, 159–62, 164, 167

208-9; optimizing, 2, 8, 10, 27,
102, 108, 174-204, 206, 207;
partial, 9-10, 104; prediction
with, 29-31, 58-60, 63-5, 67,
68-9, 72, 85-7, 94-5, 96, 105,
122-3, 125-8, 129-32, 133,
135, 145-6, 150, 156, 157, 162-
3, 166, 169, 170, 178-9, 195-7,
199-200, 202, 207, 208, 211-
12; reactions to, 136, 205, 210-
12; recreation, 78; residential
location, 73, 77, 78-87, 102-4,
108, 109, 112-35, 137-69, 174-
84, 192-200, 206-7, 211; retail
shopping, 5, 6, 10, 13, 32-72,
73-6, 77, 97, 102, 106, 107,
108, 114, 199, 207, 208-9; service location, 103, 113-34, 156-
62, 164-8, 199, 201, 205; singly
constrained, 32-72, 73-87,
101-2, 103, 113-36, 171-4,
193; spatial interaction, 32-72,
73-107, 108-36, 142, 145, 146,
153, 158, 171-3, 192-4, 199,
200-1, 202, 203, 205, 206,
208-9; static, 8-9, 30, 59, 105,
135, 210, 212; stochastic linear,
8, 168-9; transport, 73, 87-98,
99, 100, 185-91, 192-7, 201;
unconstrained, 98-100
money flows, 35, 48-50, 51-60,
61-7, 75
Monte Carlo simulation, 168-9
Moscow model, 125

NBER models, 206
network, shortest path through, 26
New Haven model, 207
New York model, 96
Newton-Raphson method, 121-2
Newton's Law of gravitation, 32,
98, 104
nonlinear models, 9. 10
Norfolk model, 33-7, 41
North Carolina model, 168-9

north Devon model, 186, 187-90
north-east corridor of USA model, 150, 152, 154, 164, 167-8,
170, 171, 206
north-east Lancashire model,
117-20
north-west England linear model,
166
north-west England shopping model, 37-41, 61-2
north-west Lancashire region, 19-
28
Nottinghamsire-Derbyshire subregional study, 6, 124

objective function in mathematical
programming: in general models, 192-3, 198, 199, 200, 202-
3; in linear programming, 174,
175-7, 178-80, 181, 182, 184;
in transport problems, 185, 186,
187, 192
objectives of study, 11-13
one shot predictions, 30
operational models, 1-2, 6-7, 8-
10, 207-9; Garin-Lowry, 124-
35; gravity, 60-72, 78, 87, 96-
7, 102-4, 124-35; hybrid, 205-
7; industrial location, 190-1,
195, 198, 205, 206, 207; linear,
163-8; optimizing, 182-4, 190-
1, 195-200; residential location,
78, 87, 103, 124-35, 163-8,
182-4, 195-200; shopping, 60-
72; spatial interaction, 60-72,
78, 87, 96-7, 102-4, 124-35;
transport, 96-7, 100, 190-2
optimization, 174-204; linear programming, 175-85, 186-92;
quadratic programming, 192-
210; transport problem, 185-92
optimizing consumer benefit, 198,
199, 200, 201
optimizing models, 2, 8, 10, 27,
102, 108, 174-204, 206, 207